School Leadership and Education System Reform

Also available from Bloomsbury

An Intellectual History of School Leadership Practice and Research, Helen M. Gunter

Educational Leadership for a More Sustainable World, Mike Bottery

Education in the Balance, Raphael Wilkins

Exploring the School Leadership Landscape, Peter Earley

Leading Schools in Challenging Circumstances, Philip Smith and Les Bell

Successful School Leadership, edited by Petros Pashiardis and Olof Johansson

Sustainable School Transformation, edited by David Crossley

School Leadership and Education System Reform

Edited by Peter Earley and Toby Greany

Bloomsbury Academic
An imprint of Bloomsbury Publishing Plc

BLOOMSBURY
LONDON · OXFORD · NEW YORK · NEW DELHI · SYDNEY

Bloomsbury Academic

An imprint of Bloomsbury Publishing Plc

50 Bedford Square
London
WC1B 3DP
UK

1385 Broadway
New York
NY 10018
USA

www.bloomsbury.com

BLOOMSBURY and the Diana logo are trademarks of Bloomsbury Publishing Plc

First published 2017
Reprinted 2017 (three times)

British Library Cataloguing-in-Publication Data
A catalogue record for this book is available from the British Library.

ISBN: HB: 978-1-4742-7396-1
PB: 978-1-4742-7395-4
ePDF: 978-1-4742-7397-8
ePub: 978-1-4742-7398-5

Library of Congress Cataloging-in-Publication Data
Earley, Peter, editor. | Greany, Toby, editor.
School leadership and education system reform /edited by Peter Earley, Toby Greany.
London ; New York : Bloomsbury Academic, 2017.
LCCN 2016036512| ISBN 9781474273961(hardback) | ISBN 9781474273985(epub) | ISBN 9781474273978 (epdf)
Educational leadership–Great Britain. |School management and organization–Great Britain. | School improvement programs–Great Britain.
EDUCATION / General. | EDUCATION / Leadership.
LCC LB2900.5 .S32 2017
DDC371.20941–dc23
LC record available at https://lccn.loc.gov/2016036512

Cover image: © stellalevi / Getty Images

Typeset by Deanta Global Publishing Services, Chennai, India
Printed and bound in Great Britain

Contents

Part 2 School leadership in a changing landscape

List of figures

List of tables

Notes on contributors

Sir George Berwick was headteacher of Ravens Wood School in Bromley from 1993 until 2011. Between 2003 and 2008, he was Director of the London Leadership Strategy, part of the London Challenge, which contributed to the creation of the role of Local and National Leaders in Education, and to the designation of National Support Schools and Teaching Schools. George Berwick has worked with the Cabinet Office and the Department for Education. He was awarded a CBE for services to education in 2007 and is a Visiting Professor at the UCL Institute of Education. The lessons learnt from the London Challenge were used to establish Challenge Partners, where he continues to develop the Teaching Schools model so that more pupils can benefit from the collective wisdom of the education community.

Domini Bingham is Academic Tutor and Researcher in the London Centre for Leadership in Learning (LCLL) at UCL IOE contributing to teaching and supervision on four academic leadership programmes. Her research interests are in adults and young people achieving their potential, professional development for older workforces, wellbeing in educational settings and in intercultural education and citizenship in schools. In the final stages of an EdD, her thesis addresses older workers and engagement in professional development. She was Research Fellow for the London Education Research Unit (LERU) and has a wider professional background and interest in international development, having worked at the Commonwealth Secretariat. Her book *Older Workforces: Re-imagining Later Life Learning* (Gower Ashgate) will be published in 2017.

Chris Brown is a senior lecturer in LCLL and Academic Head of Research, Consultancy and Knowledge Transfer for the Department of Learning and Leadership. He has a long-standing interest in how evidence can aid policy and teaching practice. Chris has written four books (including *Leading the Use of Research and Evidence in Schools*), several papers and has presented on the subject at a number of international conferences both in Europe and North America. Chris was recently awarded a grant by the Education Endowment Foundation to work with more than a hundred primary schools in England to increase their use of research. Previous roles include being Head of Research at the TDA. Chris received the AERA 'emerging scholar' award in 2015 and the AERA 'research to practice' award in 2016.

Sara Bubb is a senior lecturer in the Department of Learning and Leadership, UCL Institute of Education and a freelance consultant. With a long-standing interest in helping teachers develop, she has worked with state and independent schools on new teacher induction, literacy, professional development and leadership. Known for her articles in the *TES*, she has published reports, papers and articles, as well as fifteen books. Her research has been extensive, including of governor training and leadership development; school improvement projects; workload and wellbeing; as well as leading professional development. Her most recent book is *Successful Induction for New Teachers: A Guide for NQTs and Induction Tutors, Coordinators and Mentors* (2014, Sage).

Max Coates was a secondary head for twelve years. He has worked for the University of Bristol Graduate School of Education and St Mary's University College. He co-leads the MA Leadership at the UCL Institute of Education, University College London. Published works include books on personalizing learning and citizenship. His most recent book, *The Constant Leader*, explores surviving and thriving in leadership. He was the editor of *Shaping a New Educational Landscape* exploring future developments within education. He has recently been awarded a doctoral fellowship. The focus of his research was organizational and personal change.

Sir Kevan Collins has worked in public service for over thirty years and became the first Chief Executive of the Education Endowment Foundation in 2011, having previously been Chief Executive of the London Borough of Tower Hamlets. Prior to this role, Kevan led a distinguished career in education, starting off as a primary school teacher, leading the Primary Literacy Strategy as National Director, and then serving as Director of Children's Services in Tower Hamlets. Kevan completed a doctorate focusing on literacy development at Leeds University in 2005. In 2015, he was knighted for services to education.

Robbie Coleman is a senior associate at the Education Endowment Foundation (EEF) and a co-author of the Teaching and Learning Toolkit, produced by the EEF in collaboration with the Sutton Trust and Durham University. The Toolkit is a free, accessible summary of educational research for schools and synthesizes over 10,000 individual studies. Alongside his work at the EEF, Robbie teaches English at a comprehensive secondary school in London.

Ian Craig is a visiting professor at the London School of Economics (LSE) and UCL Institute of Education, where he is also a Senior Teaching Fellow, teaching on several masters programmes. He has been a teacher, headteacher, inspector, Director of Education and England's Chief Schools Adjudicator. Subsequently, he has undertaken disparate assignments in the UK and abroad, including working for the World Bank and DfID. In 2012 he was the IOE's Interim Director of Initial Teacher Education and in 2013 Interim Executive Director of the College of Teachers (UK). His main interests are in comparative education policy, systems development and leadership, particularly related to the crossover between policy and practice. He is also Chair of an Academies Schools Trust.

Dan Gibton is Associate Professor of education policy and law, at the Constantiner School of Education and Adjunct Lecturer at the Faculty of Law, Tel-Aviv University, Israel, and visiting professor at LCLL, UCL Institute of Education. Areas of interest include school reform, legislation and school reform, the nature and emergence of education law and law-based reform and qualitative methods in policy studies. His most recent publication is *Researching Education Policy, Public Policy, and Policymakers: Qualitative methods and ethical Issues* (2016, Routledge).

Peter Earley holds the Chair of Education Leadership and Management and, until recently, was Head of Academic Affairs in LCLL at UCL IOE. His central research interests are leadership, school improvement, professional development, inspection, self-evaluation and school governance. Recent externally funded projects include leadership development of independent school heads (2016), effective headteacher performance management (2013); the changing landscape of educational leadership in England (2012) and the experiences of new headteachers (2011). His most recent books are: *Exploring the School Leadership Landscape: changing demands, changing realities* (Bloomsbury, 2013), *Accelerated Leadership Development: fast-tracking school leaders,* (IOE, 2010 with Jeff Jones) and *Helping Staff Develop in Schools* (Sage, 2010 with Sara Bubb). He was given the BELMAS Distinguished Service Award in 2015.

Karen Edge is Reader in Educational Leadership at the UCL Institute of Education and Pro-Vice Provost (International) at UCL, UK. Karen has recently served as Principal Investigator for the ESRC-funded Global City Leaders Project exploring the lives, careers and aspirations of Gen X school leaders in London, New York City and Toronto. Karen's research interests include knowledge management, system reform and policy, districts, leadership, generations and global cities.

Melanie Ehren is Reader in Educational Accountability and Improvement in LCLL at UCL IOE, researching effects and unintended consequences of accountability, evaluation and school inspection systems on school improvement and teaching and learning in schools. Current and recent works include: coordinating an EU-funded research project on impact of school inspections in six countries, and Erasmus+ funded study on 'polycentric' inspections of networks of schools in four countries; reviewing Evaluation and Assessment in Education in Luxembourg for the OECD; a Spencer Foundation scholarship to study multiple measure accountability systems at Columbia and Harvard Universities; and reviewing the inspection system in Zanzibar/Tanzania for UNICEF. She is programme leader of the MA in 'Evaluation, Inspection and Educational Improvement'.

Sergio Galdames is an educational researcher from the Pontificia Universidad Catolica de Valparaiso, Chile and a PhD student at the LCLL at the UCL Institute of Education, University College London. Sergio has worked extensively in professional development programmes for school leaders. His research interests cover school leadership, careers and creativity.

Ron Glatter is Emeritus Professor of Educational Administration and Management at the UK Open University and Visiting Professor at UCL Institute of Education. He was the founding secretary of what is now called the British Educational Leadership, Management and Administration Society (BELMAS), and later became its national Chair and is now its Honorary President. He was given the BELMAS Distinguished Service Award in 2007. He has researched and published extensively on educational governance and leadership, focusing most recently on critical analyses of structural reforms in education. He has been on the governing boards of seven educational institutions including three schools and is currently a trustee of a co-operative learning trust comprising three secondary schools in Hertfordshire, England.

David Godfrey is a lecturer, formerly a research officer, in LCLL at UCL IOE. His work covers several research and knowledge transfer projects, which are linked by a strong interest in research-informed practice in education. His PhD thesis explored research engagement in secondary schools in England. Projects include facilitating research learning communities for an EEF-funded project; looking at alternative forms of inspection and accountability models; two projects in London schools using lesson study and also looking at leadership in Further Education. Before moving into Higher Education he taught at a sixth form college, and as an Assistant Director, coordinated research activity. He has also worked extensively as an Inspector for the Independent Schools' Inspectorate.

Toby Greany is Professor of Leadership and Innovation and Director of LCLL at UCL IOE. His research interests include system reform and system leadership, school leadership and improvement and the nature and impact of evidence-informed practice. Current and recent research studies include: understanding the self-improving school system, an evaluation of evidence-based practice, effective approaches to professional development for teachers, school-university partnerships, TIMSS 2015 and conflicts of interest in academies. Before joining the UCL IOE, Toby was Director of Research and Policy at NCSL. He has worked at the Design Council, the Campaign for Learning and the Cabinet Office and has taught in Brazil, China and the UK. From 2005 to 2006 he was Special Advisor to the Education and Skills Select Committee.

Juliet Horton is a vice principal at the City of London Academy, Islington, London and a PhD student at the London Centre for Leadership in Learning at the UCL Institute of Education, University College London, UK. Juliet's research interests cover gender and school leadership.

Chris Husbands became Vice Chancellor of Sheffield Hallam University in January 2016. Prior to that, he was Director of the UCL Institute of Education, where he oversaw the merger with University College London. He has previously been Director of the Institute of Education at the University of Warwick and Dean of the School of Education and Lifelong Learning at the University of East Anglia.

Sue John was formerly headteacher of Lampton School from 1997 to 2015, one of the first academy convertors. Lampton is a National Teaching School included in the Ofsted publication – *Twelve outstanding schools succeeding against the odds*. Sue was the secondary director of the London Leadership Strategy for the London Challenge from 2007 to 2010 and was awarded a DBE for services to education in 2010. She has held directorships at the DfE, Future Leaders and Teaching Leaders and is currently Executive Director at Challenge Partners, in addition to her continued role as secondary director of the London Leadership Strategy. Sue is a member of the Sutton Trust Education Advisory Group, director at the Futures Academy Trust and is chair of trustees of the Brilliant Club.

Rachel Macfarlane is a National Leader of Education in her thirteenth year of headship. After seven years as headteacher of Walthamstow School for Girls, an outstanding 11–16 school in the London Borough of Waltham Forest, Rachel joined Ark Schools in 2011 to set up a new co-educational, all-through academy for 4- to 18-year-olds in Ilford, East London. Isaac Newton Academy opened in September 2012. Since 2009 Rachel has been Project Director of the London Leadership Strategy's 'Going for Great' (G4G) programme and has also led the 'Good to Great' (G2G) programme from 2010 to 2014. Rachel is a Visiting Fellow at UCL IOE. She also serves on the Headteacher Board for the Regional Schools Commissioner for the North East London and East of England region.

Trevor Male is a senior lecturer in LCLL at UCL IOE. He supervises doctoral theses and masters dissertations as well as leading LCLL's MBA and teaching on the MA in Applied Educational Leadership and Management. He has worked extensively in education for over forty years, including full-time employment in three universities, as an education officer in a local authority and as a teacher. His main area of expertise is in the field of education leadership. He has published extensively, including two books: *Being an Effective Headteacher* and *Doing Research in Education: Theory and Practice* and many journal articles and conference papers.

Peter Matthews is a visiting professor at the UCL Institute of Education and former Her Majesty's Inspector and Schools Adjudicator. After working in schools, higher education, local and national government, he helped establish Ofsted in 1992, becoming Head of Inspection Quality and Development. As a consultant since 2005, he has completed many evaluation projects for the UK and other governments and the Organisation for Economic Co-operation and Development. He has written widely on school and system leadership, evaluation and improvement. He was awarded the OBE in 2003.

Ioanna Palaiologou is a Chartered Psychologist with the British Psychological Society, and currently works as an independent psychologist with a specialism in child development and learning theories. Previously, she worked in higher education, and among her main responsibilities, has supervised postgraduate research students and mentored early career researchers. Her research interests and key publications are focused on ethics in research, child development and the epistemic nature of pedagogy. She is the author of the bestselling books: *Early Years Foundation Stage: Theory and Practice* and *Child Observation: A guide for students of Early Childhood*.

Vivienne Porritt is Director for School Partnerships at the UCL IOE, University College London. Vivienne's interests include working with schools to design evidence-informed, collaborative and sustainable relationships with the IOE, the strategic leadership of professional learning, including a practical approach to impact evaluation and a collaborative approach to enquiry, supporting schools to engage with and in research. Vivienne is also a founding member and a national leader of WomenEd, a grassroots, voluntary organization that connects existing and aspiring women leaders in education. She is the co-editor of *Effective Practices in Continuing Professional Development: Lessons for schools* (IOE, 2009 with Peter Earley).

Mark Quinn has been a teacher in England since 1995. He has taught in secondary comprehensive schools in London and the South East of England for over twenty years. He is currently an assistant headteacher for staff development at Chace Community School, Enfield, London, UK. He has worked on a seconded and associate basis at London Metropolitan University and at Middlesex University, and since 2014 at the LCLL at UCL IOE. He maintains an educational blog, www.markquinn1968.wordpress.com, which he contributes to the IOE Research and Development website www.ioe-rdnetwork.com.

Kathryn Riley is Professor of Urban Education in LCLL at UCL IOE and an international scholar whose work bridges policy and practice. She has taught in inner-city schools, held political office as an elected member of the Inner London Education Authority and been a local authority Chief Officer. Her international expertise includes working for the World Bank. She is the past Director of the London Education Research Unit; teaches two MA modules and leads the UCL IOE partnership with the Further Education Trust for Leadership (FETL). Kathryn's extensive publications include *Leadership of Place: Stories from the US, UK and South Africa* (Bloomsbury, 2013) and *Place, Belonging and School Leadership: Researching to Change School Cultures* (Bloomsbury, 2016).

Karen Spence-Thomas is a programme leader in LCLL at UCL IOE. She has held teaching and leadership roles in London schools and joined the IOE in 2009, working initially as a teacher educator on the Graduate Teacher Programme. She now specializes in designing and facilitating tailored professional development programmes within and across schools and other public sector organizations. She also co-leads the IOE R&D Network of schools with Louise Stoll. Recent and current projects include: Research Learning Communities; Middle Leaders as Catalysts for Change; NCTL Research Themes Project; and a leadership programme for women with Mulberry School for Girls. Her most recent publication is: 'Understanding Impact and the Cycle of Enquiry' with Carol Taylor in C. Brown (ed.) *Leading the Use of Research and Evidence in Schools* (2015, IOE Press).

Louise Stoll is Professor of Professional Learning at UCL IOE. Her research and development activity focuses on how schools, local and national systems create capacity for learning and improvement, through creative leadership, leadership development, professional learning communities (PLCs) and learning networks. Louise is a Fellow of the

Academy of the Social Sciences, OECD expert and international consultant. Her books have been translated into five languages. She is also committed to helping practitioners 'animate' research findings, and has developed PLC materials, a networking simulation, *Improving School Leadership: The Toolkit* for the OECD, and *Catalyst*, a middle leadership development card resource.

Carol Taylor is a programme leader in LCLL at UCL IOE supporting schools to embed practitioner research and enquiry into organization and individual practice. She co-led the Teaching Schools R&D national project and the 'Middle Leaders as Catalysts for Change' project. An evaluator on the 'Effective Practices in CPD' project (2010) she is co-designer of the HMC/GSA ISQAM national accredited PD programme for middle leaders in independent schools and bespoke leadership programmes for national and international contexts. Her most recent publication is 'Understanding Impact and the Cycle of Enquiry' with Karen Spence-Thomas in C. Brown (ed.) *Leading the Use of Research and Evidence in Schools* (2015, IOE Press).

Joanne Waterhouse is a senior lecturer in LCLL at UCL IOE. Joanne's research interests focus on leadership studies, particularly distributed leadership and leadership in context. She has also researched collaborative action research processes, and has published articles on the Third Space. She is involved in an international project on school autonomy and curriculum innovation and is formulating a conceptualization of contemporary curriculum leadership. Joanne co-leads the MA in Leadership and teaches on several masters courses, including an international distance-learning course for the study of applied leadership. She also facilitates for the research learning communities project. Joanne worked for over twenty years in the primary sector. Her experience includes headteacher, LA advisor, Ofsted inspector and NCSL network facilitator.

Elizabeth Wood is a senior lecturer in LCLL at UCL IOE who leads the University of London International Programme's distance-learning MA in Applied Educational Leadership and Management. She has also validated and led two MBAs in Educational Leadership. Her consultancy work has included working with the State of Nayarit in Mexico to develop and set up a state education leadership centre, developing and writing materials for the NCTL's school business management (SBM) development programmes and working as SBM programme development manager (researching, writing and presenting). She has been researching school business managers since the late 1990s and is co-author of the first book on SBMs. She has published on the impact of site-based management on schools as well as presenting at research and professional conferences.

David Woods, CBE, has been a teacher and senior leader in schools, a teacher trainer and a local authority adviser in two LAs. He was the Chief Education Adviser for the City of Birmingham before joining the Department for Education as Senior Education Adviser working closely with ministers to develop educational policy and subsequently becoming Head of the Department's Advisory Service. He joined London Challenge from the beginning as the Lead Adviser and became the Principal Adviser for the National Challenge and then Chief Adviser for London Schools and the London Challenge. His latest books, co-authored with Tim Brighouse, are *The A-Z of School Improvement* (2013) and *The Story of London Challenge* (2015). Currently, he is a consultant working with schools, local authorities and academy chains as well as being a Visiting Professor at Warwick University and at the UCL IOE. He is also the Chair of the London Leadership Strategy (successor body to the London Challenge).

Foreword

The major responsibility for resolving the long-standing problem of the inequitable educational outcomes of England's schooling system is being transferred from national and local government authorities to a new 'middle tier' comprising groups of schools organized into various types of trusts and partnerships. The policy intention is that these new structural arrangements evolve into a self-improving school system, which uses its greater freedom from government to take more collective responsibility for the improvement of groups of schools and eventually of the whole system.

As the editors point out in their introduction, many countries are watching, and some are already emulating, England's progress. That is just one reason why this edited collection of chapters, which includes commentaries on the policy ideas driving this reform, on its historical precursors, and on the implications for the development and practice of school leadership, should attract a wide international readership.

There are at least two key questions to be asked about this latest wave of English educational reform. The first is 'What political and policy imperatives are driving the reform?' and the second is 'What evidence is there that these new structural arrangements are, or are likely to be, any more successful than the prior local or national government-led efforts?'

With regard to the first question, the chapters outline the complex and conflicting imperatives that shape this reform. One imperative is managerial – the desire to drive decision-making closer to the point of implementation, to reduce bureaucratic impediments to innovation and to provide leaders with the freedom to be responsive to their local context and community preferences. But these ideas are not sufficient to explain the emphasis on *groups of schools* working together on their school improvement journeys. The second imperative is the recognition that single school improvement too often comes at the cost of neighbouring schools and that it will never deliver on the vision of *every* child succeeding on valued social, cultural and academic outcomes. The third is the desire, on the part of policymakers and educators themselves, for the profession to take a greater collective responsibility for the quality of its work. Educational leaders, and the business partners and sponsors with whom they collaborate in multi-academy trusts, are to create a self-improving system – one in which leaders can self-evaluate, and, in so doing, accurately identify, inquire into and collaboratively resolve the problems that prevent them achieving their goals.

With regard to the second question, the book presents a fascinating puzzle; for the examples it provides of dramatic improvement in groups of schools show that there is no necessary connection between particular structural arrangements and improved student outcomes. That multi-academy trusts *can* produce dramatic lifts in student achievement is indicated by the emerging evidence included in Chapter 5 on Collaboration, Partnerships and System Leadership. But just as compelling is the story of the ninety-eight schools of Tower Hamlets, which made dramatic and sustained improvements under the auspices of a local authority (Chapter 6). From these cases, and the emerging wider evaluations, it is reasonable to conclude that there is large variation within any given structural arrangements (such as multi-academy trusts in England, or charter schools in the United States), in their ability to deliver the desired improvements. What seems critical is not the structure of schooling, but the presence of a set of conditions that research is now suggesting are the building blocks of improvement at scale. While the detail differs across differing researchers, those conditions include layers of leadership that can not only articulate, but also relentlessly focus on a compelling educational vision, that can engage teachers, students and their families in its pursuit through ambitious efforts to improve teaching and learning, and that can lead and resource the capability-building that is required to achieve the ambition.

The challenge for educational leaders and policymakers is to recognize that the real work of improvement is creating those conditions, not reorganizing the structure of schooling. It may be that some structures are better enablers of the conditions than others, but the evidence in favour of any one is far from compelling. If we are to have a truly self-improving education system, then the policy system must also be self-improving. An initial focus of a self-improving policy system should be deep study of the conditions for improvement so that the policy settings can be closely aligned to them. Take, for example, the capability-building condition. There is now a broad consensus among researchers on the types of professional learning that are more or less likely to improve the outcomes of the students of the participating teachers. What policy settings, if any, are needed to help more leaders access and use this knowledge? To what extent are such policy tenets as 'teachers and schools learn from each other and from research so that effective practice spreads' (p. 11) correct? What are the consequences for the attainment of the policy goals if leaders of schools with the greatest need for improvement have the least ability to access such knowledge? Such questions would be rigorously pursued in a policy system that was modelling the processes of self-improvement that educators are being encouraged to embrace.

The fast-changing and increasingly diverse nature of the English education system means it can be hard to discern the major policy influences, pick the critical issues and keep track of the on-the-ground realities. This book helps its readers in all three respects and as such should be at the top of the professional reading list for policymakers, educators and researchers in England and in all those other countries where lessons can be learnt from the English experience.

Viviane Robinson, The University of Auckland, New Zealand

Acknowledgements

We would like to thank all the chapter contributors for their commitment to this book and to LCLL's wider work. This collection is testament to the depth and breadth of the Centre's research and impact with schools across London and beyond. Additional thanks to Monika Robak for her support in the final stages and to the team at Bloomsbury.

Publisher's note

List of abbreviations

AERA	American Educational Research Association
BELMAS	British Educational Leadership, Management and Administration Society
CBI	Confederation of British Industry
CPD	Continuing professional development
CPDL	Continuing professional development and learning
DCSF	Department for Children, Schools and Families
DfE	Department for Education
DSBM	Diploma in School Business Management
EBacc	English Baccalaureate
EEF	Education Endowment Foundation
EFA	Education Funding Agency
ERA	Education Reform Act (1988)
FSM	Free school meals
GCSE	General Certificate of Secondary Education
HEI	Higher education institution
HMCI	Her Majesty's Chief Inspector
HMI	Her Majesty's Inspectorate
HRM	Human resource management
IPPR	Institute for Public Policy Research
IOE	Institute of Education
JPD	Joint practice development
LA	Local authority
LCLL	London Centre for Leadership in Learning
LEA	Local education authority
LfL	Leadership for learning
LLE	Local Leader of Education
MAT	Multi-academy trust
NAO	National Audit Office
NCSL	National College for School Leadership
NCTL	National College for Teaching and Leadership
NLE	National Leader of Education
NLG	National Leader of Governance
NPQH	National Professional Qualification for Headship

NSS	National support school
OECD	Organization for Economic Co-operation and Development
Ofsted	Office for Standards in Education
PD	Professional development
PIRLS	Progress in International Reading Literacy Study
PISA	Programme of International Student Assessment
PLD	Professional learning and development
PwC	PricewaterhouseCoopers
R&D	Research and development
RCT	Randomized controlled trial
RSC	Regional Schools Commissioner
SBM	School business manager
SEF	Self-evaluation form
SLE	Specialist Leader of Education
SLT	Senior leadership team
SMT	Senior management team
UCL	University College London
TALIS	Teaching and Learning International Survey
TIMSS	Trends in International Maths and Science Study
TLRP	Teaching and Learning Research Programme
TES	Times Educational Supplement

Introduction

School leadership and education system reform

Toby Greany and Peter Earley

The paradox of policy and the quest for successful leadership

This edited collection arguably revolves around two interconnected challenges: a paradox and a quest.

The paradox

The *paradox* is actually a set of contradictions that sit at the heart of education policy in many school systems. Policymakers in these systems want things that, if not inherently at odds, are nevertheless in tension – freedom *and* control; tightly defined national standards *and* a broad and balanced curriculum; choice and diversity *and* equity; academic stretch for the most able children *and* a closing of the gap between high and low performers; competition *and* collaboration. In other words, they not only want their educational cake, but also want to eat it.

Having lost faith in what Barber (2015) calls the post-war 'trust and altruism' model of public service delivery, in which local authorities ran schools with minimal central oversight, policymakers have devolved decision-making power and resources to schools in the belief that this will improve quality and increase innovation. In order to incentivize these outcomes they have put in place accountability systems that combine quasi-market pressures (such as parental choice of school coupled with funding-following-the-learner) with central regulation and control.

At one level these quasi-market shifts reflect a pragmatic policy response aimed at securing improved outcomes, efficiency and innovation, founded on theories of New Public Management (Lubienski, 2009). The development of international league tables via PISA, TIMSS and PIRLS means that policymakers are now more aware than ever of how their school systems are performing. Associated studies draw on these results to try and distil the secrets of high-performing systems (Mourshed, Chijioke and Barber,

2010; Jensen et al., 2012), although such 'policy borrowing' is not without its critics (Coffield, 2012).

At another level the shift to quasi-market systems reflects a deeper change in thinking; away from seeing education as primarily a public good to seeing it as primarily a private one. According to this neo-liberal consensus, rather than valuing education because it contributes to a robust democracy, offers the chance of personal fulfilment or the advancement of knowledge, we must invest in our human capital because doing so will improve our personal and national competitiveness in a global economy (Tan, 2014). Of course, in critiquing this shift it is important to avoid romanticizing the past; a time when in many systems a small elite was highly educated, but the vast majority of children were not seen as capable of mastering anything more than the basics.

Whatever the underpinning rationale, the OECD is clear that considering when and how to grant schools autonomy while holding them accountable for their performance should be a central focus for policy (OECD, 2015). This high autonomy–high accountability model reflects evidence on the positive impact of school autonomy when coupled with accountability and capacity building measures in more developed education systems. This evidence suggests that it is school autonomy over the curriculum and pedagogical choices – as opposed to financial and human resources – that makes the greatest difference (OECD, 2011). Importantly, though, such approaches do not appear to be appropriate in all contexts. Hanushek, Link and Woessmann (2012), Di Liberto, Schivardi and Sulis (2014) and Bloom et al. (2014) all find that autonomy can have a negative impact in systems where levels of professional capacity are less developed. Suggett (2015: 17) concludes that 'school autonomy works in tandem with system capability – and it is not older style bureaucracy that is needed, but new systems that can articulate and respond to evidence-based improvement practices, and understand change management'.

This indicates the need for a sophisticated set of capabilities from those overseeing public education systems which stretch traditional conceptions of public sector governance (Burns and Köster, 2016). Particularly challenging has been how to design and implement accountability and performance management systems which provide clarity for schools, parents and government funders on what success 'looks like' and a clear assessment of whether or not schools are offering a quality service (Ehren, Perryman and Shackleton, 2014) without descending into an unhealthy 'performativity' regime (Ball, 2003). Overly tight accountability systems can flatten the very freedom and autonomy that governments want to encourage; schools can narrow learning by teaching to the test; they can look up to second guess what they think the inspectorate wants to see (rather than at the evidence base); and they can game the system through 'cream-skimming' or by massaging their exam performance through various subtle tricks (Sahlberg, 2011).

In practice, many school systems, including England, have combined school autonomy and central accountability with parallel policies on parental choice and funding-following-the-learner. These quasi-market reforms are premised on the notion that competition between schools – for students and resources – can drive improvement and innovation.

A number of studies (Glatter, Woods and Bagley, 1997) indicate that local hierarchies of schools develop in such competitive circumstances, from the most to the least popular, and it is schools in the middle of these hierarchies that face the greatest competition. Schools at different ends of these hierarchies tend to respond differently to competitive pressures, but the dominant response is for schools to try to control their intake by attracting the most 'desirable' students. This might involve anything from increasing marketing spend to developing attractive new facilities (Lubienski, 2009). As a result, the academic results of these schools are invariably higher, so they accrue ever-greater opportunities and resources which further enhance their success. Meanwhile, at the bottom of the hierarchies lie the 'sink' schools that few parents – or teachers – choose, and which are therefore the hardest to lead.

Clearly, this presents a number of challenges, most importantly the potential for increased stratification by social class and socio-economic status between schools (Gorard, 2013). A summary of research for the OECD (Waslander, Pate and van der Weide, 2010: 7) concluded that 'the effects of market mechanisms in education are small, if they are found at all'. Furthermore, the impact is often differential: some students and schools may experience positive effects while others may face the opposite, there are winners and losers. A secondary, but nonetheless existential challenge, for quasi-markets is whether competition between schools will provide the best mechanism for developing the core resource at the heart of all effective schools – high-quality teachers and leaders. The evidence on whether or not schools can equalize and supersede children's background characteristics is summarized in Gorard's (no date) reframing of Bernstein's famous 1970 article: 'Schools *can* compensate for society – a bit.' What is increasingly clear though is that it is the quality of teachers and teaching – followed by the quality of leadership – that is critical in making this 'bit' of difference, particularly for disadvantaged children (Barber and Mourshed, 2007; Sutton Trust, 2011). Developing great teachers requires strong systems for recruitment, retention and development, in which schools play a critical part by providing rich and well-scaffolded professional learning environments (Schleicher, 2011; Cordingley et al., 2015). Yet quasi-market policies can make it harder for schools to create these environments, for example, if leaders become overly focused on prescriptive accountability-driven approaches to pedagogy that militate against the development of teachers' skills and capacity. Equally, the focus on holding single schools accountable in such systems means there are few mechanisms or incentives for schools to learn from and with each other. As David Hargreaves (2010) has argued, such lateral transfers of knowledge, ideas and expertise between teachers and schools are arguably essential if they are to build their skills and capacity at scale.

These challenges partly serve to explain the policy contradictions alluded to at the start of this Introduction. Policymakers remain broadly committed to school autonomy, accountability and quasi-markets, and have some evidence to support that commitment, but they also recognize the downsides and unintended consequences that their policies produce, such as increased stratification and competition between schools. So they seek to mitigate these outcomes by either modifying the policy (for example, by increasing funding incentives for disadvantaged learners in order to reduce stratification) or by encouraging practitioners to resolve the tensions themselves.

The quest

This takes us to the second challenge, *the quest*.

School autonomy policies have placed huge power in the hands of, and pressure on the shoulders of, school leaders. They sit at the fulcrum of high-autonomy–high-accountability systems and are expected to resolve the policy paradoxes described above. So they should: exercise their autonomy to innovate in response to parental needs, while at the same time meeting centrally prescribed targets and requirements; improve literacy and numeracy scores every year, while maintaining a broad and balanced curriculum; close attainment gaps, while pushing the brightest and the best; and collaborate with their peers to develop skills and capacity, while competing to ensure that they move up the local hierarchy.

The quest is thus to understand how leaders can lead in autonomous and accountable systems in ways which recognize and resolve, or at least mitigate, the tensions that they face. Clearly, this is not about simply acquiescing in the performativity game; delivering on externally prescribed targets at the expense of children's learning and staff's wellbeing, although there are leaders who do take this approach as Ian Craig explores in his chapter on toxic leadership (Chapter 17).

Yet the opposite of toxic leadership is far from clear-cut, and so many of the chapters in this collection, in particular those in Part 2, explore different aspects of 'successful' leadership. One reason that it can be hard to distinguish 'toxic' from 'successful' leaders is that, on the surface, they both want to secure the highest possible standards of progress and attainment for all children. But whereas the 'toxic' leader may be doing this because they are fearful of the consequences of failure or because they want the personal, ego-boosting credit that comes with success, the 'successful' – or perhaps 'healthy' – leader is working within an ethical and intellectual framework that grounds their actions in a deeper moral purpose (Leithwood et al., 2006; Hopkins et al., 2014). They are focused on helping every child, whatever their background, to relish learning and to reach their potential, because this is the best chance that a child will have for a fulfilling and productive life (Chapter 7). They are rigorous in drawing on evidence in assessing the performance of the school and in addressing areas for improvement (Chapter 12). They are transformational and learning centred in their approach: able to shape a compelling vision and to enact it through a focus on constantly improving practice backed by strong organizational management (Chapters 8 and 15). They are 'good' with people and believe in the potential of any child or staff member to develop and grow, including through distributing leadership and high-quality professional learning, but this does not make them naïve: they provide challenge as well as support (Chapters 8 and 11). They are fascinated by the content and process of learning and the ways in which it can be enhanced, for staff and students (Chapters 9 and 10). They are acutely sensitive to the context of their school, and the wider context within which it operates, and they adapt their leadership to reflect that context while also working to change it, for example, by working productively with parents and other schools (Chapters 13 and 14). They are committed to the success of all children and all schools, and so think and act on behalf of all schools and as system leaders (Chapter 5). They remain optimistic, resilient, outward looking, curious, collaborative and committed to social justice, but they are also pragmatists: prepared to challenge policy where necessary, but to subvert it where that provides a better way through (Chapter 7).

Of course, this description of the skills and attributes for 'successful' leaders risks making them sound like superheroes, a notion that has been consistently discredited. As Ancona et al. (2008) have argued powerfully, all leaders are imperfect and incomplete, so it is distributed leadership across teams that makes a difference (Harris and Spillane, 2008). This includes teacher autonomy and leadership, since teachers and support staff need to feel trusted and supported if they are to develop efficacy. The role of senior leaders in such contexts is, above all, to shape the environment so that everyone in their team can and does flourish.

A further risk is that we see 'successful' leadership as inherent or finite, something that either exists or not. What is increasingly clear is that leadership agency can be shaped and grown – or diminished – by the wider context (Fullan, 2010). Leaders will quickly learn from their role models and peers whether to collaborate or compete and will respond to whether the wider framework they operate within is enabling or punitive. In systems where trust is high, where schools collaborate and share their expertise and capacity so that effective practice spreads, where leadership development and capacity building are prioritized, and where leaders have a voice in shaping policy so that they are committed to achieving shared goals, then leadership agency will be increased. By corollary, the opposite is also true, where leaders, teachers and schools are criticized and assumed to be underperforming, where they risk dismissal if the results in any given year are poor, and where they can see that the way to get on in a politicized environment is to game the system, then leadership agency will be diminished. This raises important questions about accountability and governance, including how the 'middle tier' between national policy and schools is structured and operates. These wider contextual factors are explored alongside the policy paradoxes in Parts 1 and 3.

A final theme of the book, which is addressed in Part 3, is how school leaders might respond to some of the emerging future challenges that we face in education, such as how to maximize the potential of technology, how governance and accountability systems might change to incentivize greater peer evaluation and system leadership across groups of schools, and what we can learn about the next generation of leaders in some of the world's global cities.

In summary, the focus of this book is on the paradoxes that exist in high autonomy–high accountability quasi-market school systems and the extent to which leadership can – or cannot – address these. In this sense it can be seen that the collection revolves around three core questions:

- What is the conceptual rationale for quasi-market school systems and what evidence is there of how they are developing in practice?
- How do school leaders lead in the context of high autonomy–high accountability quasi-market systems?
- What further questions, issues and potential research should we consider when we address these first two questions?

Before we outline the ways in which the different contributors approach these questions, it is worth briefly outlining the context of educational reform in England, since this provides the backdrop for most of the contributions in the book.

England's 'self-improving school system' reforms

The focus on developments in England in this collection reflects the fact that all the authors are based in, or strongly connected to, the London Centre for Leadership in Learning at the UCL Institute of Education. But the rationale for focusing on developments in LCLL's home country is more than parochial: England provides an extreme example of high autonomy–high accountability quasi-market reform while recent developments, such as the phenomenal improvements in school performance in London over the past decade (Baars et al., 2014) and the rapid expansion of independent academies and academy chains since 2010, make it a fascinating and important case study that can provide insights for policymakers, researchers and practitioners in schools and education systems around the world. This section is intended to provide a very brief overview of the key changes as a backdrop for international readers: many of the specific policies are then explored in more detail in the relevant chapters.

The education reforms since 2010, under the Conservative-led Coalition elected in 2010 and the Conservative majority government from 2015, have been radical and widespread, affecting almost every aspect of school life (Greany, 2015a). They build on more than two decades of quasi-market reforms in England, dating back to the 1988 Education Reform Act, but they take these reforms to a different level. Key changes since 2010 have included: a new National Curriculum and framework for national tests and exams; a more demanding accountability model for schools; significant changes to how teachers are recruited, trained, performance managed and rewarded; and a move towards a national funding system. Securing equity as well as excellence has been a strong theme in the government's reform, most significantly through the introduction of the Pupil Premium, which offers additional funding for each child in receipt of Free School Meals (Lupton and Thomson, 2015).

The Coalition has overseen sharp reductions in expenditure across government departments as it seeks to reduce the UK's fiscal deficit. Although education has been largely protected, it has nevertheless seen a real-terms cut, with minimal funding available for implementation of the reforms and significant reductions in funding for local authorities and national agencies. The onus has therefore been on schools themselves to respond and adapt, although this approach has arguably been driven by ideology as much as financial necessity, since a key tenet of the Coalition's 'self-improving school system' approach is that 'the attempt to secure automatic compliance with central government initiatives reduces the capacity of the school system to improve itself' (DfE, 2010: 13).

Greany (2014) suggests that there are four principles underpinning the government's approach to the self-improving system:

I   Teachers and schools are responsible for their own improvement

II   Teachers and schools learn from each other and from research so that effective prac-
      tice spreads

III   The best schools and leaders extend their reach across other schools so that all
      schools improve

IV   Government support and intervention is minimized.

Structural change has been a major feature of the reforms, increasing school autonomy through the academies programme. Academies are companies and charities that are funded directly by central government, rather than their local authority (LA). Academies have greater autonomy than LA-maintained schools: for example, they can operate their own admissions within a broad framework and are not required to follow the National Curriculum or employ qualified teachers. By early 2016 there were 5,500 academies in total, representing almost one in four schools and covering 65 per cent of all secondary schools and 18 per cent of all primaries, while the 2016 White Paper set out the government's ambition for all schools to become academies (DfE, 2016). Successful schools have been encouraged to convert voluntarily to academy status, which most have done for financial reasons. At the other end of the spectrum, schools judged to be failing by Ofsted (the schools inspectorate) have been forced to become 'sponsored academies'. This means that they are effectively taken over and run as part of a Multi-Academy Trust (MAT – or academy chain). The sponsors of these underperforming schools are increasingly likely to be successful schools which choose to form a MAT. As explored in Chapters 4, 5 and 19, academy chains have become a central feature of the system: around 58 per cent of all academies and free schools are now in a formal chain and there are thirty-nine MATs with ten or more schools, seventy-eight with six to ten schools and 517 with two to five schools (HoC Education Select Committee, 2015; Hill, 2015).

Another plank of the Coalition's structural reform approach has been to support the development of new 'free schools', Studio Schools, University Technical Colleges and University Training Schools. These new academies can be proposed and developed by parent groups and other providers that want to challenge existing provision in an area. By September 2016 there were 438 free schools open (New Schools Network, 2016).

A further innovation has been the expansion of 'system leadership' and school-to-school support, as outlined in Chapter 5. This work has consciously built on models developed during the last five years of the Labour government prior to 2010, in particular the successful London Challenge programme and the work of the former National College for School Leadership (NCSL). The rationale for school-to-school support is that credible, serving leaders and teachers are more effective in turning around struggling schools than external consultants or LA staff. School-to-school support is arguably now the primary mechanism for school improvement in England (Sandals and Bryant, 2014).

The corollary of these shifts has been a wholesale reshaping of England's middle tier, with LAs largely hollowed out but still nominally responsible for maintained schools and the emergence of a mixed economy of academy chains and DfE-appointed regional schools commissioners overseeing the academies (Greany, 2015b and Chapter 4).

Assessing progress on the Coalition's record and the self-improving system is challenging given the rapid pace and scale of change and the limited time for the reforms to bed in. The changes to the National Curriculum and associated national tests and exams have made year-on-year comparison of performance difficult. On the one hand, reports suggest that private-fee-paying schools are struggling to recruit students because the perception of state-funded schools has improved so dramatically among parents,[1] while on the other, there are reports of a 'two-tier' system developing in which strong state schools thrive but weaker ones are left struggling (Coldron et al., 2014; Earley et al., 2012) as well as significant concerns around teacher recruitment, workload and regional disparities in performance (Ofsted, 2014; DfE, 2015). The evidence that the Pupil Premium fund is proving effective in closing the gap between disadvantaged pupils and their peers is still emerging, although children on Free School Meals did improve faster than their non-FSM peers in the 2014 Key Stage 2 results (Lupton and Thomson, 2015). The 2012 PISA results suggested that England's performance against international comparators has continued to flatline (OECD, 2013).

Outline of the contributions

Part 1 focuses on the policy context for reform in high autonomy–high accountability systems and some of the emerging themes that need to be considered in policy and practice.

Kevan Collins and Robbie Coleman start in Chapter 1 by assessing the rise of evidence as a feature of school system reforms over the past few decades, asking whether this is a permanent and ineluctable shift or simply the 'next idea in line'. They argue that the outcome may be dependent on whether school leaders adopt a narrow – 'evidence for accountability' – or broader – 'evidence for improvement' – approach.

In Chapter 2 Ron Glatter poses important questions about 'leadership of and for what?', essentially probing how we conceive the core purpose of schooling. He asks whether we should see schools as 'organizations' or as 'institutions'. The former can imply that they are little more than technocratic machines, commissioned and contracted to deliver specific academic outputs. The latter emphasizes a more enduring role founded on values, educational breadth and a wider civic contribution, which may be essential if we are to maintain public trust in our education system.

In Chapter 3 Dan Gibton explores autonomy through the prism of regulation theory and democratic legitimacy. Successful regulation depends on legitimacy, deriving at root from the government's democratic mandate, but this becomes more tenuous as schools are positioned as independent contracted companies. The quasi-privatization of schooling in England has begun to shift autonomy back from the level of individual schools to the level of academy chains and regional commissioners, creating additional complexities for leaders. As a result, he argues that we have entered a third phase in the development of autonomy, passing from *naïve optimism,* to *managerialist scaffolding,* to *a crisis of legitimacy.*

Peter Matthews and Melanie Ehren map the history and current landscape of accountability reforms in England in Chapter 4, showing how this reflects wider global developments. They analyse the accountability framework for the MATs that are emerging as a central feature of England's 'self-improving' system. They show how Ofsted, England's inspection agency, has developed an increased emphasis on school self-evaluation as a basis for improvement, which has recently evolved though the development of peer review – considered in detail in Chapter 19.

Toby Greany picks up the theme of school-to-school collaboration in Chapter 5, arguing that it has become a central objective for government policy on the 'self-improving' system in England. This may seem odd, given that England is also an extreme example of quasi-market reform premised on competition, so Greany tracks the ways in which both policy and practice have evolved. There is emerging evidence that collaborative models can prove effective and he explores some of the leadership practices and characteristics that appear to be commonly involved. He concludes that the shift towards collaboration within and between hard governance federations such as MATs not only creates tensions for leaders, but also requires a rethinking of what we mean by quasi-markets once the unit of analysis shifts from the individual school to the wider chain.

Chris Brown, Chris Husbands and David Woods focus in the next chapter on Tower Hamlets, a deprived London borough that has seen phenomenal improvement in the performance of its schools since the late 1990s. They categorize the factors underpinning this success under seven headings: ambitious leadership, effective school improvement, high-quality teaching and learning, high levels of funding, integrated services, community development and partnerships, and a resilient approach to external government policies and pressure. Their conclusion is that we need to consider the features of area-based reform, not just improvement in individual schools or even school groups, since this is potentially the only way to ensure that every school improves in a system that is becoming ever more stratified.

Part 2 of the book then moves on to assess what is known about 'successful' school leadership and the issues that arise from this. In Chapter 7, David Woods and Rachel Macfarlane start by seeking to define the features of 'great' schools, arguing that these 'schools with soul' reflect a deep commitment to values and practices that go beyond the achievement of academic standards. They set out 'nine pillars of greatness' that can be seen in truly outstanding schools: shared vision, values, culture and ethos; inspirational leadership at all levels; exceptional teaching, learning, assessment and feedback; a relentless focus on engaging and involving students; personalized and highly effective continuing professional development; a stimulating and inclusive environment; a rich and creative curriculum; high-quality partnerships; and robust and rigorous self-evaluation and review.

In Chapter 8 Max Coates teases out the links and differences between vision, mission and value statements, illustrating these with examples and vignettes from real schools. He highlights the importance of culture in shaping the true nature of organizations and illustrates possible approaches to shifting culture.

Peter Earley starts by exploring the concept of leadership and its impact on educational outcomes in Chapter 9. Many definitions revolve around leadership as a process of 'influence', rather than direct positional authority, with 'values' and 'inspiration' playing a key role. Transformational, learning-centred and distributed models are consistently seen as central to successful educational leadership. The impact of this leadership on pupil outcomes remains disputed, not least because any impact is indirect, making it hard to evaluate. Earley focuses in detail on the nature and practice of learning-centred leadership, highlighting the central importance of developing people and creating a learning culture.

In Chapter 10, Toby Greany and Joanne Waterhouse focus on the leadership of curriculum improvement and innovation. They explore this in the context of the new National Curriculum introduced in England to both 'raise the bar' in terms of the academic expectations placed on children and, somewhat paradoxically, to minimize the level of prescription on schools. While there are examples of schools that are innovating their curricula, the majority appear to be taking a relatively conservative approach. The authors review the evidence on how leaders lead innovation and the conditions required. They ask why innovation is not more widespread and conclude that 'accountability trumps curriculum' as a driver of decision-making for many schools. Yet some leaders do break this mould so they explore the conditions for such agency.

Vivienne Porritt, Karen Spence-Thomas and Carol Taylor review the ways in which leaders lead professional learning and development (PLD) in Chapter 11, arguing that leaders often struggle to ensure that PLD makes a difference. They cite studies which emphasize the need for PLD designers to combine active, collaborative learning that is sustained over time and linked to follow up opportunities which apply learning in practice. Such designs also draw on external expertise, expert facilitation and formative evaluation of impact and retain a consistent focus on student learning and outcomes. Chris Brown,

Louise Stoll and David Godfrey review leadership for innovation and evidence-informed improvement in Chapter 12. They draw on notions of the 'expert' practitioner to argue that 'evidence informed practice' develops via a process of knowledge 'creation' that occurs where producers and users of formal knowledge come together to create 'new' knowledge. Such practice is arguably ever more essential in England's 'self-improving school system', and there is some evidence that schools and practitioners benefit where they adopt such approaches. The authors explore how leaders can build the capacity of practitioners to engage with research and evidence by drawing on aspects of formal organizational learning and the development of effective, quality relationships that are steeped in high levels of trust.

Kathryn Riley, in Chapter 13, and Trevor Male and Ioanna Palaiologou, in Chapter 14, all explore the ways in which leaders work within, and influence, the wider contexts of their schools. Riley draws on examples from her work on the leadership of place to ask how leaders can respond to the requirements on them to build community cohesion and to help prevent terrorism and extremism. For schools in deprived urban communities in particular, the context for this work can be fraught, characterized by acute social tensions and sometimes intense media pressure. Yet the onus is on school leaders to create safe spaces for children where they feel a sense of belonging in a fast-moving world, while also being equipped to engage critically with and change that world. Male and Palaiologou draw on a longitudinal case study of one school to explore the ways that leaders can engage families and wider communities in partnerships that support and reinforce children's learning. This is not simply about 'getting parents into school' more often, since the evidence is clear that it is at-home parental engagement that makes the difference. While practices such as engagement from the early years are clearly sensible, the secondary-school case study demonstrates that leaders can make a difference at any stage if they are adaptive and proactive in their approach and if they appreciate the power relationships involved.

Rounding off Part 2 in Chapter 15, Liz Wood draws on her own longitudinal research to explore the evolution of an important new role in England's autonomous school system, the School Business Leader or Manager. This role has become increasingly important for schools as they have taken on greater autonomy and responsibilities in areas such as budgets, human resources and estate management. The risk is that without business managers, these additional responsibilities could intensify and overwhelm the role of headteachers as leaders of learning. Yet the evolution of the new business profession has sometimes been challenging due to the need to develop a cadre of skilled professionals who can influence established cultures in schools and thereby move beyond low-level administration and into strategic roles.

Part 3 looks to the future by focusing on some of the emerging issues and challenges that leaders need to address. In Chapter 16 Domini Bingham and Sara Bubb consider wellbeing among school workforces and the key role that leadership can play. They define and analyse workload, wellbeing and stress as key interlinked factors that can impact negatively if not managed. They then assess the role of leadership in leading healthy organizations, characterized by integrity, resilience, motivation, strong role models, support, shared learning and wellbeing, illustrating this with vignettes and examples from practice.

Ian Craig's chapter on toxic leadership (Chapter 17) argues this is a minor, but nevertheless, growing phenomenon caused by the unrealistic pressures exerted on leaders in highly accountable neo-liberal systems. One outcome of these reforms has been the development of a 'cult of leadership', in which leaders are seen as the primary driver of school quality and a separate 'tribe' from teachers. The result can be a leadership style that is directive and coercive, failing to recognize the individual worth, experience and professionalism of staff. This is the opposite of all that research has shown to be effective, and while it can be hard to detect from the outside and can even lead to short-term gains in performance, it, nevertheless, becomes a poison that slowly destroys the organization. Craig is concerned that the fragmentation of the English school system is removing the controls that were previously in place to mitigate the pressures on leaders.

In Chapter 18, Mark Quinn asks – how should leaders adapt to the challenges and opportunities offered by technology? He draws on his own experience as a teacher in a north London secondary school to explore the digital world that we all, increasingly, inhabit. He describes his own school's uses of technology in five areas: teaching and learning; management of teaching and learning; management of resources; communications; and connecting to the wider education system. Yet despite vast amounts of money being spent, the evidence that technology is connected with improvements in children's learning remains mixed at best. This connects to a wider 'moral panic' that technology is rapidly degrading children's memories while growing their thumbs. Thankfully, informed commentators suggest that all is not lost, teachers do still matter and where they work thoughtfully with technology to enhance the quality of learning they can make a positive difference.

Chapter 19 addresses two important areas of policy and practice for England's self-improving system: the development of school-led networks and peer review. George Berwick and Sue John were both headteachers and key architects within the London Challenge. Through that work they pioneered two initiatives that have since become core building blocks for national policy: school-to-school support as a model for collective learning and improvement and Teaching Schools, a model for collective knowledge mobilization through school-led teacher development and evidence-informed improvement. Since the formal London Challenge programme ended they have established a national network organization – 'Challenge Partners' – that enables schools to work together through sub-regional hubs to undertake structured peer reviews as well as other knowledge-sharing activities, which they see as central to the success of a self-improving system.

Finally, in Chapter 20, Karen Edge, Sergio Galdames and Juliet Horton draw on Edge's three-year ESRC-funded study of young leaders in London, New York and Toronto to explore issues of diversity, identity and succession planning for the next generation. They provide a helpful overview of existing research on diversity in school leadership, focusing in particular on gender, race and ethnicity, where issues of discrimination overlap with challenges around work intensification, parental responsibilities, professional development and self-perception. The authors conclude that we need to broaden our conceptions of leaders and leadership if we are to capitalize on the potential of the next generation.

The volume ends with a short Postcript where the editors consider the future of leadership and education reform and in particular the intensification of leadership roles, leading the learning, and the move towards a self-improving school system.

Note

1. Headline in The Guardian '"Massively" improved state schools threaten private sector: Better behaviour and results are attracting families who can afford private school fees, says Good Schools Guide editor', 2 May 2016, http://www.theguardian.com/education/2016/feb/05/massively-improved-state-schools-threaten-private-sector (accessed 24 February 2016).

Part 1

System reform and the changing educational landscape

Chapter 1

Evidence-informed policy and practice

Kevan Collins and Robbie Coleman

Aims

This chapter aims to:

- provide an overview of the 'rise of evidence' in education
- discuss the implications of an evidence-rich system for school leaders
- present two alternative models of evidence-use in schools: *evidence for accountability* and *evidence for improvement*.

Introduction

Educational leadership is about decision-making. Given this, and the obvious corollary that school leaders' lives are affected by policy changes that alter the number of decisions they are required to make, it is natural that reforms passing responsibility for assessment, curriculum development or pay from the centre to the school commonly receive a lot of attention. Likewise, it is tempting to try to understand system change by studying leaders who are seen to have 'taken advantage' of new powers in radical ways, for example, by breaking their relationship with local education systems, innovating with technology or adjusting the length of the school day. Focusing on the parameters of decision-making enables us to conclude, for example, that English schools have become more autonomous since 2010, and judge that the variation in practice between schools has widened over this time (Greany, 2015).

An alternative analysis of educational leadership and its relationship to system change might set aside the number or type of decisions leaders are required to make, and instead focus on the manner in which leaders' decisions are made and implemented. In this chapter we take such an approach, motivated by the view that changes to the way leaders make and implement decisions – in essence the process of leadership – may have greater educational impact than structural changes that determine the range of subjects with which those decisions might be concerned. We define 'decisions' broadly, including choices that might be described as pedagogical or 'instructional' (Bendikson, Robinson and Hattie, 2012) and those affecting other types of organizational change.

We will argue that changing the process of leadership to incorporate evidence as a core component in decision-making has the potential to have a greater impact on student outcomes than any alteration to the parameters of leadership. Recognizing that it is a contested term, we define 'evidence' as knowledge generated by external research that is transparent and rigorous, for example, by using comparison groups to estimate impact (Slavin, 2002). This definition distinguishes evidence from assessment data or knowledge generated as part of the 'corporate history' of a school.

It is now commonplace to hear policymakers cite evidence as a central justification for policy choices and large numbers of school leaders state that they use evidence in their schools (e.g. NAO, 2015). The terms 'evidence-informed' or 'evidence-based' education are increasingly widely used. In this chapter, we will chart this apparent 'rise of evidence' and examine the implications of leading a school in an evidence-rich system, before assessing the likelihood that the substantial potential benefits of using evidence to support leadership are realized.

The rise of evidence

Calls for an increased role for evidence in education are not new. In 1976, British prime minister James Callaghan argued for 'a rational debate based on the facts' to help overcome the traditional fault line of 'educational freedom versus state control' (Callaghan, 1976). Two years earlier, on the other side of the Atlantic, the National Diffusion Network was established, with a mission to share information about 'exemplary [or] model programs' across the United States (Neill, 1976). What, if anything, makes the recent apparent rise of evidence different?

Most obviously, the rise of evidence in education that has occurred in recent years appears distinct because an increased demand for evidence has been met with an increased supply of high-quality research. In many countries, evidence syntheses seeking to make evidence accessible have been produced. These summaries include John Hattie's *Visible Learning* (2011), the *Best Evidence Syntheses* in New Zealand (Ministry of Education, 2015), and the *Teaching and Learning Toolkit* in England (Higgins et al., 2015). Underpinning these resources, the quantity of rigorous quantitative research conducted in schools has also increased. Connolly (2015, see Figure 1.1) estimated that in 2013 over one hundred new randomized controlled trials (RCTs) were published, compared with fewer than twenty a decade before. Organizations such as the Institute of Education's EPPI-Centre and the Campbell Collaboration have also increased the number of systematic reviews and meta-analyses being published. While education still

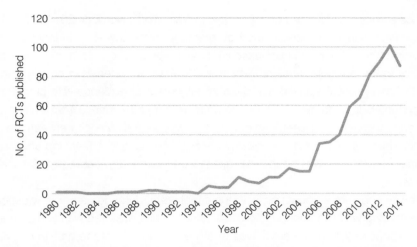

Figure 1.1 Number of randomized controlled trials in education published between 1980 and 2014. Source: Connolly, 2015.

lags well behind other disciplines in terms of the proportion of expenditure that is dedicated to research and development (NAO, 2015), the dramatic increase in the number of trials and reviews published is providing a regular stream of new knowledge to inform policymakers and professionals.

It is now beyond question that evidence can provide insights to support decision-making in schools. Where previously calls for greater evidence may have appeared abstract, concrete findings that can inform practice are being published with increasing frequency. For example, in the area of reading, at a macro level, an accumulation of evidence over many years has provided endorsement for the explicit teaching of phonics for younger readers (Higgins et al., 2015). This finding is now being supplemented by studies providing more fine-grained information about the characteristics of programmes that are effective, as well as about the necessity of combining phonics with other strategies, particular for older struggling readers (Higgins, Katsipataki and Coleman, 2014). The profession's understanding of reading is also being improved through exposure to striking individual studies that identify occasions where plausible sounding strategies have appeared to have a negative effect on learning (e.g. Maxwell et al., 2014). Evidence has also been used to challenge accepted orthodoxies, such as the idea that students who do not cross a set academic threshold should be required to repeat a year (Higgins et al., 2015), as currently occurs in Canada and some states in Australia.

In many systems, in recent years evidence has also received greater sustained political support than had previously been the case. In England, the Coalition government in power from 2010 to 2015 provided £125m of funding to establish the Education Endowment Foundation (EEF), a charity that has funded over one hundred evaluations since its launch (EEF, 2015). The Coalition also created the 'What Works Network', a coalition of organizations (of which one is the EEF) that seeks to promote the better use of evidence across several areas of public policy (What Works Network, 2014). In the United States, many trials have been funded by grants from the Investing in Innovation Fund and the Institute of Educational Sciences (IES, 2015). In addition to the dramatic increase in supply made possible by state investment, in several systems an equally important aspect of this political support has been an alignment of evidence with bureaucracies and accountability instruments. This coherence has moved evidence from a niche pursuit to the educational mainstream, and could be viewed as a difference between the recent evidence 'pushes' and previous investments such as England's Teaching and Learning Research Programme, which funded projects worth over £40m between 1999 and 2012 (TLRP, 2015).

Given its substantial impact on both the supply of and the demand for evidence, it is worth exploring why this change in political attitudes has occurred with some care. One account, popular with many advocates of evidence, holds that the growth of evidence has been inevitable. As Goldacre (2013: 7) put it: 'By collecting better evidence about what works best, and establishing a culture where this evidence is used as a matter of routine, we can improve outcomes for children.' This 'rational' argument is appealing and it is likely that for some policymakers and politicians it accurately describes their motivation to increase support for evidence. However, it does not appear to explain the timing and strength of support in all jurisdictions, and in some systems a range of more pragmatic explanations of the 'rise of evidence' are plausible. In addition, though the general trend across many systems has been towards evidence, in some countries, notably the United States (Education Week, 2015) threats to bodies responsible for generating evidence do not appear to be consistent with a straightforward account of an irreversible rise of evidence.

Most cynically, it might be argued that in some systems evidence has been reached by a process of elimination, or simply been seen as the next reform 'in line'. For example, in England, there was a marked increase in real terms in educational expenditure in the four decades to 2011–12 (Bolton, 2014), alongside radical changes to the accountability system and a range of structural and curricular reforms. However, in many areas, student outcomes remained stagnant. The attainment gap between children from rich and poor families remained stubbornly wide for many years. Thus, it is notable that the introduction of the Pupil Premium, a policy that provided additional funding for children from low-income families, has been tightly tied to the promotion of evidence. For some this is enlightened policymaking, but, uncharitably, it could be viewed as a policy of last resort.

A related explanation for increased political support for evidence might cast evidence as an *auxiliary reform*, required to enable high-autonomy or 'school-led' systems to function effectively but not valued for its own sake. From the perspective of a policymaker, for educational markets or quasi-markets to function as efficiently as possible requires participants to have access to, and the ability to use, high-quality information. This may mean creating an infrastructure that helps schools to identify which innovative practices are most likely to lead to improvements, and enables these lessons to be shared widely, with speed. Similarly, for school leaders, evidence may help fill a void created by the withdrawal of guidance or prescription from the centre that may be seen as necessary to promote school-level innovation. On this account evidence is not viewed as a necessary reform in its own right but as one that may help increase the impact of a political priority, such as the English attempt to create a 'self-improving system' (Greany, 2015).

An acceptance of alternative explanations for the political support that evidence has received in recent years could lead one to conclude that the rise of evidence is more fragile than it initially appears. Evidence might be 'next in line' but if there is a queue of other policies behind it, how long should we expect its turn to last? In many systems the existence of political factors such as a pro-autonomy consensus and the establishment of institutions that generate and promote evidence do make it unlikely that evidence will disappear quickly. But the reported threats to the Institute of Education Sciences in the United States in 2015 indicate that political support is not guaranteed to last forever. It is an open question as to how damaging the removal of support from evidence-generating institutions such as the IES might be to the pro-evidence movement. Is support wide-spread enough that evidence in education can be said to have been entrenched? Taking this line of thinking further, is it possible that maintaining political support for evidence is easier when conclusions from evidence are nascent and are not seen to challenge widely held beliefs or traditional practices?

In the next section we will examine the role of leaders in an evidence-rich system. Our contention is that the degree to which evidence will lead to any kind of long-term system change – and ultimately the extent to which it will contribute to educational improvement – will be determined by the manner in which school leaders engage with it. While it appears likely that evidence in some form is here to stay, the role that evidence should play within a system is still unclear. There is a clear difference between being an evidence-rich system and a system where evidence is a central part of day-to-day operations. Less optimistically still, it is possible to imagine systems where evidence is a mandatory part of the rhetoric, but does not lead to any educational meaningful change in the classroom.

Leadership in an evidence-rich system

In an evidence-rich system, school leaders may choose to engage with evidence in a variety of ways. Two archetypal forms of engagement might be labelled 'evidence for accountability' and 'evidence for improvement'. Which form of engagement leaders ulti-mately adopt is likely to determine the degree to which evidence genuinely contributes to system change and determine whether a meaningful role for evidence is secured in the long term.

Leaders who use evidence for accountability will view it as a tool that can help demonstrate to others that their school is fulfilling its obligations to its students. For these leaders, evidence will provide a language with which decisions can be explained and justified. Evidence will primarily be used as advertising, in the sense that it is applied to 'sell' decisions that have already been made. A school's practices may be reframed to emphasize aspects that appear to align with evidence but the practices themselves, and the leadership behaviours used to promote these practices, will remain essentially unchanged. This form of evidence-use becomes more straightforward if broad definitions of 'evidence' are used, for example, if 'evidence' is used as a shorthand term to encompass both findings from externally conducted research studies and student data generated by the school.

This portrayal of evidence for accountability is not intended to be negative. Indeed, in many education systems reacting in such a way may be a rational initial response to change. School leaders habitually use early warning signals to detect potential distractions, or to avoid investing time and effort in the latest 'fad'. Some leaders will go further and seek actively to challenge new ideas, demanding that proponents of new approaches demonstrate the value of their proposals. For others, however, a passive form of resistance through surface-level compliance will be a simpler option. Through both active and passive responses to change, leaders can serve as guardians against changes that destabilize systems without improving learning and this behaviour is particularly likely to occur in systems that have gone through periods of high turbulence and change.

The evidence for accountability approach may be pragmatic in the short term, but necessarily precludes the possibility that evidence might improve learning; clearly, practices will not become more effective as a result of being relabelled 'evidence-based' after the event. Advocates of evidence should be extremely nervous about the possibility of evidence for accountability becoming a widespread response to an evidence-rich system, and particularly cautious given that such a development would, without close inspection, appear to be a victory. The catch is that it is very difficult to agitate for change in a system when everyone purports to agree with you. A related problem occurs when genuine disagreements are impossible because they are obscured by mutations in language, as when 'evidence' is stretched to cover a wide range of practices from data use to sharing of 'best practice' and everything in between.

So what does an alternative, more positive, view of evidence-use look like? A school leader who believes evidence can support learning and school improvement would differ from one using evidence for accountability in a number of ways, affecting when, how and for what purposes evidence is used.

Most obviously, evidence for improvement requires a leader to engage with evidence throughout the decision-making process, rather than simply after the event. In this model, evidence acts as a leader's link to the outside world, both to schools within their system and further afield. It does not prescribe a specific solution to any problem but enables the leader to understand how others have sought to solve similar problems in the past, and how effectively alternative approaches have worked elsewhere. In this way evidence ties a leader to the wider profession and, notably in high-autonomy systems, reduces the likelihood that leaders are required to solve problems from first principles, or repeat strategies that have been found to be ineffective elsewhere.

Alongside turning to evidence for new ideas, a leader using evidence for improvement will recognize the ways in which evidence can support their own innovation. Education is an innovation-rich profession and teachers spend much of their time developing and honing materials and practices as they search for new ways to engage and motivate learners. The development of online platforms to share learning resources (TES, 2015) reveals the huge levels of creativity in the profession as well as its willingness to share and collaborate. The role of evidence in this process comes in supporting 'informed innovation' that explicitly seeks to build on the best available knowledge from research. 'Innovation' here can refer to both the generation of new knowledge and the development of a better understanding of how to implement strategies that have appeared to be effective elsewhere in a new context.

A further difference between a school leader engaging in evidence for improvement and another using evidence for accountability is the leaders' attitude to failure. A leader using evidence for improvement will be aware that a previous record of effectiveness can never guarantee future success, and prepare on the basis of this fact. An evidence-informed decision-making process gives power to leaders by providing the strongest justification for practices that they have investigated, implemented and found to be effective. But exceptions are necessary to prove the rule, and it is necessary for some innovations to be found to fail. A leader who uses evidence for improvement will be able to answer the question: 'How will you know if it doesn't work in your school?' Engaging with this question is important because it is based in a recognition of the necessity of pairing evidence with professional judgement. A common straw man against evidence plays on the distinction between education and other fields where evidence-use is widespread, most commonly health. It is pointed out that context matters, that not every approach works in every classroom, and that an evidence-based strategy in a school is not a pill with a guarantee. However, such an argument misunderstands how evidence in education is created, and underplays the active role the school must play in implementing and monitoring any innovation. Embracing this professional challenge, and taking ownership of the process of change, is essential for a leader using evidence for improvement.

A final necessity for leaders seeking to make evidence a central part of their decision-making process is a recognition that evidence cannot trump personal, professional or institutional values. A challenge to evidence advocates runs that evidence will diminish the opportunity for schools to develop their own ways of doing things and replace local determination with non-negotiable knowledge. Particularly in high-autonomy systems, where a diversity of school type and ethos is actively promoted, some leaders may be concerned that evidence will act as an unhelpful constraint. However, the nature of evidence in education should offer comfort to those with these concerns. The better use of evidence is consistent with an appreciation of schools developing a clear and well-articulated set of values. Rather than diminishing the importance of values, an evidence-informed approach presents new options and reveals the obligation to consider 'value judgments' as part of decision-making. For example, the evidence on setting students by prior attainment is challenging (Higgins et al., 2015). On the one hand, gathering children with higher levels of attainment together to create a 'top set' can be beneficial for this group. However, for low-attaining children setting has historically seen them achieve less well than they otherwise would have. This evidence presents a question about maximizing outcomes for the academic elite against securing progress for all students. Thus, the better use of evidence supports open debate and enables leaders to act in ways that are consistent with the values of their institution.

A choice for school leaders

In England, it is notable that policymakers and many schools have turned to evidence to support efforts to narrow the gap between students from low-income families and their peers (NAO, 2015). For leaders in these schools, evidence is viewed as a means to pursue the goal of a more equitable system. Evidence matters because they are aware of the magnitude of this challenge, and believe that it offers a more promising path than alternatives such as changing school structures or accountability arrangements in ways that have been prioritized in the past.

In this chapter we have documented the rise of evidence and noted that in many systems there currently exists a political and institutional consensus in favour of evidence that makes it easier than before for leaders to turn to evidence. However, we have presented a cautious view about the causes and security of this rise, both from the perspective of policymakers and practitioners. We have also argued that in part as a result of the consensus in favour of evidence that currently exists, it is entirely possible to imagine systems that adopt a veneer of evidence beneath which pedagogical and leadership practices remain entirely unchanged.

To go deeper, and create systems that fully embrace evidence as a tool that contributes to improvements in learning will not be easy. The ambition of positioning evidence at the heart of the education system to inform and guide the work of school leaders transcends the usual surface-level managerial adjustments and requires the development of new skills and knowledge within the leadership community. To achieve the prize of a truly evidence-informed system will require a significant personal commitment and engagement on the part of school leaders, the challenge of which should not be underestimated. Ultimately, however, it is this commitment that will determine whether evidence contributes to a new model of system change and genuine improvement in the classroom.

Implications

- What new skills do school leaders require to adopt an 'evidence for improvement' approach?

- How can policymakers ensure that evidence-informed demand from schools is met by high-quality supply? What mechanisms exist to ensure that educational research is relevant to schools and that actors in the educational market respond to evidence?

- In many systems policies to promote evidence have been tightly tied to policies promoting school autonomy. Do school leaders feel confident enough to follow the evidence, even when it means acting in ways that might be regarded as radical?

Chapter 2

Schools as organizations or institutions: Defining core purposes

Ron Glatter

Aims

This chapter aims to address the following questions:

- What are the practical implications of regarding schools and colleges as institutions as well as organizations?
- Are there substantial differences depending on which concept is preferred?
- How does this debate relate to the core purposes of schools?

This is not an erudite semantic exercise. As Lumby and English (2010: 1) have pointed out: 'Language and leadership are inseparable. Leaders traffic in language. It is language that defines problems and solutions.'

Conceptions of 'institution'

A particularly strong defence of the idea of educational *institutions* was mounted by Peter Scott in 1989. He argued that bodies concerned with education lead a double life in being both administrative and moral entities and that too much attention had been concentrated on the first of those aspects. Given that he was writing more than a quarter of a century ago, one might observe that the administrative aspect has gained ever more prominence since then, at least in a number of countries including England. An education is about more than what happens in the classroom or lecture theatre, Scott claimed. He contrasted what he called the 'public life' of institutions, as demonstrated through performance indicators, external audits and the like, with their 'private lives', 'how they work to educate people, how they successfully transmit social and cultural values, how they model the conduct of modern society' (Scott, 1989: 22). This was closely aligned to one aspect of the institution's public responsibility, which Scott termed its cultural responsibility: 'The allegiance to rationality, truth and knowledge, which all those in education must accept … . For without this primary responsiveness education would be truly a dead world. Its external utility is rooted in its internal validity, its private integrity' (Scott, 1989: 20).

Scott's formulation reflects the position of Philip Selznick who initiated institutional theory (1957, 1996). He saw institutions as infused 'with value beyond the technical requirements of the task at hand… . Values do have a central place in the theory of institutions' (Selznick, 1996: 271). This seems particularly relevant to schooling. Despite a recent strong emphasis in England and some other countries on performance indicators, particularly test and exam results, it remains the case that moral, social and cultural issues lie at the heart of education (Starratt, 2007).

In an essay Anthony Painter has argued that institutions are bodies that mediate between public and private interest and so have multiple purposes whereas organizations, such as profit-motivated enterprises, have single purposes. Nevertheless, it is not a simple public–private issue in his view as some companies, for example, co-operatives, social enterprises and 'those firms that have strong constitutional arrangements to serve the public interest have an institutional form, but not all companies are institutions' (Painter, 2014: 40). An institution must 'balance public and private values, yet still act with purpose' and must see itself not as separate from those it serves but 'a space where many different interests can interact and create new collective value' (ibid., 41). This requires a culture of openness, transparency, accountability and inclusiveness.

Commonly the notion of 'institution' is perceived to refer particularly to the most prestigious organizations in their fields, such as schools or universities at the top of their respective 'pecking orders'. However, such a limitation does not appear necessary – the designation should relate to *purposes* rather than perceived status.

Broadening the base

An educational vision that is consonant with this approach is that of 'citizen schools' as propounded by a group of authors in a publication produced by the think-tank, the Institute for Public Policy Research (IPPR). In their view a citizen school 'explicitly creates a democratic culture through its role as a civic institution'. Citizenship should 'be at the heart of the school as an institution'. All the constituencies related to such a school – typically students, staff, parents and the community – will make up a collective participatory democracy, but the powers of these groups need not be equal: 'There are powers that a headteacher and governing body must hold and enact as agents of the state, just as there will be powers that a civic community must claim themselves – this will inevitably be a balance that is constantly negotiated' (Audsley et al., 2013: 13–14).

In similar vein, Tinker (2015) proposes that publicly funded schools should be regarded as 'public interest institutions' founded on a principle of 'shared ownership' in which citizens, employees and all other stakeholders 'have a sense of belonging and control' (11). This requires inclusive democratic and participative forms of decision-making and hence 'a collegiate or shared model of leadership' (12). It goes beyond 'transactional forms of empowerment: market choice can only ever provide a thin form of power, based on choice and exit' (14). The reference to 'public interest' indicates that such institutions have purposes not just for themselves and 'their' students: they also have a wider remit in relation to their local communities and society as a whole.

Such formulations emphasizing democratic processes would not apply to all types of educational bodies that might be regarded as institutions, although it is highly relevant to the recent substantial growth in the number of co-operative schools in England (Woodin, 2015). Categories of institution unlikely to display that emphasis might include prestigious private schools, faith schools and many universities. As suggested earlier a key feature of an institution appears rather to be the commitment to a set of values *beyond* the transmission of knowledge and skills, whether these values relate to democracy, rationality and truth, the tenets of a faith, a distinct ethos or something else. Institutions embody wider educational purposes than are susceptible to the aggregation of measures of academic achievement, and in addition there is an element of continuity – a degree of protection from the instability associated with the market approach and its attendant disruptive effects.

This broader conception appears to have some international resonance. In a survey within the OECD's Programme for International Student Assessment (PISA), parents in eleven countries across three continents were asked what criteria they considered important when choosing a school for their child (OECD, 2015). Factors related to the quality of the school as an institution – reputation, climate and safety – were ranked more highly than academic achievement and this ranking was fairly stable across countries.

There are some indications that this broader view is reasserting itself and that the recent heavy emphasis on output-oriented or 'results-based legitimacy' (Woods and Simkins, 2014: 334) may be being questioned, even in policy circles in England. In late 2014 the Department of Education published guidance on promoting 'British values' in schools (DfE, 2014c). This was prompted by the so-called 'Trojan Horse' events in Birmingham where there were claims that some schools were taken over by groups with a radical Muslim agenda. The government's promotion of 'British values' proved controversial with a number of faith and other groups: for example, there was concern that the public discourse around the issue implied 'that a central purpose of teaching British values is to control and regulate young Muslims rather than to empower them' (Richardson, 2015: 45). The policy was also criticized on the grounds that the values identified, such as individual liberty, the rule of law and mutual respect and tolerance are not exclusively British. There have also been questions about whether it is appropriate for the government to prescribe or recommend the teaching of specific values (see for example Garner, 2015a). However, the episode did signal a move away from the strong official focus on academic results as the bedrock of schools' legitimacy.

Separately, there have been indications that personal attributes other than academic excellence were being given more serious attention by policymakers. During 2015, both the largest political parties in England proclaimed their commitment to 'character education' and, in particular, the attributes of grit and resilience (see, for example Adams, 2015). A plea to change the national inspection framework so that it focused as much on 'the development of key attitudes and behavior as on the more traditional academic measures' was made by a leading spokesman for the business community (see Garner, 2015b).

There are also signs of growing academic interest in this general area. The University of Birmingham, which has a specialist centre devoted to studying it, has produced a research report on character education in the UK (Arthur et al., 2015). One of the findings was that, in a survey of 255 teachers in schools across the UK, 80 per cent stated that the current assessment system 'hinders the development of the whole child'. The pervasiveness of exams was perceived to have crowded out other educational goods such as the development of moral character.

There are contentious issues here. The emphasis on 'grit and resilience' in policy circles has come under fire from some critics, who see it as an attempt to prepare people to accommodate themselves to the vicissitudes of a neo-liberal, globalized world order rather than to challenge it (see for example Evans and Reid, 2014). The Birmingham University report acknowledged this debate by distinguishing between moral and performance virtues and arguing that 'politicians and policy-makers should recognize that moral virtues such as honesty, kindness and courage are just as important as performance virtues such as resilience, self-confidence and grit' (Arthur et al., 2015: 27).

The concerns extend beyond issues of character and moral education. A study commissioned by the National Union of Teachers found that increased pressure from tests and exams and the growing academic demands of the curriculum were causing 'increasingly high levels of school-related anxiety and stress, disaffection and mental health problems' among children and young people (Hutchings, 2015: 5). A series of studies commissioned by the British Cabinet Office together with other bodies has highlighted:

- The importance of developing young people's social and emotional skills for success and satisfaction in later life
- the inequalities in these skills between children growing up in different backgrounds
- the great variability in such provision in England currently (Feinstein, 2015).

Public and other realms

The set of developments just discussed relating to democratic processes, character and moral development and the promotion of wellbeing arguably emphasize what might be called the institutional qualities of schooling as distinct from an orientation preoccupied with the measurement of outputs. Nevertheless, as Stewart Ranson suggests in his analysis of the contemporary tension in England between community and corporate governance of schools, the dominant orthodoxy appears to be that 'the model of corporate business provides the best model for school governance' (Ranson, 2012: 38). The transfer of governance, particularly in the academies programme,[1] from civil society to self-governing trusts has placed the emphasis upon private interests, such as the personal ambitions of an individual sponsor, rather than public ones. The result is likely to be a public education that has a random and arbitrary nature arising from 'the interested decisions of a corporate club or association' (ibid.: 43).

As Higham (2014) indicates, this type of development brings to the fore the question of who owns our publicly funded schools. This is an issue that has recently been taken up in a wider context by the political philosopher David Marquand. He distinguishes between three elements in society: the public realm which 'is the realm of service, equity, professional and public duty, as opposed both to the market realm of buying and selling and the private realm of love, family and friendship'. The public realm is, in his view, 'a gift of history, precious but also vulnerable... . We demean ourselves if we try to shuffle off that primordial responsibility onto others' (Marquand, 2014: 96–8). Yet the boundaries of the public realm shift over time and are constantly subject to argument and persuasion. Moreover, those boundaries are hazy. Marquand cites the example of barristers, who are market traders yet have public duties to the courts. He considers that in recent years 'the attrition of the public realm has speeded up' and that when ministers speak of the need to 'reform' the public services they mean that public institutions such as schools and universities 'should be managed as if they were private firms' (ibid.: 119–20).

Perhaps of most relevance for our discussion about institutions is the importance Marquand attributes to public trust: 'Citizens will trust their leaders if they think public institutions are governed by an ethic of equity and service... . But if the public realm succumbs to invasion by the market or private realms ... citizenship becomes an empty shell and public trust withers' (ibid.: 103). This is particularly significant in light of the evidence Marquand cites indicating that the level of public trust in Britain has fallen dramatically over the last fifty years, to a far greater extent than in many comparable countries.

Positive and negative connotations

The role of trust in relation to the idea of institutions may be illustrated by referring to bodies outside education. For example, in the commercial world it was reported that when members of the British public were asked which of thirteen well-known businesses they would trust to take care of their accounts if the firms moved into personal banking, all but one achieved thirty per cent or less support. The odd one out, John Lewis, scored more than three-quarters (77 per cent). John Lewis is a long-standing company of high repute, which is fully owned by its staff and has a fair claim to be considered an institution (Jones and Treanor, 2014). Another body which receives high scores for trust in public opinion polling is the British Broadcasting Corporation (BBC) which is also generally regarded as an institution (BBC, 2013).

However, the idea of institution can also carry negative connotations. Selznick (1996: 271) insisted that institutionalization is 'at bottom ... a neutral idea' and that leadership had a major responsibility to monitor its costs as well as its benefits. At the end of the 1980s, Peter Scott (1989) pointed out that radicals of both the left and right had tended to be dismissive of institutions, the left regarding them as stiflingly bourgeois and the right seeing them as arthritic and bureaucratic – critiques that are possibly not very dissimilar from each other. Moreover, even though stability and continuity could be beneficial educationally, there is an important debate to be had about how far the idea of institution is consonant with today's fast-paced world. In addition, 'institution' seems to imply a stand-alone school or college whereas a striking feature of recent years, at least in England, has been the formation of chains and federations made up of individual units working closely together (Chapman, 2015).

Multiple levels

The strand of analysis known as new institutional theory has a bearing on this discussion. This perspective 'enables us to understand how social choices are moulded and channeled by the institutional environment' (Lamothe and Denis, 2007: 60). A key concept here is *isomorphism,* the process of homogenization by which powerful forces in the environment cause organizations working in particular fields to become similar to one another (Dimaggio and Powell, 1983). One major influence is of course professional norms but in addition, 'all organisations operating within a common political regime are drawn toward standard practices that correspond to the political pressures and formal regulations produced by the regime' (Mitchell, 1996: 174).

A leading exponent of this approach, W. Richard Scott, has emphasized that this does not mean that organizations such as schools and colleges are unable to follow a distinctive path, and, indeed, in England and other countries policymakers have put much emphasis on the idea of enhancing autonomy, though whether there has actually been an increase in autonomy – and if so over what functions – is highly debatable (Glatter, 2012). It means simply that we need to be constantly aware of institutional context, of the 'meso-level systems that mediate between societal structures and individual organizations' (Scott, 2001: 207) and of the complex interplay between organizations and their environments.

In a striking passage, he remarks that there are multiple levels 'each constraining and empowering the other. And social structures themselves are nested, groups within organizations or networks of organizations, organizations within fields, fields within broader societal and trans-societal systems' (ibid.: 209). This fact of multiple levels requires the governors and staff of a school or college to determine its core identity, whether as an organization or an institution, according to their preferences but also by reference to the context within which it is 'nested', to use Scott's metaphor. That context includes the incentives and sanctions devised to persuade schools and colleges to act in specific ways, for instance, through the medium of inspection processes (Bell and Stevenson, 2015). So if the incentives and sanctions change, for example, by placing a greater stress on values beyond the transmission of knowledge and skills, something that as discussed earlier may now be happening in England, this could significantly affect the core identities of individual schools and colleges.

Issues and implications

The idea of institution perhaps implies that schools and colleges are more than just machines for achieving specific academic targets in the form of predetermined pass-rates and the like, an impression that policymakers have sometimes given. And yet we need to be cautious. Whether they are seen primarily as institutions or organizations, they must balance different and often competing expectations. It can be a fragile balance. The expectation for academic effectiveness is of course entirely legitimate even if it some-times appears too dominant. Moreover, as I have pointed out elsewhere (Glatter, 2006), the contemporary 'image problem' associated with the term 'organization' is somewhat accidental. To many people it has a strong mechanistic flavour and carries a sense of impersonality closely associated with the negative modern connotations of 'bureau-cracy'. This interpretation is paradoxical as the word's etymological link is with organism rather than mechanism, and much research on organizations conveys a more dynamic picture. The contemporary image probably owes a great deal to *The Organization Man*, the bestselling study of the perceived corrosive effects of the post-war corporate culture on the lives of American men (as they mostly were), published by the sociologist William H. Whyte in the 1950s (Whyte, 1956). The image has largely stuck, at least when the term is used to describe an entity rather than an activity, although I have argued and continue to maintain 'that nothing worthwhile on any scale can be achieved without organization' (Glatter, 2006: 71).

It was suggested earlier that a key distinguishing feature of an educational *institution* is a commitment to a set of values beyond the inculcation of knowledge and skills. I have not sought to deal directly here with the crucial issues of what values and whose values, since that would require a lengthy treatise, but two related issues are worth mention-ing. First, in England there has been a significant and unprecedented development of 'governance by contract' (Feintuck and Stevens, 2013) whereby a substantial proportion of schools funded by the taxpayer are contracted out under the academies programme by the secretary of state to an extremely diverse range of third parties via so-called 'fund-ing agreements'. This has placed increased focus on the process of 'commissioning' the provision of schooling. Such a process is likely to emphasize the specification and achievement of 'technical' standards rather than the less tangible, institutional qualities that have been discussed here, which may either atrophy or take controversial forms. Indeed, Selznick saw 'the intrinsic conflict between the premises of contract and those of association' as a major theme of his path-breaking work on institutions: 'The logic of contract runs up against the logic of sustained cooperation' (Selznick, 1996: 272).

Second, as is well attested in research on educational leadership and management, statements of intent by themselves achieve little. A relentless focus on implementation is crucial: as Thomas Edison is reputed to have warned 'Vision without execution is hallucination.' This is much easier said than done. There may well be good reasons for promoting a core identity as an institution. As Puusa, Kuittinen and Kuusela (2013: 165) point out in an insightful article about the construction of identity, 'A shared identity can be seen as a precondition for organized collective action' but, in fact, building a shared, coherent narrative is challenging: different sub-groups tend to have very different perceptions because modern professional organizations are generally 'loosely coupled' systems (Orton and Weick, 1990). So Puusa, Kuittinen and Kuusela (2013: 170) suggest it may be 'unrealistic to assume that members of an organization have a single coherent identity in today's kaleidoscopic organizational settings' and that assumption is particularly problematic when facing constant change because, as was suggested earlier, institutional identity requires an element of stability and continuity. However, as Leithwood et al. (2006: 11) pointed out in their review of research on successful school leadership: 'Stability and change have a synergistic relationship. While stability is often associated with resistance and maintenance of the status quo, it is difficult to leap forward from an unstable foundation.' So it makes sense for leaders to seek as much coherence as possible because 'an organization's identity is fractured when there are contrasting interpretations of what is central and distinctive to it' (Puusa, Kuittinen and Kuusela, 2013: 176).

Conclusions

In summary, conceiving schools and colleges as institutions would serve to emphasize the role of values (Hammersley-Fletcher, 2015), promote breadth in education and prioritize continuity over frequent mandated and often weakly justified structural changes and other 'reforms'. Whether you subscribe to the concept is likely to depend on how far your personal beliefs, and the collective preferences within your school or college, match these directions of travel, taking into account the expectations of your stakeholder groups, the constraints set by the wider context and the opportunities it offers.

A significant refinement of the concept is that of the 'civic institution', which arguably might apply to all publicly funded schools and colleges, and which, in addition to the other suggested hallmarks of institutions just mentioned, would acknowledge responsibilities beyond its own students to its local community and wider society and would demonstrate a strong commitment to democratic processes in its decision-making.

The issue addressed in this chapter relates to the core purposes of education, and hence of educational leadership. Starratt (2007: 182) has argued that those who practice and those who study educational leadership must always ask themselves the question 'Leadership of and for what?... Without a clear answer to that question, then all the research and theory and discourse about distributed and sustainable leadership, about restructuring and reculturing, about capacity building and professional development, will not make what goes on in schools right.'

Implications

- From your experience, is the distinction made between organizations and institutions a valid and significant one?
- How practicable is it to achieve a coherent and recognizable institutional identity within a school?
- Can the control of a civic institution legitimately be transferred from civil society to a third party through a commissioning and contracting process? Do such processes delegitimize citizen stakeholders, including parents and pupils, who are not party to the contract?

Note

1. See Introduction for a description of academies.

Chapter 3

Regulation, governance of education and the oversight of autonomous schools

Dan Gibton

Aims

School and school leaders' autonomy and empowerment have been at the heart of the debate on education policy since the 1980s. This chapter focuses on the regulation and governance aspects of autonomy. While school and headteacher autonomy exemplify educators' empowerment, the literature questions whether such empowerment might widen gaps between schools that are unable to muster autonomy and those that find it easier to succeed. The main aims of the chapter therefore are to:

- explore autonomy through the prism of regulation theory and democratic legitimacy
- position autonomy as a finite source, perhaps not unlike energy and matter.

Autonomy, school reform and policy analysis

Autonomy in education is a complex and multidimensional term. As Bolam (1993) noted in the early days of decentralization – the dimensions of autonomy: *to whom* is it delegated, in *what areas* and *in what depth and scope*, remain the cornerstones of this debate, and as time goes by, it reshapes and restructures repetitively. This is because autonomy in education is not, solely, a within-school or pedagogic process, but a deep cultural change that is linked to major cultural, political and economic fundamentals. It is impossible to talk of schools' autonomy without addressing the much wider phenomena of globalization and the globalized economy (Plank and Keesler, 2009; Stoll and Stobart, 2005), neo-liberal governance and the spread of neo-liberal philosophy and practice (Ball, 2007). That said, the role and influence of these streams, both of thought and of culture, politics and finance, are not uniform, and are sometimes incongruous to each other. In practice, the justifications and incentives for school autonomy, while derived from contradictory fields of thought, all push this rudimentary change forward. Idealistic interpretations of autonomy of the individual and the community (Higham, 2013) coincide with theories of choice (Berends, Cannata and Goldring, 2011; Raday Ben-Porath, 2010) and markets (LeGrand, 2005) and also correspond with theories on efficiency, by placing powers within the end unit – that is, the school. Research on educational leadership has also emphasized empowerment of headteachers, again from various streams of thought and empirical research that might clash epistemologically and empirically, but converge unidirectionally, towards decentralization and placing the locus of decision-making within the hands of school leaders. Again, these represent a plethora of theories and research, ranging from ideas from business administration (Heifetz, 2002), to pedagogical theories of placing responsibilities in the hands of educators (Darling-Hammond, 2010).

Present-day theories of policymaking shun linear, 'neat', rational, top-down processes, for 'messy', haphazard models (Kennedy, 1999) that have not resulted from theorization but from empirical observations of policymaking. Kingdon's (2003) now archetypal theory of policy change challenged pre-existing models of linear and rational policymaking. He built his work on the 'garbage can' classic model developed by Cohen and March (1972), which compared policymaking to a muddled process of throwing various ideas, with no discernible order, into an imaginary 'garbage can', and pulling them out at random. According to Kingdon, three prerequisite conditions are the stem of policy change, titled *Problems, Policies and Politics*. By *problems,* Kingdon refers to a misfortune, or shortcoming, that amounts to circumstances in which the public is willing to make a sacrifice to amend or remedy the situation; 'sacrifice' meaning funding or some minimizing of rights or privileges. The second condition is a *policy*, that is, an idea on how to change the situation or redress the shortcoming. This suggested solution need not promise the requested change, but it suffices that people who identify the *problem* perceive the *policy* as a possible solution. The third condition is *politics*, that is, that the problem and the suggested policy can assemble the necessary political scaffolding to overcome hindrances, for example, fears, turf wars and conflicting interests. According to Kingdon, it requires convergence of these three factors: *problems*, *policies* and *politics,* for policy change to occur.

McLendon, Cohen-Vogel and Wachen (2015) broaden Kingdon's work and link it to other theories of public policy, through three further models: *Punctuated Equilibrium* (PE) theory, *Advocacy Coalition Framework* (ACF), and *Policy Innovation and Diffusion* (PID) theory. According to the PE model, policy advances through periods of equilibrium where power games among subsystems result in stasis, and periods of disequilibrium, when 'policy monopolies are changed or overthrown' (ibid: 93). The ACF framework evolves around subsystems based on a three-tier hierarchical structure of beliefs (deep core, policy core and secondary beliefs, ibid: 96) which interact with new information and policy to bring about change. The PID theory is about how an innovative policy is diffused by one subsystem from another.

Governance, regulation and governmentality

The discussion of regulation is seldom focused on its role in achieving social justice and guarding *public interest* (Feintuck, 2010; Ogus, 2004; Yeung, 2010). Regulation is more often adopted by *private choice*-driven advocates, as a means to correct market failures.

> Regulation is the promulgation of rules accompanied by mechanisms for monitoring and *enforcement*. … Government is the rule maker, monitor and enforcer, usually operating through a public agency. The second definition keeps to the government as the 'regulator' but broadens the techniques that may be described as 'regulation' to include any form of direct state intervention in the economy… . In the third definition, regulation is all mechanisms of social control or influence affecting behavior. (Black, 2001: 20)

Yeung (2010) poses the regulatory state as a contradiction and opposition to the welfare state. The regulatory state is manifested in the New Public Management (NPM) model that first separates delivery of public services (i.e. running schools and employing staff) from commission (i.e. the organization of the system on a local or national level, enrolment policy, types of schools, etc.), and later (Gibton, 2013; Higham, 2013) separates commission from government as well, creating semi-privatized middle-tier organizations, (e.g. chains, federations) that replace elected local authorities. Yeung points to the disadvantages of political influence on regulation, which are inevitable, while recognizing that this same political influence serves as a legitimizing factor of regulation. Legitimacy *is the essence of regulation of education*. Strike (2003) discusses the role of legitimacy in education policy. He distinguishes between 'objective legitimacy' – the obvious ingredient of a legislative process (Gibton, 2013) in a parliamentary democracy such as England – and 'subjective legitimacy' that evolves in the hearts and minds of citizens and educators. Legitimacy, Strike explains, is often mistaken for economic or organizational efficiency. Yeung (2010: 78), in turn, develops this idea of legitimacy and divides the term into three categories.

> Input-legitimacy concerns the extent to which citizens have opportunities to participate in decision making; throughout legitimacy concerns certain qualities of the rules and procedures by which binding decisions are made including how collective decisions are realized in the absence of consensus, the quality of participation in decision-making, and the institutional checks and balances to guard against the abuse of power; and output legitimacy which concerns the capacity to produce outcomes that contribute to the remedying of collective problems and the extent to which decision makers are accountable.

Veljanovski (2010) refers to state legislative power as a monopoly and as its major regulatory tool. This opens the debate on the need to insulate regulatory mechanisms from political influence, by placing them in the hands of professional autonomous organiz-ations. Such a buffer might strip regulation of democratic legitimacy, and minimize the possibilities for interest groups to become involved in decision-making and the design of regulatory aims, methods and preferred results and outcomes, as well as discussion on further policy ramifications.

Perhaps a possible defence against this harmful aspect of regulation is that school autonomy enhances localization of education, and autonomous schools often rely on and seek community support that strengthens legitimacy of the school and its leaders, both within the immediate community and in the eyes of the middle and national tiers that regulate education.

Regulation, policy theory and autonomy

The takeover by neo-liberal regimes in the late 1980s in England (Whitty, 2008; Ball, 2007), and around that time in other countries, created uneasiness in terms of equity and equality, segregation and inclusion in school reform. Classic models of public education, commissioned and provisioned by national or local government (Boyd, 2003), seemed to run short of delivering on the public's expectations, hence policies of decentraliza-tion and empowering of school leaders seemed like reasonable solutions. The politics of neoliberalism and new-right regimes supported such change as part of their ideas on privatization and minimizing government involvement in public services (Ball, 2007; Levin, 2015; Whitty, 2008). These changes brought about school and headteacher autonomy that has gone through various stages and developments to this day, and can be described as transitioning through three broad phases. The first period of *naïve optim-ism* (circa 1985–98) that focused on the belief that once powers sat in the professional hands of headteachers and school staff, who are committed to improving results and serving the local community, most of the problems of schooling would be resolved. This period was followed by a period of *managerialist scaffolding* (1998–2010) and neo-lib-eral rhetoric, in which management theories, informed by the involvement of international consultancy firms, including through training programmes outsourced by the government (Earley et al., 2012), focused the core of school management on legal, financial, and organizational concerns (Gibton, 2013) and less on instructional and pedagogical lead-ership, despite researchers' calls to focus on these. Entrepreneurship was encouraged, flagged and hailed during this period, which also brought changes in school structures and the establishment of new types of schools that emphasized these traits, for example, specialist schools and city technology colleges, and finally, city academies. The third period can be described as a period of *crisis of legitimacy* in which it became clear from whatever ideological standpoint – whether social-democratic or neo-liberal – that a school cannot stand alone, not in terms of intake, not in terms of professional support and not in terms of finance. After two decades of weakening LA control over the deliv-ery and commissioning of schooling, and disenchantment with various models such as regional control, the chains and federations of academies created in England since 2010 may or may not provide the necessary middle tier, both professionally and politically, to support schools. However, such professional and political scaffolding may suffice organizationally, but it does not necessarily confer legitimacy on the wider system and may actively reduce such legitimacy, particularly where serious conflicts of interest have been identified (Greany and Scott, 2014).

After three decades of decentralization, the search for legitimacy remains a key focus for school autonomy and school leaders' empowerment. The new, current, middle tier in England, represented by organized groups of schools (academy chains and federations), does not seem to provide the necessary *output* legitimacy and *subjective* legitimacy that will link public education to schools. The public support for headteachers' authority, being servants as well as proxies of the public, might not be sustained when heads report to corporate-style chains and federations, run by a maze of commissioners and providers of education services, in which they have sometimes spent their entire career and even received their professional training.

Dean's (2010) breakthrough work on governmentality – the way we think about government – defines government 'as the conduct of conduct' in which 'the one governed is, at least in some rudimentary sense, an actor and therefore a locus of freedom' (ibid: 21). Government is 'an activity that shapes the field of action and that, in that sense, attempts to shape freedom' (ibid). This concept is therefore useful for examining the ongoing state of educational decentralization. The 'messier' models of policy-shaping as offered by Kingdon and by McLendon et al., combined with Dean's governmentality, show that educational leaders' viewpoints and feelings about autonomy, shape, in turn, government policy, both directly, through advice and consultancy of 'superheads' (Gibton, 2013; Earley, 2013) and groups of leading heads; and indirectly, through the solidifying of a cohort of the same headteachers who run large secondary-level academies and/or free schools. These 'leading leaders' become the focus of media and public interest and champions of change, innovation and success, whether evidence based or assumed faddism.

Headteachers' views on government, whether as a critical friend, owner and operator of schools, as a source of democratic legitimacy or as a regulator, shape their understanding and therefore their actions. These actions include moving the school into 'charter type' (academy, free) status and further by enrolling as sub-units within a chain or federation, owned and run by a business, a third or fourth sector organization, for example, a denomination or other type of non-government or non-public entity. The shifting landscape changes the vocabulary and feasible choice of models and reactions. Thus 'superheads' who criticized academies fiercely in 2006 became heads of such schools by 2011 and chief executives of chains, federations or their training facilities by 2015 (Woods, Woods and Gunter, 2007; Gibton, 2013).

However, the principal assertion of this chapter is that there is a delicate balance between the levels, scopes and areas of decentralization offered earlier by Bolam (1993). Autonomy can be compared to energy – a finite reservoir, leading to a situation where autonomy is no endless resource to be distributed among the various levels in various areas and various degrees of scope according to the distributor or present bearer of power. An additional interesting question is from whom autonomy is taken, what degree is minimized, what scope is narrowed and finally, who grants it. The finite quality of autonomy determines that solidifying the autonomy of one type of actor, or system tier, results in reducing that of others. The empowerment of headteachers may, therefore, have been developed at the expense of the autonomy of LAs, the immediate next upper level, and perhaps also of teachers, the immediate subordinates. This is also an issue of proximity and of scale. The capability of government to interfere with the work of a single teacher is much less than that of a headteacher. Moving into policy areas of inclusion, and multicultural education, weakens LAs, as does organizing schools into chains and federations. Therefore, mapping the subtractions of autonomy becomes a vital role of research, no less than studying the additions and progressions of empowerment. The gradual shift of school leaders into what Hopkins (2005) labelled as 'system leadership' raises the question of what part of the system is now less powerful, less influential, in what areas and to what degree or scope.

A solid body of knowledge points at headteachers' crucial role in contributing to developing equity tools, and providing education in multicultural societies, organizing schools for change, strengthening professionalism and supporting staff. Additionally, leaders represent the school towards the community and political agencies, mustering them to support the school and promote their pedagogical and instructional agenda. This includes the head's pivotal role of leadership in turnaround schools and in linking communities to school turnaround (Bangs et al., 2011).

Paradoxically, granting headteachers autonomy and placing them in the hub of school-level decision-making and control, placed them also in a new position in the field of educational policy and politics, both within the local – (LA) – and national levels, as well as in the third and fourth sectors whose growing influence on education policy is remapping the education arena. Higham (2013) provides a synoptic overview of autonomy, education policy and leadership, complementing the work of Glatter (2006), in providing a profound and updated notion of autonomy:

> I have argued that, after a period of intense concentration on ideas connected with leadership and management, we should consider a re-orientation of the field in order to renew its concern with ideas associated with organization, which include viewing organizations as complex adaptive systems and taking an institutional perspective. (Glatter, 2006: 79)

Higham's sombre review of recent changes in the landscape of leadership in England, casts a shadow on the early ideas of autonomy and headship (Levacic, 1995). Under 'competing pressures' (Higham, 2013: 16) from other tiers and groups in the system (e.g. the ministry, LAs, interest groups, parents) 'school leaders may talk the language of vision but the space in which they can lead may be narrow'. This may perhaps reveal a type of 'strategic compliance' (Lacey, 1977) rather than full-hearted adoption and real identification with the 'charter culture' as a truly autonomous one.

The deregulation of the system and the weakening of democratic legitimacy that replaces democratic control and public-interest regulation (Barber, 2008; Feintuck, 2010) with economic regulation raise concerns about the quasi-privatization of public education. Quasi-privatization (Levacic, 1995) is a term that describes how the rules of the market are imposed upon a system that is not essentially wholly privatized, for instance, by introducing corporate-like structures and high-stakes competition. Although public education remains government-maintained, shifting democratic legitimacy into third- and fourth-sector-controlled chains of schools is problematic in terms of public control over publicly financed schooling. Levin (2015) explains that:

> explaining the term educational privatization is less straightforward than it might appear because almost all forms of education have both public and private components. The term *private* refers to the provision of schooling for and by individuals, groups, institutions, or entities that is primarily devoted to meeting the private goals of both the school clientele and the institutional sponsors. In contrast, the term *public* characterizes entities and purposes that are dedicated to a broader societal impact beyond that conferred upon the direct participants, and is usually (but not always) associated with a government role. Given these working definitions ... there is considerable overlap between them in their application in the educational arena. (ibid.: 412)

Levin goes on to offer five dimensions that build the public–private spheres of education: sponsorship, governance, funding, production and outcomes, each of which needs further exploration in the discussion of autonomy and leadership.

Wong (2015) determines that the tension between decentralization and equity remains a basic dispute in education policy. Accountability seemed to be a tool, or partial tool, for bridging the gap and easing the tension between the two terms. Earley (2000, 2013) points at the inconsistency between the fundamental changes in the policy and structural physiognomies of the scene in which schools and school leaders dwell and operate, and the perhaps outdated or currently insufficient capacities and qualities of school governance and governing bodies. These were established in their current form in the second stage of school autonomy (i.e. roughly after 2000) as part of a vision of a stand-alone LA (then LEA) school: perhaps as a Foundation (previously Grant Maintained) school, run by strong independent, self-sufficient leaders, whose leadership is mainly instructional and hopefully distributed within the organization (Spillane, 2007). Governing bodies were imagined to provide public support (Radnor, Ball and Vincent, 1998), as well as local, community supervision and deliberation between the school and its immediate stakeholders, on the one hand, and assisting in lessening outside agencies' pressures, on the other hand (Earley, 2013; James et al., 2011). This hierarchic, linear structure is all but gone in the majority of academies,[1] and has been replaced by a maze of charities, ownerships, operators, some part of globalized organizations (Ball, 2007). This phenomenon is evident in other countries (e.g. the United States, see Spillane, 2007; or Israel; Gibton, 2011). The common characteristics of such systems are that they are heavily segmented (Spillane, 2007), over-politicized, and marketized (Ball, 2007; Gibton, 2013). This is labelled by Malen and Cochran (2015: 5) as an:

> unfulfilled promise of greater discretion. ... It has become clear that whatever 'new authority' was decentralized could be re-centralized. ... Thus site actors do not appear to have more extensive or more dependable degree of freedom.

Headteachers in this 'charter culture' are in the midst of complex struggles among and between powerful agencies that have reshaped the system, moving from a vision of schools as isles of calm with themselves as pillars of tranquillity and instructional and pedagogical professionalism, isolated from the turbulent struggles on governance and regulation. But evidence mounts that many heads fall short of attaining this goal, and the powerful force of system reform limits their autonomy and recentralizes it under new, and perhaps stricter, burdens which can interfere with their work. Perhaps paradoxically, parents expect tougher measures of inspection and superintendency as the middle tier becomes less connected to democratic control and legitimacy, while commissioning, not only delivery, shifts more and more into the hands of non-governmental agencies and bodies, whose accountability to the public is less direct and more obscure and entangled. Mayorization of school districts is the United States is one response to this changing landscape of commissioning and delivery (Edelstein, 2015) as is the move of power from elected school boards to elected mayors (Wong, 2015) and sometimes to appointed boards and superintendents. This is what Edelstein (2015) coins as *division of autonomy*. This contemporary term is useful for understanding the current streams in educational autonomy rather than the zero-sum notion of unidirectional transference of power from one tier in the system to another.

Earley's (2013: 74–5) list of ongoing and amplified challenges for school leaders points at the conflicting tasks that characterize their work; on the one hand, tasks that require, perhaps, isolation to allow for dealing with delicate volatile issues like inclusion, racism, managing teacher workforce, and on the other hand, growing concern with multiple providers, school reform and abundant legislation.

> I'm accountable to parents, governing bodies, the LEA, countless government agencies. My immediate boss, well, you see I'm hesitating – sometimes I talk to myself. I guess I have to be accountable to the governors but I have to say the relationship we have with the LEA is a real partnership; although we have to write reports, it doesn't feel like a top-down heavy-handed approach. My school inspector comes and works alongside. They have to be responsive to the needs of the schools with public–private partnerships. They discuss with you. We are lucky. But some schools that are not doing so well may feel the LEA is more heavy-handed and not so supportive. I think the move to Ofsted inspection had a huge impact on how we operated. (London Headteacher, 2006)

Conclusion

The landscape of school governance (James et al., 2011) is changing gradually in the light of the second and third (current) stages of school autonomy. Beginning with Local Management of Schools (Levacic, 1995), school autonomy has moved (Earley, 2013; Earley et al., 2012) from schools being offered self-regulation and autonomy to complete overhaul of the school system in which schools have transformed not just pedagogically and leadership-wise, but also in their status, organizational and legal affiliation. The regulation of education is therefore less linear and less democratically legitimate and representative, and more corporatist, commodified and managerial (Ball, 2007).

The main contribution of the chapter is the identification of the finite nature or quality and character of autonomy. This means that, perhaps similar to energy, autonomy has a finite amount, in this case in the world of education. Thus, adding or subtracting autonomy from one level, group or institution within a given system, necessarily shifts, redefines and retransforms the autonomy of all its other components. This makes understanding the role of governance and regulation especially elusive and, simultaneously, crucial. This 'charter culture' is not limited to the UK but can be found in other countries, especially in the United States (Bifulco and Bulkley, 2015; Wong, 2015). The path between centralization, decentralization and autonomy is multidirectional.

Implications

- Since the 2000s there has been a shift towards recentralization and reassigning some of the powers passed on to school leaders in the 1990s, back to the recently established middle tier, and even to central government.

- It will be interesting to see how this shifts, both locally and globally, in the near future, and how the role of school leaders adapts.

- School autonomy should be re-explored, and hence redefined in light of the new roles of regulation in education policy, and the shift of the middle tier away from democratic legitimacy. Measures to protect schools from further corporatist influence should be sought after.

Note

1. In 2016 academies constituted two-thirds of the secondary sector and roughly a fifth of the primary sector in England. See Introduction for a description of academies.

Chapter 4

Accountability and improvement in self-improving school systems

Peter Matthews and Melanie Ehren

Aims

The aims of this chapter are to:

- summarize the evolution of high-stakes school accountability in England
- consider the momentum in England towards a self-improving school system and implications for school accountability, particularly peer evaluation
- discuss accountability in relation to managed networks of schools and a new middle tier
- consider how accountability is reflected in a changing evaluation and assessment framework.

The evolution of modern accountability for schools in England

There is a complex relationship between attainment, autonomy, collaboration and accountability.

House of Commons Education Committee

School autonomy and accountability have been key drivers for education system reform in many countries over the last decade. An OECD (2011b) study confirms that school autonomy is an international phenomenon which is particularly noticeable, for example, in England, the Netherlands, the Czech Republic and Macao-China. The study also reported a strong relationship between school autonomy and accountability, finding that this combination can succeed in raising student performance.

Origins

School autonomy was introduced in England by the Education Reform Act 1988 which gave schools managerial responsibility for delegated budgets and the opportunity to leave local authority control. The act also established a national curriculum and assessment arrangements and allowed parents to choose schools. These sweeping changes inevitably increased the focus on school accountability. The 1992 Education (Schools) Act introduced the regular independent inspection of all schools in England[1] (and Wales) and prescribed the annual publication of quantitative performance information for every school. The purposes of these external accountability measures include:

- assisting parents in school choice
- increasing public awareness of the quality and educational standards of schools
- ensuring that money is well spent
- encouraging schools to improve and diagnosing what needs improving
- ensuring that arrangements for safeguarding children and young people are effective. (See section 16 of the 1992 Act and Ofsted 2015a: 5)

Since 1992, the evaluation and assessment framework in England has evolved to include not only inspection and performance indicators – together with 'floor standards' – but self-evaluation, performance management and a focus on formative assessment and target setting.

Accountability pressure and its effects

The accountability regime for schools in England is seen by many schools as high-stakes because:

- Published inspection reports state whether the effectiveness of the school is judged to be 'outstanding', 'good', 'requires improvement' or 'inadequate'. The description remains until the school is next inspected once every three years for 'good' schools; more frequently for 'requires improvement'. 'Inadequate' schools are also subject to other types of intervention and support. Most 'outstanding' schools are exempt from inspection unless their academic performance deteriorates (see Ofsted, 2015a).
- Performance tables (Department for Education) include trends in pupils' attainment and progress compared with national and local averages, the relative progress of pupils of different abilities and socio-economic circumstances, value-added and financial data.[2] All schools are expected to exceed national 'floor standards', which can be challenging for 'coasting' schools or those in difficult circumstances. From 2015 to

2016 these benchmarks relate not only to raw outcomes but also to the progress students make relative to their earlier attainment.

- Schools are also subject to other types of scrutiny, for example, by sponsors of under-performing academies, boards of multi-academy trusts (MATs), regional schools commissioners (RSCs), governing boards and local and religious authorities. Later, we shall consider the accountability of such bodies.

Comparing seven European inspection systems, Altricher and Kemethofer (2015) found that the pressure to do well on inspection experienced by headteachers (accountability pressure) was greatest in England, followed by the Netherlands and Sweden, and least in Austria and Switzerland. Such pressures are related to systems with more challenging elements such as thresholds for distinguishing failing schools, sanctions for low-performing schools and reports on individual schools to the general public. School leaders who feel more pressure to improve say that more development activities take place in their schools. School leaders in the English system were found to be 'consistently more active with respect to improvement processes and more attentive to inspection expectations and stakeholder responses' (Altricher and Kemethofer, 2015: 51). Accountability pressure can also have unintended consequences. Examples in some schools have included teaching to the test, manipulating performance data (cheating), adding expert teachers to the staff for the inspection and finding other ways of 'gaming' the system.

Strengths and weaknesses of inspections and published performance data

The impact of inspection systems has been subject to a wealth of research (e.g. Matthews and Sammons, 2004; Ehren and Visscher, 2008) and Ofsted is not immune to significant criticisms of its practice. One recent example relates to the validity and reliability of inspection judgements (Waldegrave and Simons, 2015), a second is the assertion that Ofsted and its inspectors have espoused preferred teaching styles (Christoloudou, 2013). Ofsted, disturbed by these assertions, has responded to the first by abolishing the outsourcing of inspections and the evaluation of individual lessons, and to the second by ensuring that its inspection criteria relating to teaching and learning avoid pedagogical advocacy (Ofsted, 2015d).

The impact of publishing school performance data has attracted much less research attention than the effects of inspection regimes. Publicly available performance data can have considerable leverage in promoting social equity and raising standards. Research has attributed a significant deterioration in GCSE performance in Wales to the decision by the Welsh Assembly in 2001 to stop the publication of school performance data or 'league tables' (Burgess et al., 2010).

The rise of school self-evaluation

The strong external accountability arrangements for schools in England represent a centralized and 'done to' model of school accountability. Responding to evidence from the first cycle of inspections that self-evaluation was one of the weakest aspects of school leadership, Ofsted promoted school self-evaluation through a landmark document *School Evaluation Matters* (Ofsted, 1998). From 2000, schools have completed a pre-inspection analysis of their own effectiveness, which in 2003 became a prescribed 'self-evaluation form' (SEF). This asked schools to evaluate themselves in each of the areas covered by inspection. The validation of these self-evaluations by school inspectors incentivized schools to become proficient in gauging their own effectiveness. A number of studies suggest that the accuracy of school self-evaluation reflects the leadership and management competence in the school (e.g. Matthews and Sammons, 2004) and relates to the overall improvement of schools (Nelson, Spence-Thomas and Taylor, 2015).

Schools in England must still undertake self-evaluation although they are now free to record findings as they wish. This freedom allows schools to choose specific topics and approaches for their self-evaluation. Despite advocacy of more bottom-up approaches, many schools still choose to base their self-evaluation on the aspects covered by inspection.

The emergence of peer evaluation in a self-improving school system

The 2010 education White Paper *The Importance of Teaching* (DfE, 2010) set a new policy course for education. The main theme was less central direction and more self-determination in a publicly funded school system. The paper, and the Academies Act 2010 which reflected it, introduced a range of reforms to promote greater school autonomy. These included:

- the expansion of new school types, such as free schools and academies (see Introduction for details)
- the endorsement of system leadership and school-to-school support (see Introduction and Chapter 5 for details).

The drive for a self-improving school system has led to increasing engagement in peer evaluation, a key step towards self-regulation. Schools are taking greater ownership of their quality assurance, not only through self-evaluation but by exposing their work to the perceptions of trusted peers.

Internationally, peer evaluation is rare. In a recent comprehensive survey of assessment and evaluation in twenty-eight countries, the OECD (2013) found a general pattern of growth in school evaluation, both external and internal, *but little evidence of peer review*. The report identified developing school evaluation capacity 'as a priority for school improvement' and advocated the promotion of peer learning, especially in systems where there is a high degree of autonomy.

> A starting point could be with school leadership teams working together to identify common challenges, devising common strategies and approaches to peer evaluation. The process would benefit from the appointment of an external facilitator or critical friend chosen and agreed by the school principals themselves. Within systems there are schools with more developed self-evaluation processes and there could be great benefits in finding ways to involve their staff in supporting and training colleagues in other schools. (OECD, 2013: 468–70)

A growing number of peer evaluation initiatives have arisen in England since 2010. Secondary schools in Bradford, for example, have undertaken peer reviews since 2010. Reviews are rooted in self-evaluation and lead to reports which shape areas for development and provide external verification of the accuracy of self-evaluation. Schools are revisited in the summer term with the same team to review actions taken. Other early examples include an initiative by a group of special schools led by the Mulberry Bush school in Oxfordshire.[3] Six schools took part in a pilot from 2011 to 2012. The following year the number expanded to schools providing for children with behaviour, emotional and social difficulties across five local authorities (LAs), and expansion has continued. The peer review system aims to provide a reflective self-evaluation process, giving insight into individual schools' effectiveness in agreed areas, provided by peer colleagues in their adopted role of critical professional friend. Each review involves a visit to each school by two colleagues followed by feedback. Other peer review systems are being promoted by headteachers' unions and other educational organizations as well as some MATs, LAs and teaching school alliances.

A mature system of peer reviews

The most established system for peer review in England is Challenge Partners; a co-operative group of over 300 schools clustered around twenty-nine outstanding 'hub' schools (see Chapter 19). By December 2015, Challenge Partners had undertaken over 700 such reviews. The reviews are staffed by senior leaders from partner schools and led by Ofsted-trained evaluators who manage and quality-assure the review and write the report. These lead reviewers act much more as facilitators than inspectors. They guide and coach the reviewers (who work in tandem with an equivalent number of senior leaders in the school being reviewed), quality-assure the review process, nurture relationships with the school and take responsibility for the quality and objectivity of the report. The peer evaluations differ from Ofsted inspections in several important respects. They are conducted in partnership with the school, facilitated (not directed) by an expert evaluator, and result in non-judgemental evaluations of 'what went well' and 'even better if ...'. The evaluation report is owned by the school.

A research study (Matthews and Headon, 2015) highlighted how partner schools valued having an *annual* external appraisal of their quality and standards, particularly of the effectiveness of school improvement strategies; teaching, learning and assessment; the achievement of pupils and an area of excellent practice proposed by the school. The school can also put forward other areas for review. The research also found that the peer review process leads to powerful professional development and reciprocal benefits for reviewers and their schools. The joint involvement of senior staff from the reviewed school with peer reviewers from other partner schools creates a *multiplier effect* that distinguishes Challenge Partner quality assurance reviews from external inspections and other peer review approaches. Matthews and Headon (2015) describe how, over time, the annual QA review process can give all appropriate senior leaders access to reviewer training and internal and external evaluation experience that is universally regarded by them as providing exceptional professional development. On their return from reviews, the experience and professional learning of reviewers are invariably discussed at senior leaders' meetings in their home schools. This often leads to the adoption of improved practice and further communications or visits between not only the reviewed and reviewers' schools, but also between the schools of members of the review team.

The approach has overcome the introspective and defensive culture engendered in many schools by inspection and has succeeded in 'stimulating collegial networking, peer exchange, sharing and critiquing of practice, and fostering a sense of common direction' as advocated by OECD (2013: 470). This has required the development of trust, the glue that binds together the network of schools involved in peer review and a key characteristic of their leadership.

The defining characteristics of Challenge Partners provide an interesting model for developing a peer review informed self-improving system:

i   reviewers are drawn from beyond the school's locality, local authority, local partnership or network, which gives them greater independence and objectivity

ii   the ability of peer evaluators to leave their own school contexts behind and assess evidence and other practice impartially in terms of its impact

iii   the equal involvement of senior leaders from within the school, working in tandem with external reviewers, which develops evaluative capacity and gives the review findings greater acceptance

iv   the reciprocal benefits to reviewers and their schools in terms of professional development and knowledge transfer

v a well-developed quality assurance strategy for reviews

vi a range of mechanisms for following up and providing support to schools after their review

vii a lead reviewer who is an independent Ofsted-trained inspector, and who safeguards the validity and reliability of the review.

School self-evaluation and peer reviews together provide a basis for a self-improving school system to take greater ownership of accountability, that is, be a self-accounting, even self-regulating, school system. But two further issues remain. One concerns the accountability of the multi-school cluster, such as a MAT. The second relates to the changing middle tier: the diminishing local authorities (see Greany, 2015) and the new RSCs who act for education ministers in respect of academies and academy chains. Although all lines of accountability lead to the Department for Education, the pathways vary from one type of school to another and generally involve a middle tier: LAs or alternative entities such as MATs.

The accountability of multi-school entities and the new middle tier

The rapid proliferation of academies and absorption of the majority into MATs raises the question of how the MATs are held to account. Ofsted undertakes 'focused' inspections of MATs under existing legislation and terms set out by the secretary of state (DfE, 2015b). Local authorities are also subject to focused inspections.

Focused inspections of MATs and LAs

Focused inspections involve visiting selected schools in a MAT or LA within a period of one to two weeks. A telephone survey of other schools in the group is also undertaken. Decisions on which MATs or LAs should be prioritized for a focused inspection are based on what is known about the performance and inspection outcomes of constituent schools. The inspections of both types of network lead to letters from the inspectorate which comment on matters such as how well the organization knows its schools and their strengths and weaknesses, how it uses this information to tackle issues and what impact such actions are having on improving the quality and standards of schools. These letters are published on Ofsted's website. Ehren and Perryman (forthcoming) have examined more widely the inspection of 'polycentric' school systems.

From 2014 to 2015, Ofsted inspected the arrangements for supporting school improvement in eleven LAs and four underperforming MATs and interviewed some leaders of

MATs that have a track record of improving schools. Table 4.1 summarizes Ofsted's main findings.

Comparisons of mean data for each local authority with national averages are published annually. Since 2013, Ofsted has published local authority tables showing the proportions of pupils that attend 'good' (or better) primary and secondary schools (Ofsted, 2013). The DfE does not yet publish a summary of performance at academy

Table 4.1 Strengths and weaknesses of some LAs and MATs in school improvement (after Ofsted, 2015b)

Multi-school organizations	Effective characteristics	Shortcomings
Common to both LAs and MATs	• clear vision, purpose and direction regarding school improvement • use assessment information well to target and drive improvement and arrange intervention or support • know their schools well, accurately identify those causing concern and provide suitable intervention	• not undertaking sufficiently rigorous checks on perform-ance or arrangements for safeguarding pupils • lack of clarity or understanding by key partners or schemes of delegation between trust boards and local governing bodies
Local authorities	• understood by key stakeholders • impact of school improvement work checked by management • funding decisions robust, trans-parent and provided good value for money • good coordination and co-opera-tion with external strategic partners such as RSCs and the DfE • accurately identified schools caus-ing concern and provide suitable intervention	• lack of effective consultation about school improvement strategies • arrangements to support school improvement lacked coherence • school-to-school support not always based on clear and well-understood operational plans • good schools not sufficiently encouraged to work together to improve further • approaches to building leader-ship capacity across the system varied in effectiveness • examples of good practice not identified quickly enough or shared effectively
Multi-academy trusts	• culture of continual improvement • successful leaders of academies in MATs embrace culture of high accountability	• lack clear rationale for selection of schools into their MAT or strategy for creating coherent clusters • do not always provide or commission specific support

chain level. Summarizing the performance of MATs presents challenges which have been described in a statistical working paper (DfE, 2015c). Nevertheless, academies and MATs are subject to scrutiny to ensure they meet their funding agreements with the DfE. The Education Funding Agency (EFA) distributes £54 billion to schools (2015–16). A number of investigations of academies and MATs have been undertaken by the DfE audit investigation team on behalf of the EFA when there are concerns about possible breeches of their agreements.[4]

Monitoring of MATs by RSCs

When academies or MATs cause concern, RSCs, acting on behalf of ministers, can remove the academy from its sponsor and broker its placement with another sponsor (commonly a MAT) or can prevent the further expansion of an overstretched MAT. The role, performance criteria and accountabilities of RSCs are described in detail in the report of a House of Commons (2016) enquiry. Ehren and Perryman (forthcoming) describe how regional school commissioners will use 'soft intelligence' to ask regional HMIs to flag up focused inspections of struggling academy chains or to prioritize inspections of potentially failing academies who do not receive or accept the adequate support of peer schools or their governing body. Ofsted's non-executive role in relation to schools is to evaluate and report on them and recommend to schools, their 'parent' organizations and government what improvements are needed. There is some overlap in such functions because the DfE and RSCs also have access to their own advisers who visit and report on the performance of academies.

An evolving accountability framework

As the self-improving school system matures, it follows that the national evaluation and assessment framework will need to adapt. Although the different elements of accountability – external and self-evaluation, assessment of students and appraisal of teachers – may all play a part, the balance needs to change for two reasons. The first is to allow greater self-regulation. The second is to encompass the two powerful new elements: peer evaluation and the evaluation of system-leading organizations such as MATs as well as the impact of RSCs and LAs. The evolving accountability framework is depicted in Figure 4.1.

Several authors have equally argued for removing (or decreasing) one or more of the other layers of school accountability. Writing on school accountability in a self-improving school system, Christine Gilbert – former HM Chief Inspector – for example, suggested that 'if Ofsted were to take a different approach to the inspection of those schools that had undertaken a strong self-evaluation process, tested out laterally with peers, change would be dramatic' (Gilbert 2013: 16).

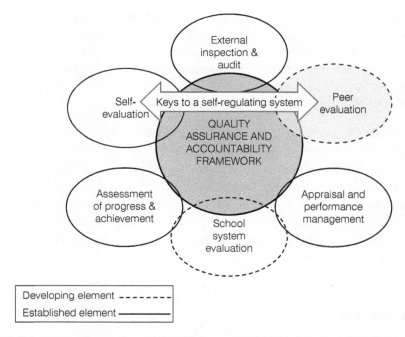

Figure 4.1 Schematic representation of the evaluation and assessment framework in England.

The inspectorate

Ofsted is changing and seems committed to building such closer partnership with schools. Examples of how this is taking effect are:

- most 'outstanding' schools are exempt from inspection, unless their performance deteriorates

- good schools are inspected for a day approximately once every three years, unless there are concerns or they are better than good, in which case extra inspectors are summoned to gather more evidence

- inspection attention is focused on 'inadequate' schools and those 'requiring improvement'

- practising headteachers and senior leaders are trained to be Ofsted inspectors and are included on the enlarged inspection teams. The inspection training provides them with evaluation skills of benefit to their school leadership, while inspections benefit from an injection of their insight and their immediate knowledge of school practices.

Rigorous ongoing self-evaluation, externally validated, is at the heart of an authentically self-improving school. As the OECD Education Policy Outlook states:

A strong focus on self-evaluation holds the basic premise that schools are best placed to analyse their own contexts, performance and areas for improvement. The provision of a comparable evidence base to all schools allows critical reflection on where each school stands in comparison to other schools. Where there is a strong evidence base for school evaluation and an established mechanism for external school evaluation, external evaluators can focus on how a school conducts its self-evaluation and uses the results to improve student learning, or could even collaborate with the school to validate its self-evaluation and improvement plan. (OECD, 2015: 130)

Peer evaluation is emerging as the preferred means of validating self-evaluation. If a self-improving school system is to be a self-reviewing system, critically scrutinizing and benchmarking current performance and developing evidence-based approaches to further improvement is essential. Ofsted could do more to promote effective intrinsic accountability if inspectors took account not only of self-evaluation evidence but also the steps taken by the school to have their findings externally validated. The lesson to be learnt from the history of self-evaluation is that schools quickly became far more adept when Ofsted took serious account of it.

Implications

Accountability in the evolving self-improving school landscape in England presents new challenges at school and system level. How can a school system in which accountability has been driven by high-stakes inspection and performance indicators be more authentically self-regulating? Can robust and regular peer evaluation provide a systemic means of validating school self-evaluation and reduce the need for inspection, so long as other indicators point to the school's effectiveness? Can MATs and LAs rise to the challenge of demonstrating their effectiveness as umbrella organizations and their efficacy in improving the quality and standards of their constituent schools?

'Ultimately, accountability rests with the professionals' as argued by Matthews (2014: 28). 'The more they can manage their own quality control and continuing improvement, the less need there should be for external inspection.' Fullan, Rincón-Gallardo and Hargreaves (2015: 14–15) reach similar conclusions when considering internal accountability as a mechanism for building professional capital.

> It should be clear that the system has a role in both internal and external accountability. Relative to the former, policy makers will need to make a major shift from superficial structural solutions to investing in and leveraging internal accountability and building the professional capital of all teachers and leaders throughout the system. Once started, this is an investment that keeps on giving and, most of all, results in all levels of the system doing the work of day-to-day accountability. Furthermore, the more internal accountability takes hold, the more schools and districts [c.f. networks such as LAs and MATs] will seek and use external input on how well they are doing. … Great accountability improves the present as it shapes the future. It invests in, grows and circulates professional capital throughout the system.

In England, embedded self-evaluation, growing commitment to peer evaluation, the criteria and benchmarking provided by Ofsted and performance information, and the opportunities and freedoms of a relatively autonomous self-improving school policy environment provide the ingredients for school and system accountability and enhancement.

Notes

1. Inspection in England is the responsibility of Her Majesty's Chief Inspector (HMCI) who leads the Office for Standards in Education, Children's Services and Skills.
2. See www.education.gov.uk/schools/performance/
3. http://www.mulberrybush.org.uk/our-training/peer-review-new-school/
4. For investigation reports on MATs, see https://www.gov.uk/government/collections/academies-investigation-reports

Chapter 5

Collaboration, partnerships and system leadership across schools

Toby Greany

Aims

This chapter focuses on the development of school-to-school support, networks and partnerships and the leadership practices associated with these, focusing in particular on developments in England. It aims to:

- analyse the rationale for school partnerships and system leadership in decentralized school systems
- review the development of collaboration, partnership and system leadership in England's 'self-improving' school system
- summarize the evidence of impact from such partnerships
- assess the leadership practices and qualities involved
- explore the implications for policy and leadership practice.

Introduction

This chapter explores the development of school-to-school support and partnerships in England. These partnerships have become a defining feature of what the government calls the 'self-improving, school-led' system (see Introduction). Most schools engage in partnerships that are informal and emergent, based on shared interests, concerns or simply personal relationships. Even partnerships that do have a more formal basis sometimes face fraught political and interpersonal adaptive challenges (Kamp, 2013). The focus here, however, is on more formal arrangements that are structured through a policy-driven process. These generally fall into one of the following non-mutually exclusive categories:

- structural governance models, such as multi-academy trusts (MATs) or academy chains and federations

- designations based on formal criteria, such as National Leaders of Education (NLEs) and Teaching Schools
- role-related partnerships, such as where an executive head oversees two or more schools (but not in a formal federation).

Key to this development has been the emergence of a cadre of what are called 'system leaders', broadly defined as leaders who work beyond their immediate school to support the improvement of the wider system (Fullan, 2005).

The need for such lateral school-to-school partnerships has become apparent in the face of evidence that neither top-down centrally imposed change, nor pure competition and marketization can achieve sustained improvement across school systems (Burns and Köster, 2016). Instead, the aim has been to 'unleash greatness' by asking school system leaders to work together in ways which transfer knowledge, expertise and capacity within and between schools, so that *all* schools improve and *all* children achieve their potential. There is emerging evidence that such models can prove effective in addressing underperformance and improving outcomes, in particular in some of the most challenging schools. But England's 'self-improving' system also faces significant challenges, at both conceptual and practical levels, which this chapter reviews.

The limits of quasi-markets for system improvement

Granting schools autonomy to determine how they secure improvement while holding them accountable for their performance has become an increasingly central tenet of international thinking and policy on school system reform (OECD, 2015). Such approaches are frequently associated with wider quasi-market reforms, such as giving parents the right to choose which school they prefer for their child, backed by funding models which reward more popular schools. The argument for granting schools autonomy is that it will free them up from hidebound bureaucracies and make them more responsive to their parent 'customers' (Institute for Government, 2012). Quasi-markets are thus clearly predicated on *competition* between providers as the primary driver of improvement (Lubiensky, 2009). Of course, in practice, public education systems are not markets in the true sense of the word, since the consumer does not pay and failing providers (i.e. schools) are rarely allowed to close altogether.

As outlined in the Introduction, England is recognized as an extreme example of high school autonomy–high accountability quasi-market (or neo-liberal) reform by international standards. The 1988 Education Reform Act (ERA) introduced parental choice and gave school governing bodies responsibility for resources while holding them accountable for performance, and successive Conservative and Labour governments have sustained this policy direction. By the time of PISA 2009, schools in the UK were judged to be among the most autonomous in the world[1] (OECD, 2011). Few would argue that they are also among the most accountable (see Chapter 4). Given this focus on quasi-markets, competition and vertical accountability, it may seem strange that England now sees networking and collaboration as central to the success of its 'self-improving school system'. How and why has this happened?

One way to assess this is through an historical lens, mapping the trajectory of policy thinking over the past fifteen years. While subscribing to the broad tenets of the ERA, New Labour's approach to reform from 1997 was markedly top-down. This was epitomized by the National Strategies for Literacy and Numeracy, which did secure initial improvements in pupil outcomes but then stalled in the early 2000s (Alexander, 2011). This led to a gradual re-evaluation of the approach and a recognition that lateral networks of schools overseen by system leaders might offer more sustainable and effective ways of addressing underperformance and developing and distributing innovation between schools (Higham, Hopkins and Matthews, 2009). Michael Barber, a former adviser to New Labour, first articulated the idea that for school systems to move from 'Good to Great', the policymakers must 'unleash greatness' by trusting front-line professionals and fostering lateral networks (Barber, 2007; Mourshed, Chijioke and Barber, 2010). These ideas were then picked up by the centre right Coalition government elected in 2010, which adopted the 'self-improving system' label, as described below.

Another way to assess England's journey from a purist focus on competition towards a greater focus on networking and collaboration is in the context of wider evidence and thinking on school system reform. This has revealed the limits of pure market mechanisms to secure improvement: quasi-markets make only a minimal – and often differential – impact on outcomes, as outlined in the Introduction. Similarly, while there is evidence that school autonomy coupled with clear accountability can support systemic improvement, such models do have pitfalls and can lead to a narrowing of learning and unhealthy competition between schools, as explored in the Introduction, Chapter 4 and – from the perspective of toxic leadership – in Chapter 17.

This leads us to a third, arguably more existential, challenge for the quasi-market model: Is competition the best way to develop the core resource at the heart of all effective schools – high-quality teachers and leaders? Research is increasingly clear that it is the quality of teachers and teaching that makes the greatest difference in outcomes, particularly for disadvantaged children (Barber and Mourshed, 2007; Sutton Trust, 2011). Developing great teachers requires strong systems for recruitment, retention and development, in which schools play a critical part (Cordingley et al., 2015). While it is possible for single schools to provide such contexts, in a highly competitive system there are few mechanisms for schools to learn from and with each other. This limits the potential of such systems to improve at scale, so it is arguable that the negative effects of competition need to be tempered by collaboration.

School partnerships at the core of a self-improving system in England

Hargreaves' thinking on self-improving systems has influenced thinking and practice in England (2010, 2011, 2012a, b). He argues that simply freeing schools up and holding them accountable will not, in itself, ensure a self-improving system. Instead, he proposes moving beyond the existing architecture of single self-managing schools by putting in place four 'building blocks':

- clusters of schools (the structure)
- the local solutions approach; and co-construction (the two cultural elements)
- system leaders (the key people).

Hargreaves argues that by working together in deep partnerships these clusters – or families – of schools can realize benefits that individual self-managing schools cannot, although he acknowledges that building deep partnerships based on trust and reciprocity is challenging. He argues that school leaders should start by fostering cultures of applied professional learning – Joint Practice Development – between teachers across schools as a means to develop trust and a shared sense of endeavour.

The Conservative-led governments elected in 2010 and 2015 have accelerated reform in two directions (Lupton and Thomson, 2015). On the one hand, school autonomy has been radically increased with the extension of academy 'freedoms' to all schools (see Introduction). By 2016, almost one in four schools, including the majority of secondary schools, had either chosen or been forced to become an academy, while the government has announced its intention that all schools must become academies (DfE, 2016). The second shift introduced since 2010, and described in more detail in the following section, has been an expansion in the level of school-to-school support and partnerships, most significantly through Teaching Schools and Multi-Academy Trusts.

Based on an analysis of the White Paper (DfE, 2010) Greany suggests (2014) that the government has four core criteria for the self-improving system:

- Teachers and schools are responsible for their own improvement
- Teachers and schools learn from each other and from research so that effective practice spreads
- The best schools and leaders extend their reach across other schools so that all schools improve
- Government support and intervention is minimized.

While the first and last of these could be seen as taking existing quasi-market reforms to their logical conclusion, the middle two are arguably innovative, in that they seek to mitigate the negative impact of competition through a parallel focus on collaboration between schools, with successful system leaders acting as the mechanism for structuring these partnerships.

The development of partnerships and emerging evidence of impact

Until the early 2000s, while there were individual examples of successful school partnerships in England, there was no one model of partnership that had proved consistently successful in terms of securing improved outcomes for children or addressing significant underperformance in schools (HoC Education Select Committee, 2013). This was despite the Labour government providing significant funding for partnership-based programmes such as Networked Learning Communities, Excellence in Cities, Education Action Zones and Beacon Schools. Part of the reason for this lack of impact may have been that these programmes tended to have broader aims than addressing school underperformance and often adopted a model of successful schools transferring their 'best practice' to other schools, leading to resistance and weak knowledge mobilisation (Brown, 2015). Nevertheless, it is possible to argue that these programmes laid the groundwork for collaborative cultures to emerge between schools after the fierce competition of the 1990s (Higham, Hopkins and Matthews, 2009).

The journey towards a more system-wide focus on school collaboration was given shape and momentum by the London Challenge programme, which ran from 2004 onwards (Baars et al., 2014; Greaves, Macmillan and Sibieta, 2014). Faced by the need to address systemic underperformance in the capital's schools, the London Schools Commissioner, Sir Tim Brighouse, persuaded some of the capital's most successful headteachers to support the 'keys to success' schools that had been identified as needing most improvement. The rationale for this approach was that support from credible, serving leaders and teachers would be more effective than that from external consultants (Matthews and Hill, 2010). These 'consultant heads' did not work alone; they drew on the capacity and resources of the staff in their home schools to support the weaker schools (Earley and Weindling, 2006). The brief for these staff was to co-design solutions with staff from the supported school, thereby enabling Hargreaves' 'Joint Practice Development' rather than imposed 'best practices' (Ainscow, 2015).

The 'consultant head' model was scaled up nationally by the then National College for School Leadership through the National Leaders of Education/National Support Schools (NLE/NSS) and Local Leaders of Education (LLE) initiative. These headteachers and their teams were designated against a clear set of criteria and then brokered to support schools deemed to be underperforming (whereas seriously failing schools tended to be closed and reopened as sponsored academies). Importantly, the core remit of these system leaders was to provide temporary support – 'mooring alongside' – withdrawing once the supported school was back on its feet (Matthews and Hill, 2010). By June 2014 almost 1,000 NLEs had been designated. Evidence to date does indicate that outcomes improve faster in NLE-supported schools than in a matched sample (NCTL, 2013) and that NLEs increase the rate of improvement for children on free school meals (FSM) (Rea, Hill and Sandals, 2011; Rea and Dunford, 2013).

Muijs' (2015) robust mixed methods analysis of the impact of school-to-school support partnerships brokered between high- and low-performing primary schools in one LA has identified the positive impact achieved: 'Pupils in partnership (primary) schools outperformed their peers in matched comparison schools, with the strength of the relationship growing over time... . This suggests that the relationship is more beneficial for the supported schools, though it does not appear to have had any negative impact on supporting schools and may at best show a small positive relationship' (ibid.: 575).

Meanwhile, other strands of policy and practice were coming together to demonstrate the potential of other forms of partnership. Federations involve a more permanent relationship between two or more schools than in the NLE/NSS model, whereby the schools effectively amalgamate under one governing body. The model was enabled by Labour's 2002 legislation, but it took several years before significant numbers of schools had adopted it. Research for the National College indicated a positive federation effect on pupil outcomes over time, most significantly in the case of 'performance federations' (i.e. strong and weak schools together) and where an executive head was in place (Chapman et al. 2009; Chapman, Muijs and MacAllister 2011).

Academy chains, which are groups of academies overseen by a single MAT, have emerged since 2010 as the dominant structural model for school partnership. The government has played an active role in brokering underperforming schools into academy chains, generally run by successful schools. By March 2015 over half (58 per cent) of all academies and free schools were in a formal chain (HoC Education Select Committee, 2015b). By 2015 there were thirty-nine MATs with ten or more schools, seventy-eight with six to ten schools and 517 with two to five schools (Hill, 2015).

Hill's reports on academy chains (Hill, 2009; Hill et al., 2012) flagged some of the challenges for policy and practice in this area: most obviously the rapid pace of growth in some of the larger chains. An analysis by Hutchings, Francis and Kirby (2015) found that the majority of the more established chains they studied were performing around the mainstream average for improvement and/or attainment for disadvantaged pupils, but with small numbers of both higher- and lower-performing chains and some evidence of a gradual 'pulling away' of outlier chains at opposite ends of this spectrum. Salokangas and Chapman (2014) use case studies of two academy chains to illustrate the very different ways in which governance and leadership models can evolve, with differing balances in terms of central and local school-level control and resulting differences in culture and approaches to school improvement.

Teaching School Alliances represent a different type of policy-driven partnership to those described above, both because the partnership remains voluntary for alliance members and because the alliance remit is broader than just addressing underperformance.

Launched by the 2010 White Paper (DfE, 2010) Teaching Schools are 'outstanding' schools that play a leading role in co-ordinating initial and continuing professional development, school-to-school support and research and development across an alliance of partner schools (Matthews and Berwick, 2013). By June 2014, 587 Teaching Schools had been designated. The evaluation (Gu et al., 2015) reflects considerable progress overall and indicates the sheer diversity of organizational forms and approaches emerging. It also flags a series of challenges for the Teaching School model, ranging from the unreasonable and unsustainable workload required to establish the alliances, to a lack of robust peer challenge between partner schools.

This section has outlined the key types of policy-driven partnerships and some of the evidence of impact associated with them. The next section focuses on the emerging evidence of how system leaders lead these partnerships.

System leadership: Evidence on how leaders lead differently in partnerships

Matthews (2007, cited in Higham, Hopkins and Matthews 2009) had a formal role assessing and evaluating many of the first NLEs. He set out a summary of the qualities and practices that he observed, including: 'strong and principled moral purpose', 'thoughtful and systematic', 'earn trust … through consulting, valuing and developing the people with whom they work, and having belief in them', 'build confidence, capability and self-esteem in the people with whom they work, as well as institutional capacity through growing other leaders', 'inordinately high expectations, great optimism', 'decisive and prepared to take unpalatable decisions', and 'find innovative and often unorthodox solutions'.

This list suggests that the early pioneers of system leadership were driven, charismatic, even maverick, individuals, undaunted by the challenges of taking on underperforming schools, often in the most deprived socio-economic circumstances. Subsequent evaluations of the early academy chains (Hill, 2009, 2012), Teaching Schools (Gu et al., 2015) and wider partnerships (Chapman, 2013) have produced similar lists. Similarly, the heads observed by Robinson (2012: 168) in her study of primary system leaders

> had very different personalities and worked in different contexts, (but) were charismatic. … They tended to dominate the agenda, needed to influence others and had strong conviction regarding the integrity of these beliefs. They expressed high ideals of the success of the organisations and confidence in the staff to follow these ideals. While they had some freedom at the margins, they were also … simultaneously constrained to work within centrally determined policies.

Of course, one person's inspirational leader is another person's empire builder, and system leaders have consistently faced the charge that they are first and foremost interested in their own power and prestige. While Coldron et al. (2014: 398) do not see it so simplistically, they nevertheless recognize the complexity of motives expressed by the 'well positioned heads' (who, importantly, are often but not inevitably synonymous with system leaders) in their study who:

> tended to take a pragmatic view of how to respond to the changes, a logic of action that could be characterised as aiming to accumulate prestige ... while recognising its precarious nature and maximising their own room for manoeuver, taking charge of their own destiny as far as possible.... . Being graded by Ofsted as at least Good and preferably Outstanding was what mattered most.... . The headteachers we interviewed thought it was inevitable that the weak would get weaker and the strong stronger. They felt that increasingly competitive local fields are creating winners and losers.

This is not to suggest that system leadership is all about single heroic individuals. The most successful models are clearly about teams working together across multiple levels of the traditional school hierarchy. What successful system leaders appear to be able to do is create the conditions for this collaboration to happen, in particular through their ability to read and respond to different contexts and to engender trust and reciprocity within and between schools (Higham, Hopkins and Matthews, 2009; Robinson, 2012). That said, as Chapman (2013) observes, while system leadership can be seen as liberating by some staff, for others it can be seen to increase constraints and pressures as they are required to focus internally on the daily grind of school improvement.

Turning to the specific practices that system leaders undertake – at one level, their work can be very hands on, dealing with immediate crises in failing schools and finding ways to apply learning on school improvement from one context to another (Robinson, 2012). For example, Mujis' review (2015: 575) identified that: 'Effective partnership working entailed intensive intervention by the supporting school.... . A lot of the successful models revolved around doing very concrete delineated activities, based on clear and limited goals.... . This intensive action was characterised by intervention in three main areas: leadership development, development of teaching and learning approaches, and generating quick wins.'

Equally though, it is becoming increasingly clear that some system leaders are moving beyond the day-to-day leadership of learning in a single school. Senior leaders in larger MATs – the largest of which might have annual turnovers of £200m or more – are increasingly seen as chief executives: strategic leaders who must understand all aspects of business development, organizational design and risk management (Hill, 2012). It is too early to say whether certain MAT leadership approaches – or even whether certain MATs – are consistently more effective in this than others, or how MAT leadership might evolve once the founding generation of heads move on and the sector begins to mature to reach a steady state.

Discussion and summary

The evidence presented so far indicates that system leadership and school partnerships are developing at pace in the English context, in parallel with further deregulation through the expansion of academies. The initial driver of NLE-style school-to-school support models was that struggling schools are best 'turned round' by serving leaders who understand the issues and the context and can offer direct expertise and capacity. Equally, Teaching Schools appear to have been a response to a political desire to increase the role of schools in Initial Teacher Education and a recognition that, as central infrastructure and support were stripped back after 2010, there was a need to ensure lateral learning between otherwise autonomous schools. While initially focused on turning round failing schools, MATs are evolving into a more widespread solution for the 'self-improving system' – a way of aggregating schools into manageably large groups that have organizational coherence and accountability across 21,000 schools. Meanwhile, many schools are developing their own partnership arrangements, often with significant infrastructure and sophisticated processes for supporting school improvement, such as the Challenge Partners model described in Chapters 4 and 19.

The implications of this for leaders and leadership appears to be that they must choose either to remain as a stand-alone school, accountable for their own performance and competing with other schools in their locality, or they must join one or more networks. These networks might offer support and security in return for some loss of autonomy. Few networks operate on a purely financial purchaser/provider basis – most will ask the member school to contribute skills and ideas in kind, while offering support and capacity if things go wrong.

The choice between competition and collaboration is by no means straightforward for leaders and most appear to be balancing a mix of both (Earley, 2013). It is clear that different schools in different contexts face different choices, with phase, geography and the history of competition and collaboration in an area all playing a role. Equally, the way that the local authority conceives and enacts its changing role will influence school decisions (Greany, 2015c), as will the development of new 'middle tier' structures such as the DfE's Regional Schools Commissioners (see Chapter 4).

The policy decision to aggregate schools into MATs and similar collaborative structures (such as Charter Management Organizations in the United States) may seem like a logical development for quasi-market systems that want to mitigate the negative impacts of competition by creating structures that can foster collaboration between schools within the group, while at the same time sustaining a healthy level of wider competition and parental choice between MATs (Croft, 2015). Such a decision seems to move the unit of measurement from the individual school to the group, effectively creating 'quasi-super-markets' in which individual schools may become little more than retail outlets for their wider chain. Of course, many would argue that removing LAs and replacing them with MATs is simply 'moving the structural deckchairs' while reducing local democratic oversight, with little impact on the technical core of teaching and learning in classrooms (Hatcher, 2014). Others, including Ofsted (2013), are concerned that we are seeing increasing fragmentation and a two-tier system developing in which some schools and regions thrive, but others languish (Earley and Higham, 2013; Coldron et al., 2014; Greany, 2015a, b).

The priority for leaders in England is to develop partnerships that genuinely enhance the richness and quality of learning for teachers and children, since this offers the potential for genuine improvement. The challenge is to keep and realize this goal in the face of so many other political and practical challenges. If partnerships become little more than administrative structures to replace LAs, then their impact will be minimal, and could in fact be negative if leaders become distracted from their core focus on learning. What is undoubtedly clear is that school leaders in England must become more adept at working in an environment that requires collaborative as well as competitive approaches.

Note

1. The OECD's three-year international benchmarking study, Programme for International Student Assessment (PISA), asks school principals to indicate who makes decisions regarding the school: the school itself, an external authority (such as the District) or a mixture of the two. A series of questions on specific aspects of school organization are categorized into two broad areas: i) resource allocation, including staffing and budgets; and ii) curricula and assessments.

Chapter 6

Leadership to transform outcomes in one deprived urban area

Chris Brown, Chris Husbands and David Woods[1]

Aims

This chapter aims to:

- tell the story of remarkable educational improvement across one deprived urban local authority – Tower Hamlets, in London – between 1997 and 2013
- analyse the factors that underpinned that improvement
- assess the implications for school system reform more widely.

Tower Hamlets in context

Tower Hamlets covers an area of less than eight square miles in east London, bordering the Thames and the City of London financial district. In the nineteenth century, the area was synonymous with poverty, overcrowding and disease, dominated by warehouses and the docks, and known – pejoratively – as the 'East End'. During the Second World War, bombing devastated much of the area, while the post-war period saw the decline of traditional dock industries, leaving substantial areas of land and buildings derelict. Part of the borough was designated as an economic development zone, and since 1980, there has been massive expansion of new industries and employment. Nevertheless, Tower Hamlets remains one of the poorest boroughs in the UK.[2] For example, 57 per cent of the borough's children were entitled to Free School Meals (FSM) in 2011.

Tower Hamlets has a diverse multicultural population, but the Bangladeshi community is the largest ethnic group: for example, 55 per cent of all children and young people come from a Bangladeshi background. In 2012, there were over 65,000 children and young people, of whom 89 per cent were classified as belonging to an ethnic group other than White British, with three-quarters (74 per cent) speaking English as an additional language.

There are ninety-eight schools in the borough. Of these, seventy are primary and fifteen secondary, along with a pupil referral unit and six special and short-stay schools. Early Years provision is delivered through the private and voluntary sector in over fifty-three settings and there are six local authority–maintained nurseries.

Deprived urban communities around the world often perform poorly in educational terms, yet Tower Hamlets reflects a remarkable story of educational improvement. The story begins in September 1997 with the appointment of Christine Gilbert as the borough's new director of Education. The educational 'legacy' inherited by Gilbert was 'dire': earlier that year the borough had been positioned 149th out of 149 local education authorities (LEAs) in terms of its performance. A damning Ofsted Inspection of Tower Hamlets followed in September 1998. The inspection report noted that only one-quarter (26 per cent) of pupils gained five or more higher-grade general certificates in secondary education (GCSEs) (the national qualification taken by sixteen-year-olds), compared to a national average of 43 per cent; and only 47 per cent of pupils achieved level four in the key stage 2 English tests (at age eleven), compared with 63 per cent nationally. Returning to the borough two years later, Ofsted found a great deal had been achieved (Ofsted, 2000): although pupil test results remained below the national average, the gap had started to narrow at each key stage, and there had been some significant achievements in raising standards. The report concluded that in a relatively short space of time Tower Hamlets had gone from having significant weaknesses to delivering what was required of it at least satisfactorily and often well.

By 2005, the 'Annual Performance Assessment' of Tower Hamlets found dramatic improvements. Attainment at key stage 1 and 2 was well above that of statistical neighbours, as was the proportion of pupils gaining five A*-C grades at GCSE. Attainment gaps too were narrowing although still below national averages. Tower Hamlets was providing a service that 'consistently delivered well above minimum requirements for users' and inspectors awarded the borough the highest grade possible. The last 'Annual Performance Assessment' of Tower Hamlets was written in December 2008 before this system of monitoring was scrapped: the borough maintained its rating, along with the judgement that it 'consistently delivered outstanding services for children and young people'.

In a space of less than ten years, Tower Hamlets had moved from a position where it was heavily criticized for a lack of strategic planning and the poor management of its services, to one in which it was praised for its high-quality services, sustained improvement in education outcomes, excellent partnership work and being highly ambitious for its children and young people.

Although there has been no overall inspection since December 2008, the story of improvement continues in the borough's school data, as well as in wider official documents. The 2012 performance data for its secondary schools, for example, illustrates that Tower Hamlets (in attaining an average of 61.4 per cent) had exceeded the national average by over 2 per cent (in terms of pupils achieving five A*-C GCSE grades, including

English and Maths). Similarly, in terms of expected progress between key stage 2 to key stage 4, the borough had exceeded the national average by 4 per cent in English and by 5 per cent in Maths. Encouragingly, the most deprived pupils (those eligible for FSM) also performed very well: over half (54 per cent) achieving five A*-C GCSE grades, including English and Maths compared to 36 per cent nationally, meaning that Tower Hamlets had reduced its achievement gap to only 7 per cent compared to a national gap of nearly one-quarter (23 per cent). In addition, and quite remarkably, by the spring of 2013 every secondary school in Tower Hamlets had been judged either 'good' or 'outstanding' by Ofsted inspectors (with seven out of fifteen ranked as 'outstanding': over twice the national average). Tower Hamlet's primary schools also exceeded both London and national averages at key stage 2 and level 4, with attainment in English at 89 per cent, in Maths at 86 per cent and in English and Maths combined at 82 per cent.

Explaining success

Ambitious leadership

Tower Hamlets became an education authority in 1990, following the abolition of the Inner London Education Authority, at the same time as a corporate reorganization of the council took effect, delegating decision-making and service delivery to seven neighbourhoods, a reorganization which was said in the 1998 Ofsted report to have been a 'disaster' (Ofsted, 1998: 11). Between 1990 and 1997, costs spiralled, the authority became concerned with securing adequate numbers of school places in the face of a serious deficit and then, between 1994 and 1997 'came largely to a standstill. The work of individual services was not given impetus and focus by clear leadership from the centre' (Ofsted, 1998: 13). Despite this, the damning report ended with a note of optimism: the borough understood the scale of the challenge and had appointed a new director of Education, Christine Gilbert, who had already put a new education development plan out for consultation.

Hargreaves and Shirley (2009) argue that Gilbert combined 'visionary' leadership with a concomitant strategy to raise performance by establishing goals that were deliberately designed to be just out of reach (Hargreaves and Harris, 2012). Ofsted (2000: 4) stated that 'much of the LEA's success in implementing the recommendations and improving its support to schools can be attributed to the high-quality of leadership shown by the director and senior officers. Headteachers, governors and members all expressed their confidence in the management of the LEA.' Kevan Collins took up his post as director of Children's Services in Tower Hamlets in 2005 when Gilbert was appointed chief executive. His initial assessment was that primary schools had already closed the gap 'dramatically', but that secondary schools were still lagging, with GCSE performance across the borough at 30 per cent. Nevertheless, he felt that the borough still needed to 'turn the screw' on primary schools, sending bespoke letters about their results, intervening strongly to agree programmes of work needed to secure targets and, as he puts it 'establishing the rhythm' of expectations at a time when England's National Strategies were stepping back.

The borough developed an in-depth knowledge both of its schools and the communities they served. Hargreaves and Shirley (2009) note that the borough built trust with its schools and developed deep insight about what was happening (more so than could be gleaned simply from performance spreadsheets). There were important significant early changes: not only was the advisory service restructured and brought closer to schools, but Gilbert insisted on a separation between inspection and support. Ofsted (2000) suggest that a key feature of the borough's leadership was the development of effective working partnerships with schools, but these were based on tough decisions. Officers, headteachers and advisers were trained in a rigorous and systematic way.

Very effective school improvement

The Ofsted report of 1998 was critical of the performance of schools and the borough's inspection and advisory service. It reported that the service was poorly regarded by schools with an overemphasis on monitoring and inconsistent levels of support. By 2000 Ofsted noted that a radically restructured advisory service had been put into place with not only clear strategies for supporting and developing schools but also monitoring and intervention where required. In this period the number of schools in special measures and serious weaknesses was a major concern and challenging targets were set to reduce this number. Over the next few years schools causing concern were monitored and reviewed very closely with appropriate support as required. For the primary schools the highly focused implementation of the literacy and numeracy strategies was paramount, and for all schools, leadership was under particular scrutiny. Where headteachers were found wanting, decisive action was taken. Indeed the data demonstrate that between 1998 and 2012, out of forty-eight schools causing concern or in Ofsted categories, forty-two heads were replaced. Crucially, the director of Children's Services and senior officers were closely involved with the appointment of new headteachers and did not hesitate to use their powers to prevent an appointment where they thought the governors' recommendation was inappropriate.

The LA also invested in the development of its leaders, creating a cohesive approach. In such a small borough, with less than one hundred schools, the authority knew its schools well and established a range of consultative forums to make sure that policies were explained and that the views of heads and other stakeholders could be taken into account. The shared intelligence about schools enabled the authority to support where required and to challenge appropriately. Over time a spirit of 'collaborative competition' seems to have developed – or what Hargreaves and Harris (2012) call 'an additional twist of friendly rivalry' – with success in some schools spurring on other schools to do just as well. Schools were also encouraged to work together, for example, with two Teaching School Alliances operating after 2010.

This action by the borough reflects the central importance of effective school leadership for school improvement, as explored in more detail in the following sections. As Leithwood and Seashore Louis note: 'To date we have not found a single documented case of a school improving its student achievement record in the absence of talented leadership' (2012: 3). The impact of school leadership is verified by examining the Ofsted performance data for Tower Hamlets between 2005 and 2012, which suggests that the overall effectiveness of schools is highly correlated to the effectiveness of its school leaders and management in embedding their ambition to drive improvement ($r^2 = 0.912$); similarly outcomes for individuals and groups of children appear to be strongly correlated to the effectiveness of the leadership of its schools and the management of teaching and learning ($r^2 = 0.999$) (see Woods et al., 2013, for methodology). Over time, Ofsted inspections have seen a steady improvement in the grading awarded for the leadership of teaching and learning.

High-quality teaching and learning

A massive teacher shortage was experienced in the mid-1990s with the result that teachers were recruited from abroad. Successfully reversing this position and attracting and retaining high-quality teachers is cited as a major feature of Tower Hamlet's approach to improving its educational performance (Hargreaves and Shirley, 2009).

The Tower Hamlets leadership realized that positive effort was needed not only to counteract the negative publicity which might flow from working in one of the most challenging and lowest performing of local authorities, but also to build an esprit de corps around teaching in and driving change for children. Specific initiatives were focused on recruiting and retaining high-quality staff; encouraging and supporting local people into education and maximizing work-based routes to qualified teacher status; improving the recruitment of newly qualified teachers; improving access to housing for teachers and professional development of teachers.

Of particular note was the desire to find out what attracted people to Tower Hamlets, what encouraged them into teaching and what persuaded them to stay in the borough. Extensive work was done on stressing the positive advantages of working in the borough – of being part of radical change, so that working in and for Tower Hamlets was 'the place to be' for those committed to urban education. Attraction packages often carried a requirement to stay in the borough for at least a defined period as a condition of accepting the package. This was underpinned by a high-quality continuing professional development offer at all levels and an explicit commitment to career development and to promotion from within. The borough ran a master's degree programme in close partnership with a university, and, at a time when many councils were closing theirs, kept a Professional Development Centre.

Intensive work was done on the recruitment of newly qualified teachers. Less high-profile, but just as important in building strong community cohesion, was the work on encouraging and supporting local people into education roles. An extensive programme with special courses for training teaching assistants was developed. The ultimate aim was to develop a clear progression route into teaching for these staff, the vast majority of whom were local people.

No doubt as a result of these and related initiatives, the inspection data for 2005–12 indicates that the overall effectiveness of schools in the borough was highly correlated to the quality of teaching ($r^2 = 0.926$) (see Woods et al., 2013, for methodology).

High levels of funding

No account of the education transformation in the borough can overlook resources. Tower Hamlets was well funded, with almost 60 per cent more resource per pupil than schools across England and higher levels of resourcing than almost all other London boroughs. Christine Gilbert contrasted Tower Hamlets with her experience as director of Education in Harrow, where money was always tight. Moreover, as schools in Tower Hamlets improved, so the council became yet more willing to invest in education: improvement drew in more resource.

It could be argued that the transformation of schooling in Tower Hamlets was simply a consequence of high levels of funding. But this argument runs into obvious flaws. If the performance of schools in Tower Hamlets was simply a consequence of funding, the 1998 Ofsted report would never have been written. It is undeniable that Tower Hamlet schools were well resourced – far better than most schools elsewhere – but money needs to be spent wisely and well. What Tower Hamlets began to achieve after 1997 was a highly effective return on levels of investment. If the Tower Hamlets story makes a strong case for high levels of education spending, it also makes a case for targeting that spending intelligently, for linking investment with outcomes, for monitoring the impact of spending and for building the case for investment.

Integrated services

The annual performance assessments of services for children and young people conducted by Ofsted between 2005 and 2008 regularly reported that the council made an outstanding contribution towards improving outcomes in all five areas of its Children and Young People Plan (see below). The priorities were firmly rooted in a community planning process, which involved all key stakeholders including children and young people. The authority's use of benchmarking to review performance and to set challenging targets was identified as good practice and the track record of successful partnership with other agencies identified as a clear strength.

The council's services were often described as making an excellent or outstanding contribution to improving the *health* of children and young people. Joint multi-agency strategies were judged to be very effective with a strong emphasis on prevention and detailed needs analysis. By the end of 2007 the authority had exceeded national targets for achieving 'Healthy Schools' status. Similarly, during these years the outcomes for the *safety and care* of children were described as outstanding with very strong and clear systems for information sharing and cross-agency working ensuring that the needs of vulnerable children were being met. In terms of *making a positive contribution*, there were excellent contributions to improving outcomes enhanced by collaborative work with a number of partners, including the youth offending team, the police and the voluntary sector. Opportunities for young people to have a say were provided through local youth partnerships, and the Tower Hamlets Youth Partnership and the Youth Parliament. In terms of *economic wellbeing*, the authority was very successful in making substantial reductions in the number of young people not involved in education, employment or training through targeted, innovative approaches. The proportion of young people achieving level two and level three qualifications at age nineteen was below the national average (200*), but increasing at a faster rate than nationally. The final area, *enjoying and achieving*, is covered elsewhere in terms of the sustained improvements in educational outcomes. A particular feature to note though were the excellent outcomes for vulnerable children, including looked-after children and those with learning difficulties and/or disabilities.

Community development and partnerships

Tower Hamlets has a powerful local identity shaped by history and experience. The first community plan was launched in May 2001 and produced by the local strategic partnership. There were three strands to this partnership – local area partnerships, community plan action groups and a partnership management group. In both, *Performing Beyond Expectations* (2012) and *The Fourth Way* (2009), Andy Hargreaves, Dennis Shirley and Alma Harris argue that community development was central to the success of Tower Hamlets as a 'turned-around district'. They argue that while most local authorities had endeavoured to deliver more children's services to disadvantaged and other communities, Tower Hamlets had gone further and had worked hard to create new capacity to strengthen community relations and engagement. For example, it had worked with faith-based organizations and made formal agreements with the Imams from this largely Muslin community to counter the effects of children taking holidays for religious festivities and extended holidays in Bangladesh during term time.

A particular feature of community relations and engagement in Tower Hamlets are the school- and community-based projects used very effectively to promote citizenship and community cohesion. For example, peer mentors were trained to improve relationships between younger and older residents. Activities promoted through the interfaith forum promoted community cohesion and interfaith understanding across schools. The youth service reached impressive numbers of young people through a range of community-based services and the youth participation team ensured that children's voices were heard.

A resilient approach to external government policies and pressure

Hargreaves and Shirley (2009: 67) argue that a key factor in Tower Hamlets' success was 'a resilient but not reckless approach to external government pressure and policy – accepting the importance of testing and targets, but deciding to set their own targets and resisting the politically motivated pressure to build new high school academies since the authority already had high-trust relationships with its schools that now performed very well'.

The low point in education outcomes in Tower Hamlets coincided with the coming to power of the Labour government in 1997. One part of Gilbert's recovery strategy was to engage directly and positively with the government's agenda. For example, Tower Hamlets became a pilot for some early initiatives and then robustly implemented the National Strategies setting their own ambitious targets for improvement. Collins (quoted in Woods et al., 2013: 46) put it like this: 'We did not set out to be innovative or to reinvent education. We adopted the national secondary strategy. We adopted assessment for learning and we set out to be brilliant at implementation. Implementation was what we set out to be good at. We wanted to do basic, basic stuff and get it right.'

Conclusions and implications

The achievements of Tower Hamlets and its schools after 1998 were exceptional: across the borough, all schools improved. The educational outcomes for all groups of pupils were substantially improved. Beyond this, the borough embedded a shared commitment to high standards and high expectations across the community, the council and schools. By any measure, the achievement is considerable. In this final section we ask: What were the key factors in Tower Hamlets' improvement? What are the lessons for policy and practice? And, at a time when governments across the world continue to drive change in education, what are the implications for global educational practices?

It is our contention that the transformation of schooling in Tower Hamlets depended on a number of linked factors: committed political leadership; challenging professional leadership; a robust approach to selecting from, and then rigorously managing, external policy imperatives; the engagement of schools; the judicious spending of generous levels of resourcing. We cannot answer counterfactual questions with precision, but it is our belief that while different approaches might still have seen improvement in some schools, the coherent, area-wide improvement would not have been possible without strong political and professional leadership within the authority.

Charles Payne's account of American school reform – So Much Reform, So Little Change (2008) is subtitled 'the persistence of failure in urban schools'. His account of the failure of repeated waves of school reform to bring about significant improvement in America's urban schools is compelling reading. Payne is dismissive of reform, which is disconnected from the daily realities of urban schools, dismissive of grand theories of change, and concludes that 'there is no one lever we can move which will give us the purchase we need' (Payne, 2008: 47). Payne argues that successful reform depends on what he calls 'five fundamentals':

- instructional leadership
- professional capacity
- establishing a learning climate[3]
- family and community involvement
- the quality of instruction.

Moreover, successful school reform is 'comprehensive, sustained and intense'. Payne's book ends with a coruscating denunciation of what he calls 'liberal and conservative theories of school reform' – the one arguing that school reform is impossible without serious assaults on poverty and the circumstances which create failure, and the other that circumstances do not matter, that incentive structures alone can drive change (Payne, 2008: 192–3). Both, he argues, are extremely damaging to children. In practice, says Payne, we know a great deal about successful reform, and he concludes his book with a mantra for effective reform.

> Give them teaching that is determined, energetic and engaging. Hold them to high standards. Expose them to as much as you can, most especially the arts. Root the school in the community and take advantage of the culture the children bring with them. Pay attention to their social and ethical development. Recognise the reality of race, poverty and other social barriers, but make children understand that barriers don't have to limit their lives. ... Above all, no matter where in the social structure children are coming from, act as if their possibilities are boundless. (ibid.: 211–12)

It is possible and useful to look at Tower Hamlets in the context of what we know about effective school improvement and reform across the world. For too long, the assumption of research and policy has been that effort must be focused on reforming and improving individual schools. But school reform at scale – successfully improving areas and districts – is more challenging. It is always possible for individual schools to improve – either by accident or design – by subtly altering their intake or shifting their relationships with neighbouring schools. In the long run, all this does is to move failure around the system. It is not a recipe for serious or sustained improvement.

Tower Hamlets is therefore a very important case study because of what it tells us about *area*-based reform. This is important for any number of reasons. If we can move our reform and improvement efforts from schools to areas, we have the prospect of improving the life chances not for sub-sets of children – important though this might be – but for all children and young people. If schools and their communities can bring about systemic improvement, then all benefit, and not simply a fortunate few who have found their way into more successful schools. It is the achievement of Tower Hamlets that it has made significant progress on that score.

The research is clear that there are some essential ingredients for school reform at scale. Heather Zavadsky's detailed study of five North American school districts (2010: 272) is clear that the initial ingredient, on which all else depends is 'climate or culture' – the buzz which leads to belief that success is possible and, eventually establishes trust. Beyond this 'reform needs to look different' depending on the community – though standards and expectations need to be high and consistent. In the same way, Levin's conclusions on 'how to change 5000 schools' set out some simple but – to those seeking to lead and manage change – far from obvious propositions: focus on a few key student outcomes that matter most and are most understandable; put effort into building capacity for improvement; build motivation by taking a positive approach; and work to increase public and political support for reform (Levin, 2008: 234–6). These were the lessons learnt in Tower Hamlets, and, it is worth noting, learnt before Payne, Zavadsky and Levin had synthesized their own understandings of the nature of successful urban reform.

The experience of Tower Hamlets since 1998 is inspirational. It shows that improvement is not only possible but achievable, that improvement in some schools does not need to be bought at the expense of others and that improvement, once attained, can not only be sustained but surpassed. As a result, it is not unreasonable to argue that what Tower Hamlets has created are some of the best urban schools in the world. This is a genuinely exceptional achievement, worth celebrating, worth understanding, but above all, worth learning from.

Notes

1. This chapter is an edited version of a longer study by the same authors published in 2013 entitled 'Transforming Education for All: The Tower Hamlets Story' (IOE Press).
2. See, for example, http://www.standard.co.uk/news/london/children-in-tower-hamlets-are-poorest-in-uk-with-42-per-cent-living-below-breadline-8502616.html; http://www.bbc.co.uk/news/uk-16483257;
3. In the text which follows, Payne clearly means 'learning climate' to 'include[e] ... the degree to which students perceive high expectations' (Payne, 2008: 46).

Part 2

School leadership in a changing landscape

Chapter 7

What makes a great school in the twenty-first century?

David Woods and Rachel Macfarlane

Aims

This chapter aims to:

- define and illustrate what being a 'great' school means in the twenty-first century

- explore the characteristics and features of great schooling through a model developed by the London Leadership Strategy's 'Going for Great' programme – The Nine Pillars of Greatness

- reflect on the different dimensions of great schooling identified.

Introduction

You can mandate awful to great but you cannot mandate greatness – that has to be unleashed.

Joel Klein

The purpose of this chapter is to consider the range of characteristics that define great schooling in the early twenty-first century. Dictionaries offer various definitions of great and greatness but the ones that could best apply to schools relate to 'remarkable achievements', 'exceptionality', 'excellence', 'superior character and quality' and 'impressive and striking effects'. The research literature is very extensive on good schools but there is much less written about great schools. This may be a question of terminology. In the descriptions of great schools, the terms 'world class', 'outstanding' and 'excellent' are often used interchangeably. For the purpose of this chapter, we will assume that these terms can be used to describe various areas of great practice.

But there is another dimension to great schools, connected to the broader purposes of education: a deeper sense of what is worth learning in the twenty-first century. 'Schools with soul' prioritize spiritual, moral, social and cultural education along with character development; for them, compassion is the key organizing principle promoting the highest collective values.

Great schools ask the question: 'By the time children finish school, what do we hope they will have become?' The answer to this might vary in different stages of schooling, but most of us would agree that they would be fluent, decent, self-driven achievers who live up to altruistic ideals and values; and that they would be compassionate individuals who care for each other and for the planet. Great schools should be places where everyone tastes the confidence that comes with success and where all children are aware of their potential to achieve almost anything if they invest the required effort and hardwork.

Of course, great schools vary in age range, size, context, locality, tradition and many other characteristics. Each school will have its own DNA, with unique and distinctive features. However, we would argue from the literature and the practical experience of working closely with great schools that they do share a number of key ingredients. A caveat is that we are writing at a particular time and future developments, particularly in learning technologies and the organization of schooling, may transform our concept of great schooling later in the coming decades.

What does the literature say?

An influential publication in the debate about great organizations and schools is Jim Collins' 2001 study of companies in the United States that were said to have progressed from 'good to great'. His contention was that 'good is the enemy of great – and that is one of the key reasons why ... we don't have great schools, (is) principally because we have good schools' (Collins, 2001: 1). He refers to organizations needing to 'transcend the curse of competence and complacency' and describes a range of characteristics of these great companies, including:

- 'level 5 leadership' (building enduring greatness through a blend of personal humility and intense professional will)
- confronting the brutal facts
- getting the right people in the right places
- being driven by core purpose
- having a culture of discipline to sustain great results
- the harnessing of technological accelerators.

His final concept of the flywheel reminds us that good-to-great transformation never happens in one fell swoop – there is no miracle moment but rather a predictable pattern of build-up, increased momentum and breakthrough. Some of Collins' concepts have been applied to studies of schools both in the United States and England, although with the recognition that the business and education sectors have different purposes and different success criteria (Gray and Streshly, 2008).

Michael Fullan was an early critic of Collins' model, pointing out that the concept of moral purpose, which was absent from the study, is a vital characteristic of great schooling. This is something that Fullan has reiterated in several books, while stressing the complex and ever-changing environment of schooling and the need for schools to constantly learn from each other to meet new challenges and to sustain high performance (Fullan, 2008).

In 2009, Andy Buck published *What Makes a Great School?* (updated in 2013), applying some aspects of the Collins model, along with the work of Fullan and others. He argues that great schools:

- are those that consistently perform at an outstanding level for a sustained period of time across a wide range of indicators
- have a deeply embedded set of strongly held values and traditions understood and lived by all staff, children and parents
- are outward looking both in terms of system leadership and the way that they are keen to learn from others.

Other commentators have referred to specific characteristics of great schools. Stephen Covey, in 'The Speed of Trust' (2008), reflects on successful organizations, saying that an essential element of a great school is that it has a high level of trust between staff members and between staff and students, where energy is released in a productive and efficient way, allowing for great progress towards goals (Covey, 2006). George Berwick, in 'Engaging in Excellence' (2011), sets out the building blocks of great schooling, exploring a theory of action based on effective knowledge management, encompassing moral, social and organizational capital (Berwick, 2011). Alistair Smith, in his study of high-performing schools in 2011, uses the analogy of performers in the circus arena to introduce a three-tiered model of school improvement: senior leaders (high-wire walkers), middle leaders (human pyramid) and classroom teachers (trapeze artists) (Smith, 2011). Tim Brighouse and David Woods in several publications have stressed the importance of a sustained culture of improvement – 'The very successful school has to juggle the past, present and future; it's juggling all these three components that marks out the continually outstanding school. For the outstanding school, "if it ain't broke" is just the very time to start fixing it. The outstanding schools anticipate' (2008: 135). For them the route to greatness lies in moral purpose: 'The determination, brought to reality, that all members of the school community should behave in a way that is mindful of each other' (Brighouse and Woods, 2008: 151).

There are many other publications that concentrate on particular aspects of great schooling, particularly with regard to students' learning and progress. Guy Claxton and Bill Lucas have written extensively about building learning power and how the science of learnable intelligences is changing education (Claxton, et al. 2011). David Hargreaves has reflected on the 'Four Deeps: deep learning, deep experience, deep support and deep leadership' (Hargreaves, 2008). The literature stresses the importance of schools developing a 'growth mindset' mentality (for example, Dweck, 2006). For students, teachers and school leaders, the central message is that success is possible for all, but it comes from a long-term developmental process, with improved performance resulting from rich, instrumental experiences and extensive practice.

Most recently there have been a number of publications from data derived from serving and recently retired headteachers describing how schools can become 'great' (Little, 2015; Coates, 2015, West-Burnham and Harris, 2015). Of particular interest is Roy Blatchford's 'The Restless School' (2014) with its emphasis on 'Excellence as Standard' for schools with an embedded culture of thinking and doing and a passion to be the best they can be. The quest for excellence becomes their habit and their purposeful practice.

In this brief and selective review of the literature, much of it practitioner-based, it is important, at least for English schools, to consider what the national inspection framework regards as outstanding schooling, although the term 'great' is never used. Over many years, Ofsted have published examples of outstanding practice in schools, but also stressed that great schools are more than the sum of their parts. Ofsted surveys and reports reflect key characteristics such as:

- strong values and high expectations that are consistently applied

- outstanding and well-distributed leadership

- sustained excellence

- highly inclusive culture

- having particular regard for the educational progress, personal development and wellbeing of every student

- constantly looking for ways to improve further (Ofsted, 2009, 2010).

The Framework for Inspection (2015) has grade descriptors for outstanding leadership and management including: governance; outstanding teaching, learning and assessment; outstanding personal development, behaviour and welfare; and outcomes for pupils (Ofsted, 2015).

International studies by McKinsey stress the key characteristics of great schooling as world-class teaching and learning underpinning excellent performance. This involves recruiting and retaining the right people, developing effective teachers who teach consistently well and establishing systems and support to ensure that every learner is able to benefit from excellent teaching (Barber and Mourshed, 2007; Barber, Chijoke and Mourshed, 2010).

Studies by Fenton Whelan (2009) and Andy Hargreaves and Denis Shirley (2009), as well as the work of Michael Fullan (2014) in *The Principal*, reflect on great schooling and systems in Canada, the United States, Finland and the Far East in particular. John

Hattie, in his meta-studies of educational research throughout the world, *Visible Learning* (2008) and *Visible Learning for Teachers* (2011), sets out the major school influences on educational outcomes as well as those interventions that do not appear to work. In *The Politics of Collaborative Expertise* he argues that in the best schools it is the excellence of teachers, the support of such excellence and an open debate about the nature of growth towards excellence that matters and that 'the possibility of attaining excellence is available to any student regardless of their background or prior achievement' (Hattie, 2015).

In 2009 the London Leadership Strategy, as part of the London Challenge, established a 'Going for Great (G4G)' programme for outstanding (in Ofsted terms) secondary schools. One of the major aims was to encapsulate the key features and qualities of schools which are consistently outstanding in order to better understand how outstanding schools become great schools. This programme, involving leaders from each of the G4G schools attending four seminars each year, focused on exploring the nature of greatness in schools by sharing and discussing experiences and research, setting up peer excellence visits, listening to and debating with keynote speakers and writing a case study showcasing great practice in each school. Over the six years that the programme has run, six practitioner case study publications have been written, encompassing some 130 studies (Macfarlane and Woods, 2010, 2011, 2012, 2013, 2014 and 2015).

The programme directors, in response to and influenced by the research literature, the G4G discussions, school-to-school visits and the case studies written by delegates, produced a model of great schooling, published as *The 9 Pillars of Greatness*. The rest of this chapter will focus on these nine pillars, to support our description of a great school in the twenty-first century.

The nine pillars of greatness

Pillar 1: A shared vision, values, culture and ethos, based on the highest expectations of all members of the school community

We could argue that a school cannot be great without a clear vision, understood and shared by all and underpinned by the school's values, philosophy and ethos. In the best schools, everyone is able to articulate their collective values and beliefs and their attention is focused on working to a common ideal and shared goals. The vision and aspirations of the school are optimistic and based on a 'growth mindset' philosophy. There is no ceiling on the expectations of the performance of any member of the school community.

The school's culture and ethos result from the application of its vision and values and manifest themselves in customs, rituals, symbols, stories and language. They are successfully expressed through the ways that members of the school community relate to each other and work together, through the organization of the school's structures, systems and physical environment and through the quality of learning for both pupils and adults.

The culture and ethos are embedded in the basic assumptions and beliefs that are shared by all members of the school community and are the 'glue' that holds everyone together. There is a commitment to excellence, to remaining open to new ideas and to thinking in new ways. Leaders at all levels act in a way that is consistent with the vision and values of the school. The collective vision permeates the whole institution and is felt by everyone who visits (Hargreaves and Shirley, 2009).

Pillar 2: Inspirational leadership at all levels throughout the school

A characteristic of great schools is that they grow and develop great leaders as well as great teachers, through coaching, mentoring, role modelling and providing a range of leadership opportunities. Great schools practice 'invitational' and 'distributed' leadership based on the belief that all have potential for growth and development (including students) and that everyone has a different profile of leadership qualities. Some of the G4G studies focused on strategies to build leadership capacity and manage talent within schools.

Other studies refer to transformational leadership, particularly from heads and senior leaders seeking to transform attitudes and beliefs and unleash the motivation to drive success. This is leadership that is visionary, inspiring and value based, where leaders are able to develop and share a compelling view of what a great school should be and communicate this effectively to the entire school community. Here leaders are enthusiasts, forecasters and cheerleaders. There is, however, a recognition that in great schools transformational leadership goes alongside excellent operational leadership, where leaders are planners, organizers, resourcers, technicians and deliverers, paying attention to detail and getting results through being resilient and determined (Leithwood et al., 2006, Fullan, 2014).

Leadership characteristics widely observed in the leaders of great schools include a sense of moral purpose, optimistic personal behaviour, clear communication, role modelling, transparency and trust, conviction and consistency. In every context, leaders need to lead through example with high expectations, enthusiasm and encouragement, to generate maximum effort and energy (Brighouse, 2007).

Pillar 3: Exceptional teaching, learning, assessment and feedback to support the highest levels of attainment and achievement

In great schools the promotion of high-quality learning is at the heart of the school's endeavours. There is an agreed school policy about the practice of teaching and learning which is subject to continuous review. This will be founded upon values and beliefs about the complexities of learning and the craft of teaching, underpinned by the highest of expectations, with a shared philosophy and a shared language transmitted effectively into every area of the curriculum (Smith, 2011; Robinson, 2011).

The leadership team will prioritize the careful selection, induction, training and retention of a consistently high calibre of teaching staff, with excellent subject knowledge and a passion for their curriculum area. Staff will routinely provide stretch and challenge to all students they teach and employ excellent classroom management and organizational skills.

Staff members will consider collectively what constitutes great learning and put in place effective processes and practices to maximize achievement and attainment. A variety of learning technologies and resources, which encourage independent thinking and learning, are used highly effectively and imaginatively across the curriculum (Claxton and Lucas, 2010).

Students are taught to learn independently so that homework becomes an effective opportunity for learning through practice, preparation, elaboration and exploration, paving the way for future learning and seamlessly linking one lesson's learning to the next.

In the classrooms of great teachers, assessment for learning is very well developed and consistently utilized, with regular opportunities for learning dialogues, self and peer assessment and diagnostic and developmental feedback based on accurate and robust pupil performance data. Great schools have carefully thought through the purpose and place of assessment, be it formative or summative, and testing is designed to inform and refine future teaching (Black, 2003). In great schools, curriculum enrichment is every pupil's entitlement: opportunities to learn beyond the classroom inspire and motivate pupils and lead to outstanding achievement.

Pillar 4: A relentless focus on engaging and involving students

In great schools, the students are involved in leading, managing and planning their educational experience at all levels. Everyone is considered a learner and it is emphasized that all members of the school community have a responsibility to support and motivate each other in their learning. This includes encouraging risk-taking, pushing oneself beyond one's comfort zone and embracing mistakes as an important part of the learning journey.

In great schools, student voice is strong throughout the school: through the student council and student leadership teams but also through day-to-day opportunities in every classroom, such as student surveys, feedback and evaluations which capture every voice on school matters. Students co-plan schemes of learning and co-construct learning activities with staff. Some of the G4G case studies have described initiatives whereby students have become teachers: writing schemes of learning, delivering them to their peers or younger students and evaluating them with staff.

In schools that are truly student focused, the students play a key part in the appointment of staff, edit and contribute to school publications and communications, observe and evaluate learning, are represented on school working parties and the governing body and its committees, and act as ambassadors in representing the school within and beyond the institution. Student focus groups research, investigate and report back on school issues, such as marking, homework, sanctions and rewards. Peer counsellors, mediators and mentors are used to aid behaviour management and maintain and rebuild student relationships where they have gone wrong (Coles, 2015).

Pillar 5: Personalized and highly effective continuous professional development within a learning community

Continuing learning for everyone is central to the notion of a great school. There are some powerful manifestations of this, such as establishing learning communities within the school, setting up a dedicated resource area for professional development, having a comprehensive system for electronically recording staff feedback on courses, conferences or visits to other schools, together with the use of teaching blogs and Twitter to exchange ideas. Great schools have regular publications of practitioner case studies of the best practice in learning and teaching, based on action research, with an expectation that all staff will wish to contribute. Great schools possess the crucial ingredient of collegiality among their staff, initiating support, and sharing and sustaining the best learning and teaching. In great schools the collaboration is not left to chance or even goodwill but structured through the development of teams and teamwork, study groups, reference groups and collaborative planning, teaching and assessment (Bubb and Earley, 2010; Hattie, 2008, 2011 and 2015). As part of staff development there will be organized coaching and mentoring involving pairs or small groups of staff working together. Great schools will have identified their outstanding practitioners and skilfully matched them to other staff. Action research and professional reflection is the norm rather than the exception: the school is enquiry minded and geared to innovation and research. The school is a knowledge-creating institution which fully mobilizes its intellectual capital to produce excellent educational outcomes.

Pillar 6: A stimulating and inclusive environment and climate for learning

Great schools have consistently high expectations of the behaviour of children, young people and adults and the relationships between them, based on mutual respect, honour, trust and kindness. Students are taught about healthy lifestyles, how to avoid risky behaviours, build successful relationships, manage emotions and act responsibly as mature citizens.

Considerable attention is paid to the whole school environment and the quality of the daily experience of those who work and learn in the school: the entrance foyer as a welcoming area, the playground, lunch facilities, toilets, corridors and social spaces as bright, safe and quality places that enhance the climate. A stimulating visual backdrop to learning is created by the public presentation of pupils' work, learning walls, whole school displays and exhibitions, the use of photographs, pictures, quotations and plasma screens. Displays reinforce the love of subjects and learning, celebrate achievement and progress and raise aspirations.

There is a high-quality infrastructure in place to support learning – for example, the library, resource bases and personalized spaces. Individual classrooms and learning areas are planned to encourage pupils' autonomous learning, their ownership of and responsibility for spaces and risk-taking within a safe environment. The use of digital technologies – both within and outside the classrooms and schools – enhance learning (Brighouse and Woods, 2013).

Pillar 7: A rich and creative curriculum, within and beyond the classroom, fully meeting the needs of individuals and groups of students

Great schools have a carefully considered curriculum, based on the vision, values and aims of the institution, where all subjects and stages interlink meaningfully and coherently. The curriculum will be concerned with the acquisition of knowledge and understanding, the development of learning skills and the fostering of positive character traits. It will support the development of lively, enquiring minds and the ability to question and argue rationally.

In great schools the curriculum helps pupils to understand the world in which they live, and the interdependence of individuals, groups and nations, enabling them to enter the wider world as active and responsible participants in society. Pupils have the opportunity to learn and practice skills that will prepare them for careers in a fast-changing world. The curriculum provides memorable experiences and rich opportunities for high-quality learning and wider personal development. Students are provided with cultural opportunities beyond their prior experience and their horizons are widened by a comprehensive programme of trips, activities, speakers, fieldwork and extracurricular sessions.

Learning and teaching will be personalized throughout the curriculum through pathways and tailored programmes for a wide range of pupils with differing needs, so that all are able to participate, progress and achieve (Robinson, 2001; Waters, 2013; Brighouse and Woods, 2014). The best schools will be at the forefront of successful and innovative curriculum design.

Pillar 8: High-quality partnerships with parents and the community, other schools and networks, locally, nationally and internationally

In the context of great schooling, comparatively little has been written about high-quality partnerships (see Chapters 5 and 14). We do not believe that a school can truly be called great unless it is also a system player and change agent, contributing to and sustaining knowledge and understanding of education and school systems locally, nationally and internationally. In a stimulating global world widening horizons is crucial. Great schools have a range of international partnerships for a variety of purposes, such as curriculum projects, learning languages and learning about different cultures. Locally, a great school should recognize its responsibilities for supporting the education of children and young people throughout the area, working closely with agencies such as social services, health, housing, as well as promoting sports and the arts. It should also develop partnerships with other local schools, helping to identify and disseminate best practice through excellence visits and shared professional development (Brighouse and Woods, 2013).

A great school seeks to build positive interactions with all parents and carers. It will prioritize links with families with specific needs and those who may be hard to reach. The school understands that community links are about mutual enrichment. It believes that all students, supported and encouraged by the school, should contribute to and positively impact the community. Its facilities and resources are fully used by the local community. Through these strong links, the school's excellent ethos will also permeate the local community and assist in promoting community cohesion.

Pillar 9: Robust and rigorous self-evaluation, data analysis and collective review

All great schools practise quality assurance and have developed a culture of self-evaluation. In England, this is likely to involve learning walks, lesson observations, evidence reviews and book looks, as well as the regular and forensic analysis of performance data, leading to creative discussions about strategies for improvement. In essence, the school learns its way forward, building in time for collective enquiry and continually striving for betterment. In particular, great schools practise appreciative enquiry – they appreciate the best of 'what is' in terms of current strengths, ask what it could be like if they could develop more of the good things identified, develop a vision of a preferred future and plan accordingly. Appreciative enquiry promotes creativity, questioning and dialogue, fostering a growth mentality.

In great schools there is continuous reflection, implicit in the way that all within the school community talk about their work and learning. Self-evaluation is grounded in sophisticated, accurate and open analysis and is used to compare performance against the most demanding of benchmarks. The school regularly seeks feedback and takes full account of the views of students, staff, governors, parents and the community as a whole (MacGilchrist, Myers and Reed, 2004).

Great schools do not restrict quality assurance to internal self-evaluation. They make good use of external critical friends. A school may need a range of critical friends for different aspects of school life and they may call upon the leaders of other schools to perform the role in the form of peer review (see Chapters 3 and 19). In great schools, evidence for self-evaluation is collected as a matter of everyday routine and in a culture that develops and sustains critical reflection, enquiry and intellectual curiosity, leading to continuous improvement and ensuring consistently high standards.

Summary

Reviewing the literature on great schooling and the nine pillars of greatness together we conclude that a great school in the twenty-first century will have the following characteristics. Most importantly a school cannot be called great without a clear vision and set of values understood and shared by all, and underpinned by inspirational leadership at all levels. A great school is thoughtfully outfacing, seeking and sharing best practice, as well as being a system player and a change agent. It is never satisfied with the status quo, always building on the present to secure an even better future. In great schools, the promotion of high-quality learning and teaching is at the heart of the school's endeavours, with very high levels of exceptional and consistent practice within a rich, innovative and inclusive curriculum. Great schools constantly harvest and harness knowledge, talent, creativity and energy, thriving on appreciative enquiry and quality assurance. A great school is future-proofed: reliably, rigorously, robustly and relentlessly doing the right things with the right people at the right time.

Remaining questions

This chapter concentrates on the experience of schools in England and it will be important to research great schooling in other countries, cultures and education systems.

- How far do definitions and characteristics of great schooling vary within different communities and societies?
- What is the impact of regulatory and inspection systems on great schooling?

Chapter 8

Setting direction: Vision, values and culture

Max Coates

Aims

This chapter aims to consider a number of issues around setting direction. More specifically:

- Leadership and culture are inextricably linked and their formation requires careful analysis and engagement
- Working definitions are offered for mission, vision and value statements
- Schein's (2004) analysis of 'culture' is considered
- A model for effecting cultural change is advanced.

Introduction

Whenever we engage with human groupings, we encounter culture. There are behaviours, attitudes, values and procedures that serve to delineate a particular group. Sometimes these are overt, declared and enforced, as for example, in a military context. In many organizations they are multilayered and amorphous. Consider for a moment a school that you might know. It will have stated aims and objectives; it will have structures such as a leadership hierarchy and a timetable. It will also have a pecking order and interconnectivity among staff and pupils which has not been mapped out in a handbook.

Often, when leading a school there is pressure to get on with the 'real' business. There is a need to write a strategic plan, perhaps to restructure, to secure the budget and to create the curriculum. However, to neglect a considered and structured response to culture is perilous to the point of being foolhardy. This is adroitly captured in the comment made by Peter Drucker in a conversation with Dick Clark, the CEO of Merck, that 'culture eats strategy for breakfast'. Schein (2004: 11) again stresses the importance of creating and managing culture: 'The only thing of real importance that leaders do is to create and manage culture. If you do not manage culture, it manages you, and you may not even be aware of the extent to which this is happening.'

This chapter argues that not only is generating the appropriate culture a high priority for leaders but that the concept has a synergy with mission, vision and value statements. If the three statements are afforded a centrality and engaged with consistently then they become powerful tools to explore and shape culture.

The big three

Many, probably most, schools have a statement, which purports to encapsulate its nature, activities and intentions. These often feature 'buzzwords' such as: achievement, potential, respect and community. There is often an uncertain journey from print to practice with the statement having little reference to the pragmatic operation of the organization. An example of this mismatch emerged from research into the development of Co-operative Trust Schools (Coates, 2013). Over the last few years the co-operative movement has provided a route to autonomy for schools by supporting them in becoming trust schools. Schools making this transition were required to commit to the very explicit statement of values that underpin the co-operative movement. The research undertaken indicated that for a number of these schools lip service was paid to these values and the change to becoming a Co-operative Trust School was merely badge engineering. A senior manager when asked, what difference does it make to be a Co-operative Trust Academy, replied 'absolutely nothing' (Coates, 2013: 17).

These aphorisms are usually presented under one of three headings: the value statement, the mission statement or the vision statement. This trio are not, however, synonyms. Equally, they are not alternatives so it is not helpful to select one in preference to another. It is suggested that each provides a specific focus and also serves a particular purpose. The following are not offered as being ex cathedra definitions but rather more working explanations to support developmental thinking.

Values statement

This is concerned with what the organization holds to be the correct way to behave as individuals and so ultimately how this is demonstrated collectively. It can serve as a lens through which to review policy, deployment of budget, inclusion and exclusion, relationships with other schools and the emphasis given to different aspects the curriculum. The list is almost endless. Used effectively it can become the forum for appeal in evaluating decision-making, behaviour and the formulation of policy. Consider the following example of a value statement from Corelli College in South London. This is a Co-operative Trust School which featured in the research mentioned above (Coates, 2013). The college emphasis on their stated values and the translation of these into their actions. Their unequivocal statement is:

ounded on a set of values called the Co-operative values which many organiz-
.cross the world use as their guiding principles. We chose these values because
we . .ieve they will enable our students to become active and responsible citizens and make Corelli College a happy and productive learning community. Everything we do is based on these values: self –help, responsibility, democracy, solidarity, equality and equity. (Corelli College, 2015)

Mission statement

This has a present tense dimension to it. It is very much about what the organization currently does or is attempting to do. It can be the case that platitudes and clichés used in such statements can obscure intentions and lead to the production of a form of words that is anodyne, even meaningless.

Consider the mission statement from The Sacred Heart Catholic School in South London: 'Our school strives to be a Catholic community in which Christian principles of care and respect are valued, with emphasis on the development of the individual through academic achievement and personal development' (Sacred Heart, 2015).

This statement makes some good points; it uses inclusive language, it makes its faith basis explicit and places both the status of the individual and the expectation of achievement at a high level. Less obvious is the connection between the mission statement and the school's declared specialisms. The school is also a specialist Mathematics, Computing and Language College. The Department for Education expects that such agreed specialisms will receive focus, resources and demonstrate excellence. Clearly, the school believed these two areas to be important and yet they are not noted in the school's mission statement. This should be taken as an observation and is certainly not intended as a judgement of the actual operation of the school.

Of course, mission statements are invariably framed in both positive and acceptable terms. To date no school or academy has dared to capture its activities in this way: 'Our school is focussed on examination results to the exclusion of the development of personal creativity. We apply covert selection procedures to secure pupils of a high ability. Staff are driven relentlessly within a climate of coercion and fear. Obtaining a good Ofsted judgement and excellent GCSE and A level results take priority in every decision that we take.' (Chapter 17 on toxic leadership picks up some of these themes.)

Vision statement

Here the tense becomes a future one. Of the big three, this can be the most problematical, generating more of a wish list than a direction. It is in such statements that phrases such as 'helping every child achieve their potential' or 'striving to be the hub of our local community' can become commonplace. Many of these sound worthy but are either intangible or rely on something outside the school for their realization. What happens if the local residents have their own ideas as to where they want the community hub to be located?

One school that captures the concept of a vision statement is that of St. Stephen's Primary School, Bristol. These are two statements drawn from the full suite of six: 'Imagine a school that inspires and nurtures all individuals to become confident and adaptable learners for life, a school that builds resilience and challenges each person to realise their full potential.' 'Imagine a school that embraces the uniqueness, curiosity and creativity of all children, a school that prepares children to invent the future and to achieve their goals' (2015). An extended account of St. Stephen's development of its vision statement is contained in the vignette.

Vignette

Evolving a vision statement: St. Stephen's Infant School, Kingswood, Bristol

The current head, Tim Ruck, was appointed in 2006. One of the first things that he did was to work on a vision statement for the school and to explore how it could develop real traction in the life of the school community.

In September 2006 he initiated the first vision-setting day. The meeting included teaching staff, support staff, parents and governors. The focus was 'What do we want our school to be like?'. This session resulted in a working group that formulated their first vision statement around the ideas of being happy, healthy and eager to learn.

The vision statement is now part of a three-yearly review when it is revised and then followed by extensive consultation with parents and carers as well as staff and children. The head did say that with the children their initial focus seemed to be more about chocolate and the size of the playground.

They have just finished their third review. It has become altogether more sophisticated. A major feature is a review of the previous three years. Small groups of stakeholders are asked to consider aspects of the vision statement using evidence including data, video, photomontage and parental questionnaires. These are evaluated using a traffic light system; green for 'on track', amber for 'perhaps faltering a little' and red for 'in need of attention'. They can also 'park' issues, which they want to discuss later.

The head also feeds in ideas and developments which he considers important. In 2012 the University of Bristol's 'Effective Lifelong Learning Inventory' was included. Using animal symbols this has had a significant impact on developing the pupils' engagement with learning. Other additions have included developing an understanding of neuroscience for four- to seven-year-olds, growth mindsets (Dweck, 2006) and 'teamship' rules. The latter are an annually signed agreement by staff around the expectations about being a team member and focus on behaviours and attitude.

> How has this impacted the school? The vision statement review together with its annual 'mini review' shapes the strategic planning of the school, which is also annual. It has generated community connection such as infant age children undertaking community service and developing global links with other children. The vision statement is very much part of the induction of new staff. Members of the school's strategic leadership group are identified with different areas of the vision statement and leading in these areas.

That future focus is captured by that word 'imagine'. It is resonant with Copperrider's statement that: 'Human systems have an observable tendency to evolve in the direction of those positive images that are the brightest and boldest, most illuminating and promising' (2003: 12).

The quoted vision statement also has an action focus in that it is explicitly linked to the 'Effective Lifelong Learning Inventory' (Crick et al., 2013). Underpinning key words such as 'resilience', 'adaptable' and 'curiosity' are research-based constructs, which provide an established route to support the school's intentions.

The above gives an overview of the differences between these three statements. Regrettably they often lack impact and cynicism or indifference within the organization robs them of their potential contribution, while ambiguity renders them ineffectual as an agent of transformation.

The significant issue for any of the statements lies in their actualization. The following account illustrates their all-too-frequent emasculation. I was coaching two Year 10 pupils who were under imminent threat of permanent exclusion. Between the two appointments I was standing in the corridor watching the arterial flow of the school day. Suddenly, I saw a young girl ejected from a nearby classroom. The door was slammed after her with such violence that plaster fell out from around the architrave. The girl, probably in Year 9, stood stifling sobs. She had her hair braided and beaded and I thought that might be a good entry point for a conversation. I commented that her hair must have taken a great deal of time and was it for a special occasion? The answer was four hours and that she was a bridesmaid at her sister's wedding the following weekend. I observed that the lesson did not seem to have gone too well. I was told that she had taken a mirror out of her pocket to have a quick look at her hair. The teacher had told her to put the mirror away and get out. As she was leaving the teacher announced 'she might think that she looked beautiful but she needed to know that she wasn't'. It struck a discordant note with the school's value system prominently displayed in the entrance. This claimed their foundations were courage, honesty, learning and respect. This was a spectacular piece of 'rug pulling' by that staff member.

There is a need to move beyond marketing straplines. The American ethicist Hauerwas (2001) suggests that there is a requirement to thicken words and ideas. This he understood as being a need to add layers of meaning and interpretation, to consider the implications of the statement in a real-world context. The filing cabinet is not the preferred location for mission, vision and values statements; rather they must become reference points for decision-making, strategic intent, evaluation and organizational dialogue.

Culture and values

The chapter started with a mention of Schein (2004). He is a time-served writer on organizational culture and has provided a model for working with cultural analysis and formation. Of course, his is not the only framework but it does offer a pragmatic approach to a subject, which can all too readily become somewhat esoteric. For Schein the culture of a group can be defined as: 'A pattern of shared basic assumptions that the group learned as it solved its problems of external adaptation and internal integration, that has worked well enough to be considered valid and therefore, to be taught to new members as the correct way to perceive, think, and feel in relation to those problems' (2004: 17).

Schein offers a three-tiered analysis of culture: artefacts, espoused beliefs and values and the third tier, basic underlying assumptions. They are often presented in diagrammatic form as an iceberg. The metaphor being used to reinforce the message is that much of culture is below the surface and the deeper you go the harder it is to articulate and define. It is summarized here as a table and the values, vision and mission statements have been mapped on to Schein's model. The examples and the mapping have been developed by the author.

Table 8.1 Summarizing levels of culture and relating these to mission, vision and values statements (Schein, 2004)

Levels from Schein's model	Manifestations	Statement
Artefacts (Evident)	Rituals, timetable, myths and legends, architecture, uniform, dress code, setting, documents, notices, assemblies, CPD, parking arrangements, arrangement of pupils/students by age, reporting, assessment, curriculum structure options	Mission
Espoused Beliefs and Values (Rational)	Views on intelligence, appropriate pedagogy, accountability, equity, community, academy categorization, gender	Vision
Basic Underlying Assumptions (Affective)	Motivation, racism, sexism, limited aspirations, hierarchy, trust, honesty, integrity, respect (by whom for whom), confidentiality ·	Values

The argument advanced so far is that culture – whether positive or negative – will enable or disable the success of the school. Changing that culture is challenging and time-consuming: 'In the best of schools, with the best resources and the most skilled leadership, the timeframe for transforming culture, structure and belief and practice is years' (Evans, 2001: 27).

To change culture, content and process must be conjoined. They always remain as being work in progress. St Stephen's vision statement (see Vignette) is time-limited, running from 2015 to 2018. It may well be that an existing statement has to be developed as new thinking and engagement emerges. Like other areas of organizational development, a carefully conceived and time-lined plan is paramount. These can be bespoke; Schein (2010) offers a ten-step model. Kotter's 'Eight Step Change Model' (1996) could also be utilized. This ascending staircase model is a useful tool to support the implantation of linear change. In this case it is offered for consideration as a means to engage with culture reform.

Step 1: Establishing a sense of urgency

Put another way, if the arguments for engaging with culture have not been convincing it is best not to start changing it. There is a need for relentless engagement. If your focus changes, then the identified priorities will automatically slip off the agenda as they are perceived as being no more than the leader's latest initiative. Of course, culture will still be the backdrop of every other development.

Step 2: Forming a powerful guiding coalition

The option is to work with a larger organizational group or a smaller change team. The latter could be the senior leadership team or a cross-sliced group drawn from across the organization. The decision here is not clear-cut and may well depend upon the size of the organization, its maturity and its willingness to participate.

Step 3: Creating a vision

This is where the statements start to be crafted. The two of choice are either the mission statement or the values statement. The mission statement is easier to formulate and subsequently communicate. If the values statement is selected, then this clearly underpins every aspect of the operations of the school. It is however harder to communicate and those who will do this must feel confident that they have explored how they will model this. It may well be that an external facilitator will be beneficial here. There will be three outputs from this stage:

- The statement itself, which will be relatively brief but not such that its meaning is not clear and applicable

- A carefully crafted story that supports the statement. This is essential and should be around three minutes in length
- A reasoned rationale complete with evidence and perhaps statistics. This will be needed at some point but should be available if asked for.

Step 4: Communicating the vision

The classic approach is the staff presentation perhaps followed by meetings with pupils and parents. The challenge here is that such meetings tend to impose rather than invite. A more viable method is to use coaching conversations. Engagement with individuals using the triple strand of coaching of empathy, listening and questioning is more likely to broker understanding and 'buy-in'.

The guiding coalition literally divides those to whom the vision must be communicated into groups and speaks to each person individually. After this a more formal presentation could follow.

Step 5: Empowering others to act on the vision

Again coaching should be considered as being central to this stage of the process of change. The very act of listening serves to empower staff. If coaching is used during this stage it will also surface the specific professional development needs of the individual. If these are addressed and the individual gains confidence in an area where they are perceived to be weak, they will gain in personal confidence and be more likely to identify with the organizational intentions and narrative. Individuals lacking in skills and confidence are more likely to defend themselves by denigrating the organization and its leaders. In one academy chain involved in the research it was decided to implement the current Singaporean approach to mathematics. This was imposed but in fairness was supported by extensive professional development. The latter lacked personalization and made large assumptions around the mathematical ability of non-specialist primary teachers. The training did not engage with the teachers' fears around their personal competencies and so in some cases these staff reverted to their earlier approaches.

Step 6: Planning for and creating short-term wins

Many individuals do not cope with deferred gratification while others suffer a transfer of attention to other issues. The impact of the statement must be demonstrated and sooner rather than later. Examples of good practice resonant with the statement must be showcased. This could be through a newsletter, a spotlight on practice in a staff meeting, an information slot in a governors' meeting or a featured display in a prominent part of the school. This sends the message that something is indeed going on and also that this is an ongoing initiative, which is being afforded high status.

Step 7: Consolidating improvements and producing more change

This is the point where not only does monitoring take place but it also provides the opportunity for inclusion. The majority can edit the statements and not only increase their breadth but secure a greater level of identity.

Step 8: Institutionalizing new approaches

The statements become routinely used in devising policy. They are brought into meetings to support prioritization. Crucially, they become embedded in documentation so that their centrality is reinforced.

In outlining Kotter's (1996) change model, coaching has been mentioned a number of times. It is suggested that this is a key skill in both embedding mission, values and vision statements and also in challenging extant culture and developing fresh culture. Schein (2010) tends to support such a coaching approach with his advocacy of using questions rather than instruction. He does, importantly add the caveat that ultimately culture must change at the level of the group and not the individual.

Conclusion

My wife and I went to the cinema recently and I was astonished to see after the advert for Calvin Klein a video extolling the virtues of a local academy. I had got used to seeing the hoardings on the back of buses but this took marketing schools to a whole new level. A neo-liberalist model of education will almost inevitably generate marketing by schools. It is, however, a travesty if 'strap lines' become substituted for carefully articulated statements of intention. Statements of mission, vision and values are key tools in shaping a culture of achievement. Of themselves they are not a magical incantation but rather an output of a dynamic process of organizational change. Used properly they support alignment and define direction. When they are carefully crafted and consistently used as a focus they generate motivation. They can be plaited into a threefold cord.

When leaders tackle culture – whether to dismantle dysfunctional culture or to evolve a more appropriate culture that supports its aims – consistency must be preeminent. Schein (2010: 237) argues:

> The most powerful mechanisms that founders and leaders, managers and parents have available for communicating what they believe in or care about is what they systematically pay attention to. This can mean anything from what they notice and comment on to what they can measure, control, reward and in other ways deal with systematically. Even casual remarks and questions that are geared to a certain area can be as potent as formal control mechanisms and measurements.

There can be no 'downtime' in cultural formation but if Schein (2004) is to be believed, then engaging with culture is not an adjunct to leadership, it is actually the breath of leadership itself. To change focus away from cultural formation is by definition to direct the attention of others in the organization away from the things, which have been designated, of crucial importance. The very act of inconsistency in working with culture will undermine its formation and create a parallel track. In the 1990s, schools in England began to engage with strategic planning. Nowadays, its lack would be seen as a culpable deficit. There is a need to develop a similar process to generate a culture that will sponsor outstanding learning, teaching and formation. In the same way that DNA classically has two strands, our school leaders should have strategic planning and cultural development connected like a double helix.

Chapter 9

Conceptions of leadership and leading the learning

Peter Earley

Aims

This chapter aims to:

- define leadership and note its impact on student outcomes

- discuss notions of learning-centred leadership and leadership for learning (LfL)

- consider leading the learning and how leaders develop people and enhance the quality of teaching and learning

- present the case why LfL matters even more in high-stakes accountability systems.

Numerous research studies and reports state that leadership is a crucial factor in organizational effectiveness and the key to success and improvement. It is now widely acknowledged that high-quality leadership is one of the key requirements of successful organizations and that leaders can have a significant positive impact on organizational goals, or in the case of education, student outcomes (Day et al., 2009, 2011; Robinson, 2011).

This chapter begins with a brief discussion of the concept of leadership and its impact on educational outcomes. Next, models of school leadership, in particular, LfL or learning-centred leadership, are considered. Such notions of leadership have continued to gain primacy over other conceptions of leadership of schools (Hallinger, 2012). The main facets of LfL and how learning-centred leadership is enacted, especially in developing people and creating a learning atmosphere or culture, are also considered. Considering how leaders undertake such leadership is the main subject of this chapter; however, the notion of 'learning' is problematized which is seen as particularly relevant within high-stakes accountability systems.

Defining school leadership

The range of popular and academic literature on leadership is extensive; there has been substantial interest and research into what effective leadership looks like, with as many as 65 different classification systems developed to define the field and over 300 definitions of leadership (Bush and Glover, 2003, 2014). Northouse (2009), in a comprehensive review of the leadership literature, notes the wide variety of theoretical perspectives and points to the fundamental differences between trait, behaviourist, political and humanistic approaches or theories. He points to the emerging view that leadership is a process that can be observed in the behaviours of leaders and the need for leaders and followers to be understood in relation to one another and as a collective whole.

With reference to the education sector, Earley and Weindling (2004) note the changing discourse of the relevant literature from an emphasis on management to one of leadership. A number of typologies are offered and leadership theory is categorized chronologically under five headings: trait, style, contingency, influence and personal trait theory, the latter seeing effective leadership as superior individual performance centred on notions such as emotional intelligence. Dominant conceptions of leadership in education are seen as transformational, learning centred and distributed and these and other notions of leadership are discussed in Bush and Glover (2014). Recent thinking sees leadership operating at all levels of an organization with leaders working to create an environment in which everyone can grow and talent is developed. In fact, a simple definition of a leader is someone who creates an environment in which everyone can flourish!

The importance of leadership has long been recognized but as a concept, it is elusive and there is no clear, agreed definition of it. Definitions are both arbitrary and very subjective but the central concept is usually 'influence' rather than authority – both are dimensions of power, with the latter usually associated with a formally held and recognized position (Yukl, 2002). Northouse (2009: 3) in synthesizing the research offers a definition of leadership as 'a process whereby an individual influences a group of individuals to achieve a common goal'. The notion of 'influence' is neutral, however, and leadership is usually linked with 'values' – leaders' actions are clearly grounded in personal and professional values.

Effective school leaders have a strong sense of moral purpose and social justice. They influence others' actions in achieving desirable ends. The process of leadership is also 'intentional' in that the person seeking to exercise influence is doing so in order to achieve certain purposes. Another I is for inspiration – rarely is this notion not found in conceptions of leadership. Leadership is also often associated with 'vision' which provides the essential sense of direction for leaders and their organizations (Bush and Glover, 2014).

How leaders influence organizational outcomes

Day and Sammons (2013: 3) in a review of successful leadership note that 'international examples of original research provide consistent evidence that demonstrates the impact of leadership on school organisation, culture and teachers' work'. Such research they state offers substantial empirical evidence that the quality of leadership can be a crucial factor in explaining variation in student outcomes between schools. Karen Seashore Louis, who has been involved in many impact studies over the years (e.g. see Louis et al., 2010), remarks:

> Although leaders affect a variety of educational outcomes, their impact on students is largely indirect and is relatively small compared to other factors. While formal leaders interact with pupils in many circumstances, the impact of schooling on students occurs largely through more sustained relationships that occur in classrooms and peer groups. (2015: 1)

The effect of leaders is largely *indirect*; what leaders do and say, and how they demonstrate leadership does affect pupil-learning outcomes, but it is largely through the actions of others, most obviously teachers, that the effects of school leadership are mediated. Achieving results through others is therefore the essence of leadership and it is the 'avenues of leader influence' that matter most (Hallinger and Heck, 2010). For Southworth 'effective school leaders work directly on their indirect influence' (2004: 102).

A major British study into the impact of school leadership found that school leaders 'improve teaching and learning and thus pupil outcomes indirectly and most powerfully through their influence on staff motivation, commitment, teaching practices and through developing teachers' capacities for leadership' (Day et al., 2009: 2). They also refer to the importance of school culture and trust. However, they also state 'the question of the size of leadership effects and how they operate (directly or indirectly) to raise student outcomes remains a subject of debate' (ibid.: 3). They suggest that school leadership influences student outcomes more than any other factors, bar socio-economic background and quality of teaching. They cite the 'New Leaders for New Schools' report from the United States which states that 'nearly 60% of a school's impact on student achievement is attributable to principal and teacher effectiveness with principals accounting for 25%' (ibid.: 19). However as Osborne-Lampkin, Folsom and Herrington (2015) systematic review of the empirical studies published between 2001 and 2012 on the relationships between principal characteristics and student achievement in the United States suggests, it is not a simple matter to research and correlation does not imply causality. Although perhaps it is unwise to attempt to quantify the exact effect size, there is little doubt that the research evidence reinforces the earlier point that leadership matters. What is more, it is suggested that LfL or learning-centred leadership matters most. It is to this model of leadership that we now turn.

Leadership for learning

Bush and Glover (2014) helpfully divide models of leadership into eight types: instructional leadership, managerial, transformational, moral and authentic, distributed, teacher leadership, system leadership and contingent leadership. It is the first model, that of instructional or pedagogic leadership, that has developed into LfL. Hallinger (2012) notes how instructional leadership has been reincarnated as a global phenomenon in the form of 'leadership for learning'. Timperley (2011: 145) states that leadership that is focused on promoting effective teaching and learning has had a number of terms 'as with any idea that gains currency in education, the labels for this kind of leadership abound and have usually taken an adjectival form of instructional, pedagogical or learning-centred leadership. Alternatively it is expressed as leadership of or for something, such as leadership for learning.' Learning-directed learning is another term used.

Timperley goes on to say that Murphy et al. (2007) summed up the essence of the ideas expressed in these multiple labels when they said:

the touchstones for this type of leadership include the ability of leaders

a to stay consistently focused on the right stuff – the core technology of schools, or learning, teaching, curriculum and assessment, and

b to make all the other dimensions of schooling (e.g. administration, organization, finance) work in the service of a more robust core technology and improved student learning. (2007, cited in Timperley, 2011: 146)

In broad terms, whatever its label, it is an approach to leadership 'whereby the leader helps foster a learning climate free of disruption, a system of clear teaching objectives, and high teacher expectations for students. Elements include principal leadership, clear mission, teaching expectations, and opportunities to learn' (Osborne-Lampkin, Folsom and Herrington, 2015: 2).

This form of leadership is highly concerned with improving student outcomes, where the focus is on learning and leading teachers' professional development. For example, Southworth (2002: 79) states that 'instructional leadership is strongly concerned with teaching and learning, including the professional learning of teachers as well as student growth'. Southworth has contributed significantly to the debate about learning-centred leadership and has developed a model which includes the strategies of modelling, monitoring and dialogue (Southworth, 2009; Earley, 2013). For Southworth, learning-centred leadership is about 'the simultaneous use of these strategies in ways which mutually reinforce one another. It is their combined effect which creates powerful learning for teachers and leaders and which, in turn, inform teachers' actions in classrooms and lead to improved teaching and student learning' (ibid.: 101).

Learning-centred leadership emphasizes the centrality of teaching and learning and suggest that leaders' influence on student outcomes is via staff, especially teachers. MacBeath (2006: 39) agrees with Southworth (2003) saying that, 'instruction is no longer our guiding star; rather it is learning. If learning is our primary goal, then we should think of leadership being "learning centred" rather than instructional.' LfL has also been conceptualized as a combination of pedagogic and transformational leadership (Day and Sammons, 2013; Robinson, 2011). If this is the case, then how can leaders lead the learning? How might this form of leadership be operationalized in schools and classrooms?

Leading the learning: Making it happen

This section considers how leaders can act as learning-centred leaders, especially their role in developing people, enhancing the quality of teaching and learning and having a positive impact on student outcomes, broadly defined.

As mentioned above, Southworth (2009) discussed the learning-centred leadership strategies of modelling, monitoring and dialogue to which West-Burnham later added mentoring as underpinning all three (Earley, 2013). For the OECD, LfL was about focusing on supporting, evaluating and developing teacher quality which included 'coordinating the curriculum and teaching program, monitoring and evaluating teaching practice, promoting teachers' professional development, and supporting collaborative work cultures' (Schleicher, 2012: 18). For Levin, leaders must see leading learning as their main responsibility, 'to which they devote a considerable amount of time and attention and which takes priority over other competing pressures' (2013: 6). Rhodes and Brundrett (2010: 156) argue that senior leaders need to help teachers – who are leaders of teaching and learning in classrooms – 'to improve their own practices by enabling teachers to continue to learn themselves'.

In order to keep a focus on learning it is important to visit classrooms and participate in professional development, initiate and guide conversations about student learning, keep up to date and share learning with others, make pupil learning a focus for performance evaluation, establish teaching and learning as central topics for school-wide staff meetings, analyse data about student learning and use it for planning and to set goals for improvements in learning and then review progress in relation to these goals (Levin, 2013).

Southworth has made a number of suggestions of how systems and structures can support learning-centred leadership. These include planning processes – for lessons, units of work, periods of time, classes and groups of students, and individuals; target setting – for individuals, groups, classes, years, key stages and the whole institution; communication systems – especially meetings; monitoring systems – analysing and using pupil-learning data, observing classrooms and providing feedback; roles and responsibilities of leaders – including mentoring and coaching – and policies for learning, teaching and assessment and marking (2009: 102).

The work of Robinson and her colleagues in New Zealand (Robinson, Hohepa and Lloyd, 2009; Robinson, 2011) has convincingly demonstrated how leadership related to teacher development has by far the greatest impact on student outcomes. In their meta-analysis of the five factors underpinning effective leadership 'Promoting and participating in teacher learning and development' was found to have the greatest influence on student outcomes. Such leaders ensure an intensive focus on teaching-learning relationships; promote collective responsibility and accountability for student achievement and wellbeing; and provide useful advice about how to solve teaching problems (Robinson, Hohepa and Lloyd, 2009). The central message of the research was clear: 'The more leaders focus their relationships, their work and their learning on the core business of teaching and learning the greater their influence on student outcomes' (Robinson, Hohepa and Lloyd, 2009: 201). Vignette 1 outlines this further.

Vignette 1

Leadership where it counts: making a bigger difference to your students

Robinson's book *Student-Centred Leadership* (2011) provides research-based guidance on the leadership practices associated with increased learning and wellbeing of students. At its core is a meta-analysis of 30 research studies which have examined the links between various types of school leadership and students' academic and social outcomes. The five leadership dimensions associated with successful leadership are:

1 Establishing goals and expectations

2 Resourcing strategically

3 Ensuring quality teaching

4 Leading teacher learning and development

5 Ensuring an orderly and safe environment.

For Robinson 'making a bigger impact requires moving beyond a "general idea" about the importance of these five dimensions, to a more precise understanding of how they work to improve the quality of teaching and learning'.

● The first dimension of student-centred leadership involves setting and communicating clear goals.

This 'requires gaining commitment of all those involved by linking goals to values which people hold dearly; ensuring that staff have or can acquire the capabilities needed to achieve the goals and using evidence about current levels of student achievement to set important and realistic targets'.

● Once these goals are established, the second dimension of effective leadership – resourcing strategically – comes into force. 'Scarce resources – money, time on the timetable, teaching materials and staff expertise – are allocated in ways that give priority to key goals. ... Strategic resourcing and strategic thinking are closely linked.

Strategic thinking involves asking questions and challenging assumptions about the links between resources and the needs they are intended to meet.'

- The third dimension 'involves ensuring the quality of teaching'. In schools 'where teachers report that their leadership is heavily involved in these activities, students do better'. For Robinson this form of leadership 'requires a defensible and shared theory of effective teaching that forms the basis of a coherent teaching programme in which there is collective rather than individual teacher responsibility for student learning and well-being'.

- The fourth dimension of leadership aims to 'develop the capacity of teachers to teach what students need to learn, while being open minded about what that is and how to achieve it'. Crucial here is leaders' 'knowledge of the types of professional development that are more and less likely to make an impact on the students of the participating teachers'.

- For Robinson although the third dimension scores the highest 'effect size' it is the fifth dimension which provides a foundation for all the rest. 'Effective leadership ensures a safe and secure environment for both staff and students. Teachers feel respected, students feel their teachers care about them and their learning, and school and classroom routines protect students' learning time. Strong ties are developed by bringing relevant cultural resources into the school and classrooms and by more direct involvement of parents in the educational work of the school.'

Robinson notes that while the five dimensions tell leaders where the biggest difference to student outcomes can be made, they say little about 'the knowledge, skills and dispositions needed to make the dimensions work in a particular school context'. She points to the importance of three interrelated capabilities:

(a) using deep knowledge of teaching and learning to (b) solve complex school-based problems, and (c) building relational trust with staff, parents and students.

Robinson notes that is unrealistic (and unhelpful) to expect a single school leader to do all this and 'it may lead to unrealistic conceptions of heroic leadership and deny the reality of distributed leadership in schools' arguing that 'a more useful exercise is to involve the whole senior leadership team in a discussion of the emphasis currently given to each of these dimensions'.

However the five dimensions and the three capabilities are used, for Robinson 'the yardstick for progress should be their impact on the learning and well-being of students'.

(Source: *School Leadership Today*, 2013, 5.2, 63–68)

MacBeath and Swaffield's LfL project conducted in a number of countries suggests such practice requires leadership that is shared and accountable, supportive learning environments are created and teachers are given every opportunity to grow and explore new ideas in the classroom (Swaffield and MacBeath, 2008). Their colleagues at Cambridge have gone further and more recently argued that 'principals have a key role in creating the conditions for enabling teachers to have a voice and to contribute to the development of policy and practice' (Bangs and Frost, 2016: 97).

A willingness to take risks in practice and to innovate are critical to creating a learning-centred or learning-enriched community that learns and reinforces continuous improvement (Bubb and Earley, 2010). Seashore (2015) sees learning-centred leaders as fostering what she calls 'professional community' and they act in very specific ways:

> They observe classrooms and ask questions that provoke teachers to think; they give 'power' over curriculum priorities and school practices to teachers; they consult teachers before making most important decisions; they ensure that all students have equal opportunity to have the best teachers; they use staff meetings to talk about equity and instruction, not about procedures; and they ask all teachers to observe each other's classrooms. In other words, teachers assess the effects of their principals by pointing to specific behaviors rather than generalised personality characteristics.

For her school leaders shape the school culture 'in ways that make its members more productive as well as more satisfied' (ibid.). The social conditions that staff encounter in a school are crucial and for Seashore these are grounded in professional community, or 'the stimulating relationships that they have with other teachers that create effective individual and collective learning environments that support change'. Her research suggests that school leaders have a major effect on whether or not supportive and challenging work environments exist. They exert influence in the following ways:

- Affect working relationships and, indirectly, student achievement (*instructional leadership*)
- When influence is shared with teachers, they foster stronger teacher working relationships (*shared leadership*)
- Create a culture of support for teachers that is translated into support for student work (*academic support*). (Seashore, 2015)

Promoting a learning culture and encouraging teacher leadership is important for, as the OECD note, 'teachers who report they are provided with opportunities to participate in decision-making at a school level have higher reported levels of job satisfaction in all TALIS countries and higher feelings of self-efficacy in most countries' (OECD, 2014, cited in Bangs and Frost, 2016: 99). Frost argues that 'with the right kind of support, teachers everywhere can experience a reigniting of their professionality and enhancement of their sense of moral purpose' (ibid.: 103). Such re-ignition is crucial at a time when teacher motivation may not be at its highest (Carr, 2016).

Although leadership of learning at all levels is important, headteacher leadership remains the major driving force and underpins the school's effectiveness and continued improvement. Such leadership 'serves as a catalyst for unleashing the potential capacities that already exist in the organisation' (Leithwood et al., 2006 cited in Day and Sammons, 2013: 34).

The research of Day et al. (2009) revealed that headteachers recognized the importance to the success of their schools of widening the participation of staff, consulting with them regularly and, in some schools, involving pupils in school-wide decision-making. As Day and Sammons note of this research study: 'There was evidence also of much effort to reshape and broaden the senior leadership team into a group which represented more strongly the "core" business of raising teaching and learning standards. ... Organisational change and development are enhanced when leadership is broad based and where teachers have opportunities to collaborate and to actively engage in change and innovation' (2013: 38).

There are some clear messages emerging from the research about learning-centred leadership or the leadership of learning, most notably that the actions of school leaders, especially headteachers, are crucial for creating that 'learning atmosphere' or organizational culture for both pupils and staff so that learning occurs. Effective leaders empower teachers and other staff to reach their potential because it is through teachers and high-quality teaching that students will be helped to reach theirs. However, it begs the question of the purpose of learning and it is to this more philosophical question that we finally turn.

Leading learning for what?

This final section presents the case why learning-centred leadership matters even more in education systems which operate within a high-stakes accountability culture. Within such systems there is a danger that learning becomes very narrowly defined and the overall purpose of education lost. It is easy in a time of measurement, targets and league tables to lose sight of what the primary purpose of schools should be. The question needs to be asked: What are the core purposes of learning and education, and hence of school leadership?

The philosopher Gert Biesta has coined the term 'learnification' which he sees as the rise of a new language of learning on education – this rise is seen in what he refers to as the number of discursive shifts: for example, all students and adults are referred to as learners; teachers as facilitators of learning, creators of learning opportunities, etc. (2016: 80). Assessment is for learning and strategies are referred to as learning and teaching strategies, leadership as learning centred and so on. 'Learning' is certainly a term whose time has come which perhaps is a greater reason for its nature and purpose to be carefully considered. As Smythe and Wrigley remark: 'In the discourse of the new leadership, even the term "leading learning" has been reduced into monitoring attainment; the complexities of social justice are viewed very narrowly through the lens of reducing attainment gaps' (2013: 156). For others the global testing culture permeates all aspects of education, 'from financing, to parental involvement, to teacher and student beliefs and practices' which has led 'to an environment where testing becomes synonymous with accountability, which becomes synonymous with education quality' (Smith, 2016: x).

For Dimmock (2012: 46) discussion about learning-centred or instructional leadership is meaningless in such a culture, where 'government policy priorities are measured by league tables and inspection regimes that are nationally defined and unresponsive to local circumstances, since the principalship is increasingly defined by the extent to which these outcome measures are achieved. There is little scope for much else.' There is a view that 'the teacher is no longer viewed as a professional, but as a labourer who simply has to follow evidence-based methods in order to secure externally determined goals' (Evers and Kneyber, 2016: 3) and that teaching is no longer the vocation it was once seen to be (Carr, 2016).

Andy Hargreaves argues that school autonomy is not always a good thing and can work against notions of LfL as it tends to lead to 'principals turning into de-professionalised performance managers and evaluators of teachers as individuals rather than builders of professional communities amongst all their staff within and across schools' (2016: 123). Education systems and schools however need reflective professionals who are able to make judgements and act upon what is considered to be 'educationally desirable'.

LfL must be leadership with a purpose. It is argued here that it must be about learning that is more than just attainment, exam and test scores and meeting central government's policy objectives. Of course attainment is important as children's life chances have little chance of being realized without knowledge of the basics, but education – and learning – must be about more than this. Glatter (see Chapter 2) raises similar concerns about the core purposes of education, and hence of educational leadership and quotes Ray Starratt (2007) who argues that practitioners and researchers alike must always ask themselves the question 'Leadership of and for what?' He suggests that without a clear answer to this then 'all the research and theory and discourse about distributed and sustainable leadership, about restructuring and reculturing, about capacity building and professional development, will not make what goes on in schools right' (ibid.: 182).

Learning-centred leadership or LfL must keep this question centre stage – leadership of learning for what? This, it should be argued, is the essence of learning-centred leadership. This is no doubt harder to keep at the core of what schools do while operating in a high-stakes accountability culture, but not impossible as other chapters in this volume show (see also Matthews et al., 2014 for a study of outstanding primary schools).

Implications and challenges

- A concern or challenge for learning-centred leaders will be maintaining the focus on learning – to concentrate their efforts on professional and pedagogic matters rather than administrative and financial concerns. The growing number of competing pressures and demands on school leaders' time will make this an increasingly difficult task and will call for even more distributed leadership where all leaders' focus is learning (Earley, 2013). It will be important to ensure that staff in charge of teaching and learning keep it as a high priority and know how to lead and effectively promulgate their vision of teaching and learning.

- Will the growth of a self-improving school system help or hinder the development of such leadership? What does a self-improving system mean for learning-centred leadership? How will leading learning play out in a federation or chain? Will chief executives become further removed from the 'core business' of schools which will increasingly be seen as the responsibility of senior and middle leaders? Will such leaders have even less 'autonomy' than under previous arrangements? Will executive heads and chief executives of academies and chains be more likely to have a business rather than an education background?

- How will leaders ensure that focusing on learning (LfL or learning-centred leadership) includes whole school discussion, including with governing bodies, about 'learning for what'? Will this help avoid schools becoming 'examination factories' (Hutchings, 2015) and discourage teaching to the test and other unsavoury practices associated with toxic organizational cultures? (see Chapter 17)

Heads and other school leaders can therefore play key roles in creating and maintaining the conditions and environment where teachers can teach (and learn) effectively and students can learn. Effective learning-centred leaders empower staff and students to reach their potential. Student outcomes can be improved and not only in relation to attainment.

Chapter 10

Leading curriculum innovation

Toby Greany and Joanne Waterhouse

Aims

This chapter aims to:

- provide definitions of key terms and summarize recent debates on the purpose and nature of the curriculum

- describe the context of curriculum and assessment reform in England over the past three decades

- set out some of the ways in which school leaders are innovating their school's curricula, and the emerging evidence for the conditions and leadership practices required for successful curriculum innovation

- discuss some of the key implications for leaders and leadership in 'self-improving' school systems.

Introduction

Curriculum leadership and innovation have become increasingly central to debates on school system reform in recent decades (Kärkkäinen, 2012; Greany and Cheong, 2016). On the one hand, policymakers have felt a need to determine and implement national curricula that reflect cultural, philosophical and/or economic priorities for development. On the other, they have recognized the need to promote flexibility at school and classroom levels so that teachers and leaders can respond to local priorities as well as rapidly changing needs and contextual requirements. This tension between centralization and decentralization is mirrored in the wider debates around school autonomy and reform reflected in Part 1 of this book; but it is also integrally linked to these debates since, in a more autonomous system, school leaders become key to the success of either approach. Of course, the curriculum's central focus on what and how children are taught means that it can attract significant additional political and public debate, making the implementation challenges all the more acute (Supovitz, Daly and del Fresno, 2015).

This chapter is written in the context of a new national curriculum that was introduced in England from 2014 onwards. Equally relevant are the radical structural reforms introduced from 2010 onwards: most notably the expansion of academies and free schools that are not required to apply the national curriculum (see Introduction for details). The new national curriculum aspires to be both more content-rich – with very few nods towards the widely held view that twenty-first-century learners require a more process-based curriculum that develops transferable skills – and also less prescriptive in terms of defining every aspect of what schools should cover and when. It appears that all schools in England – including academies and free schools – have needed to adapt their curricula to some extent to reflect the new national curriculum. This is because the new curriculum is impacting on the design of the national tests and exams that are used to hold schools accountable. However, relatively few schools appear to have used the opportunity offered by the new national curriculum to design genuinely innovative curricula. Of the schools that are changing their curricula more significantly, it does not appear that these are exclusively the academies and free schools that have the greatest apparent freedoms. The chapter argues therefore that leadership agency – or professional autonomy – as exercised by headteachers and their teams is more important than structural autonomy – that is, legal freedoms – for securing curriculum innovation.

The chapter concludes by exploring some of the leadership conditions and qualities that appear to be required for successful curriculum innovation and leadership agency as well as some implications and further reading.

Some of the core definitions and concepts that underpin this discussion are set out in Box 1.

Box 1: Defining curriculum terms

Defining 'curriculum' can be fraught with complexity, but a common definition is that it incorporates the purposes (the 'why'), content (the 'what') and processes (the 'how') of learning in schools. In practice, there is an acknowledged difference between the curriculum as planned by leaders and enacted by teachers and the curriculum experienced by students. Therefore, a simple definition might be that the curriculum is the sum total of the formal and informal learning opportunities offered by a school.

In practice this raises fundamental questions about the nature and purpose of education (see also Chapters 2 and 8), how these are determined and by whom (Marsh, 2009). Husbands (2015) alludes to these by asking whether our aim should be to:

- Pass on the best that has been thought and said – a cultural transmission model?
- Develop new attitudes towards, and new interests in, experience – a progressive model?
- Develop new skills and competencies – an applied model?

From an operational perspective, as Kärkkäinen (2012) explains, curriculum organization deals with elements such as:

- Scope – the breadth of subjects and topics offered over a given time
- Continuity – re-visitation of a theme or skill over a certain period of time
- Sequencing – deepening of a skill or concept over a certain period of time by building on a preceding one
- Integration – promoting a mutually reinforcing relationship between elements such as concepts, skills and values across the curriculum.

The evolution of the national curriculum in England

The idea of a national curriculum in England was conceived as an entitlement for pupils, helping to ensure a consistency of provision, thereby breaking down the walls of what Prime Minister James Callaghan had called the 'secret garden' of education. In practice, the process of defining the curriculum has led to a protracted and often heated debate between politicians, employers, professionals and academics about the rightful purpose and priorities for the nation's education system, resulting in regular reviews. These have required teachers and school leaders to become accustomed to remodelling their plans and reprioritizing their resources to align with external requirements, with some arguing that teachers have lost the art of designing their own curricula.

The national curriculum was introduced for publicly funded schools in 1988. It was structured into discrete subjects and organized into three 'Core' subjects (Mathematics, English and Science) and several 'Foundation' subjects, including History, Geography and Art. The curriculum structure introduced the idea of age phases for pupils across the school system. For example, Key Stage 1 encompassed pupils in Year 1 and Year 2, aged four to six years. Over the following decades there have been four major reviews prior to the most recent in the period 2011–2013 (and introduced from 2014). These reviews heralded further developments, such as the introduction of a specific Early Years Foundation Framework.

The 2014 National Curriculum for maintained schools (i.e. excluding academies and free schools) retains a commitment to 'a balanced and broadly based curriculum' which a) promotes the spiritual, moral, cultural, mental and physical development of pupils at the school and of society; and b) prepares such pupils for the opportunities, responsibilities and experiences of adult life. To some extent the curriculum review reflected a level of consensus that the previous Labour government's policies had led schools to become too focused on getting children to pass exams, rather than enabling them to become successful learners, as this quote from the Confederation of British Industry – the main employer body – suggests (CBI/Pearson Education and Skills Survey, 2013: 24):

The cult of relativism in schools has allowed too many young people to leave without achieving their full potential. Definitions of achievement based on GCSE performance are too narrow. There are lots of brilliant examples in the UK of schools with a clear idea of the outcomes they want their pupils to achieve and which embed that ambition for success in every aspect of school life, but too often this is driven by outstanding school leadership that rebels against the system.

A number of features of the curriculum review and its outcome are worth noting. First, a key requirement for the review was to 'raise the bar' so that curriculum demands in England matched those in high-performing jurisdictions (Gove, 2011). Thus the underpinning assumption was that the previous curriculum had been 'dumbed down' and needed to be made more academically rigorous as a way to stretch more able children but also provide 'core knowledge' for children from more deprived backgrounds (Hirsch, 1999). Secondly, the curriculum does very little to address the '21st-century skills agenda', a broad term encompassing both cognitive and non-cognitive skills, such as critical thinking, problem-solving, collaboration, effective communication, motivation, persistence and learning to learn (Pellegrino and Hilton, 2012). This is despite the fact that employers in England have identified the need for schools to develop qualities such as creativity, teamwork and adaptability (CBI/Pearson, 2013) and that many high-performing school systems are actually focused on enhancing this area (Greany and Cheong, 2016). Thirdly, the new curriculum is explicitly intended to minimize the level of prescription on schools and give them greater space to innovate, with minimal support for implementation (DfE, 2013). Fourthly, as in previous iterations, the new curriculum is inextricably linked with the introduction of new tests, qualifications and accountability measures for schools, which we turn to next.

Understanding the interplay between curriculum, assessment and accountability

The White Paper that introduced the curriculum review stated that: 'We envisage schools and teachers taking greater control over what is taught in schools, innovating in how they teach and developing new approaches to learning' (DfE, 2010: 40). The aspiration has thus been to reduce national prescription so that schools will engage in a deeper evaluation of how to align their curriculum with both formative and summative assessments in ways that enhance learning (Oates, 2011; McIntosh, 2015). Thus, the new, more content focused but less detailed, curriculum has been accompanied by the decision to remove the previous national framework of attainment 'levels'. Instead, schools are required to design their own 'effective assessment systems' founded on a published, national set of core principles (National Curriculum, 2014).

Thus far, however, the evidence indicates that these efforts to 'free up' schools to innovate have not succeeded, or at least have only succeeded in part. While there are examples of schools that are developing thoughtful curriculum and assessment models, these appear to be a small number of leading edge Teaching Schools (Lilley et al.,

2014). Schools more widely have either bought in commercially developed packages or created their own versions of the former 'levels'. For example, the government's official Commission on Assessment without Levels reported that: 'We have been concerned by evidence that some schools are trying to recreate levels based on the new national curriculum' (McIntosh, 2015: 4).

A survey of academy leaders by Bassett et al. (2012) indicated that the opportunity for 'educational autonomy' and 'freedom to innovate to raise standards' was a significant reason behind schools choosing to become academies (71 per cent and 57 per cent of respondents, respectively). However, only 31 per cent reported that they had actually made some changes and a further 31 per cent planned to do so. Four in ten (39 per cent) believed that the national curriculum 'already allows them sufficient freedom'. A later report from the same researchers analysed a second survey of academy school leaders: half (51 per cent) reported 'a general sense of educational autonomy' but only one-third (35 per cent) had, or planned, a varied curriculum. The authors concluded that 'academies are not fully capitalising on the freedoms they have over the curriculum' (Finch et al., 2014: 18).

Equally, innovation may come from more disruptive places (Leadbeater and Wong, 2010), for example, the new free schools have been explicitly set up to challenge existing providers and provide new curricula and pedagogical models. There are examples of free schools that have explicitly sought to do this through both highly traditionalist and highly innovative approaches. For example, the West London Free School offers 'a classical – knowledge-based – curriculum, including compulsory Latin up to the age of 14',[1] perhaps as a way to attract parents that might otherwise prefer a private education. By contrast, School21 has set out to offer 'new ways of teaching for the 21st-century'[2] aimed at developing a set of six attributes: eloquence, grit, professionalism, spark, craftsmanship and expertise. Dunford et al's (2012) study of free schools did not indicate that this level of innovation had been widespread.

Even if single schools do prove effective at innovating in their curricula, there is a related question of whether or not such innovations will be scaled up to secure wider benefits across England's 21,000 schools. An interesting example of this challenge is the teaching of Chinese, which has arisen as a new policy priority in the UK, but a difficult one to address at the level of individual schools (and even school partnerships) given the paucity of existing teachers or resources. Tinsley and Board (2014) researched the development of Chinese teaching in schools across the UK. They identified just ninety-five primary schools in England that are teaching Chinese – which equates to around 1 in 160 – while in Scotland they identified 119 such primary schools – equating to around 1 in 16. The researchers are clear that Scotland's clear strategic plan for addressing issues such as teacher training and its support for implementation in schools through Local Authority hubs is part of that country's apparent success, especially compared to England's laissez-faire approach.

In summary, it appears that national changes to exams, tests and accountability measures have preoccupied schools in England, rather than the opportunities created by the new curriculum (Greany and Waterhouse, 2016). This reflects a concern among school leaders that securing exam and national test results in order to meet the requirements of the accountability framework is more important than innovating the curriculum. This tension between apparent policy 'freedoms' that are modified in practice by structural constraints is explored in more detail in the following section.

Perspectives on curriculum innovation from schools

The sense in which 'accountability trumps curriculum' as a driver of school decision-making comes through from qualitative data that the authors have collected as part of a wider international research project. The following section is informed by interviews with school leaders participating in the Grand Curriculum Design programme – a professional development course offered by the Institute of Education and RSA (Royal Society for the Encouragement of Arts, Manufactures and Commerce). It aims to 'provide curriculum leaders with the knowledge and skills required to design curricula that are flexible, innovative and responsive to the needs of each school's students and communities'.[3] The interviewees are therefore self-selecting and it can be assumed that they are more engaged in thinking on curriculum innovation than the average.

School leaders on the programme expressed their frustrations with perceived constraints and boundaries. One secondary school teacher described the directive nature of the curriculum as a series of impositions: 'We've got to do this, we've got to do this, we've got to do that'. His reflections on the course – which aimed to encourage more autonomous thought – was somewhat dejected: 'Here, blue sky thinking, go back and it's teach and mark.' There was a strong sense of the structural constraints in the current system with three teachers each bemoaning perceived limitations:

- 'We might question compartmental subjects, but what about the staff and faculty arrangements?'
- 'We're stuck in time frames, curriculum subjects and curriculum leadership, we're in shackles'
- 'We struggle with the tyranny of the syllabus.'

Another colleague was struck by the thought that 'we're so busy providing education for the children, we're not really thinking about the children'.

Alternative voices expressed an appreciation of the freedoms and choices available. In particular, there was a strong theme of collaboration with the students to co-construct appropriate pathways through a curriculum offer that best suited an individual's needs. This included a recognition that technology was a major influence on creativity and individual learning. The teachers' comments in this regard were characterized by the expression of professional efficacy and autonomy:

- 'Whatever the curriculum is, our students will make it theirs.'

- 'We plan a creative curriculum when for accountability we weave the desirable characteristics in.'

- 'The idea of us learning from them (i.e. the children) as much as them learning from us is really important. And we shouldn't be scared of it.'

Curriculum innovation: Structure and agency in local contexts

The teachers cited in the previous section illustrate an inherent tension between structure and agency (Wermke and Hostfalt, 2014). Structure here might be real or perceived, but it broadly encompasses external requirements (such as pressure to address the accountability regime) and internal structures and processes (such as existing faculty and staffing structures) that can make change appear difficult. Agency represents the will and capacity to shape alternative responses, whether exercised by individual teachers, departments or schools. At one level, agency might be seen to stem from individual confidence and commitment among individual school leaders (sometimes called sheer bloody-mindedness!). Yet such agency will also be conditioned by other factors, such as whether leaders have the intellectual capacity and vision to imagine alternative models, and/or practical opportunities to see such alternatives operating in practice. Equally, for the teachers quoted in the previous section, their agency was enhanced through collaboration, both with each other and with students, since this gave them confidence and a moral contract to underpin their distinctive approaches. It appears that levels of teacher agency – expressed as self-efficacy – are significantly influenced by in-school factors, such as levels of trust and support from senior leaders (Micklewright et al., 2014).

At the school level, agency will also be conditioned by structures: for example, if a school is struggling to perform in accountability terms, then it may be less likely to innovate because the risk of failure is more acute, while a school that has been categorized as outstanding may feel more able to take risks. Thus, not surprisingly, as Earley and Higham's recent research has indicated (2012), school leaders in England tend to fall into roughly equal segments between Confident, Cautious, Concerned and Constrained.

There is some evidence that agency to reform curricula may also be more culturally acceptable and structurally feasible in the primary school sector. A recent report on a project focused on leading curriculum innovation in primary schools described innovative practice that was informed by effective leadership of change (Brundrett and

Duncan, 2014). As such, it was viewed as a process. This innovative process featured examples of collaboration within and between schools, the explicit inclusion of all staff in decision-making and professional development, and the use of existing structures for monitoring and review. There was a requirement for an 'ethos of change' to be created by the leadership, one which 'allows freedom for experimentation, supported risk-taking and the trialling and piloting of cross curricula approaches to teaching' (Brundrett and Duncan, 2014: 5). In particular, the authors reported that the primary principals welcomed curriculum development initiatives because 'they view the leadership of learning as central to their role' (ibid.: 5). The process was complex and culturally contingent, requiring 'a good fit' with the school's particular context. Brundrett and Duncan represent this leadership practice as a Model for Curriculum Innovation which is a four-stage process:

i   Researching, including 'environment scanning' in which leaders use their knowledge and judgement of their complete environment to plan bespoke initiatives

ii Ethos building

iii Trialling

iv Implementation.

In this way the change is both evolutionary and dynamic and led as 'an integrated, multi-faceted and whole school activity' (ibid.: 9). The authors stress the particular nature of primary schools and their leaders as a key feature: 'The community-focussed nature of successful primary schools means that primary school leaders are at the forefront of curriculum innovation' (ibid.: 9).

This is not to imply that schools in any circumstance cannot exert their leadership agency to secure an appropriate and rounded curriculum that ensures success for all children. Many of the leadership practices involved align closely with the wider research on effective transformational, learning-centred and change leadership, as set out in Chapters 7–9. Robinson (2011) develops this further in relation to curriculum leadership by arguing for clear strategic decision-making about instructional time. This means making sure that the school day and year are geared towards maximizing the desired curriculum experience, whether in the classroom or through wider enrichment activities. Aligned to this is the need for a coherent instructional programme which aligns curriculum, instructional strategies and assessment, so that together they allow for integrated and cumulative learning within and across the years of schooling. Robinson describes this as a 'lengthy and complex business' (ibid.: 86), with success relying on both a rigorous evidence-informed assessment of which aspects of the school are currently successful and which need improvement, and a commitment to collaborative and continuous learning and adaptation by teachers and other school staff so that agreed curriculum changes can be applied and improved systematically.

To conclude, Robin Alexander (2012: 13) provides a powerful and practical indication of the leadership skills and qualities that are required by primary school leaders wanting to secure successful curriculum innovation in England's 'self-improving' system:

> Evidence from research, inspection and shared experience, understanding of curriculum matters, rigour in curriculum discourse, preparedness to acknowledge that the generalist class teacher system isn't sacrosanct, a flexible approach to school staffing, a desire to share intellectual capital between schools as well as within them … all informed by an unshakeable commitment to 'a curriculum which is consistently well-taught regardless of the perceived significance of its various elements or the amount of time devoted to them': these are the name of the new curriculum leadership game, and the shift from centralised direction to school self-improvement gives our latest generation of school leaders the chance to break the mould.

Conclusion and implications

Many commentators agree that schools need to become more innovative in their curricula if they are to prepare children for a fast-changing world (Caldwell and Spinks, 2013). The assumption of New Public Management is that granting schools autonomy will lead to increased curriculum innovation and responsiveness to changes in the wider environment (Lubienski, 2009).

However, relatively few schools in England appear to have engaged in conscious curriculum innovation that goes beyond the minimum requirements. Examples of such innovation exist in both more and less formally autonomous schools. We posit that, while remaining an important influence, parental choice of school in England is a less powerful driver of school behaviour than centrally defined accountability. This finding differs from Lubienski's (2009) review of international evidence on innovation in quasi-markets for the OECD. His review also found limited levels of curriculum innovation among supposedly autonomous schools, such as charter schools in the United States, but identified the 'traditionalist' tendencies exerted by parental choice mechanisms as the primary cause. The difference here may reflect the degree to which centralized accountability through school inspection has been used as a primary driver of improvement and control of schools in England.

Interestingly, though, it appears that there are other factors at play beyond accountability and autonomy. Some leaders – in both more and less autonomous schools in England – appear to be able to meet the needs of the accountability framework, while at the same time innovating their curricula. In the words of the CBI, leaders who have the courage and determination to do this remain 'rebels against the system'. Sometimes this innovation appears geared towards meeting the needs and desires of parents (who may be more or less conservative in their expectations of education), indicating the importance of quasi-market forces as Lubienski (2009) argues. Equally, though, other examples suggest that it is the values and beliefs of school leaders, coupled with their confidence and capacity for 'breaking the mould', that drives curriculum innovation, perhaps indicating that leadership agency is as important as market forces in driving innovation. Leadership agency may be affected by individual experience, skills and values, but also seems to be influenced by the extent to which the institution and its staff remain professionally connected to other innovative schools that can provide ideas, mutual support and challenge. Lateral school-to-school collaboration may therefore be particularly important in England's 'self-improving school-led' system, where the capacity of local authorities and other intermediary bodies to influence and support school-level innovation has been significantly weakened (Greany, 2015).

This leads us to two conclusions, both of which have implications for policy, practice and research.

The first is that we need a more nuanced understanding of accountability. Vertical accountability – that is, to government – appears to have both a coercive and normative power over school leaders, in that it requires them act in certain ways (backed by rewards and sanctions) and also ingrains a sense that this is the 'only way to do things'. But that same vertical accountability may also have a normative impact on parents, telling them that only the qualifications that government deems important are worthy of consideration and that only the schools that Ofsted deems high quality are worth of choosing for their children. Thus vertical accountability may condition market accountability – that is, to parents – so that they require one and the same thing from schools – high test scores and good Ofsted judgements. In the process, innovation appears to become an unintended casualty.

The second conclusion is that we need a more nuanced notion of autonomy. Essentially we see two forms of autonomy. The first we call 'structural autonomy': this describes the extent to which the legal/policy framework formally delegates decision-making powers to school boards and/or leaders in two areas: resources (e.g. budgets/staffing) and curriculum/pedagogy. The second we call 'professional autonomy', which has some parallels with Hargreaves and Fullan's notion of Professional Capital (2012). 'Professional autonomy' reflects a view that autonomy is as much about the confidence, capacity and effectiveness of school leaders and teachers and the trust placed in them by district and national officials as it is about formal delegated powers (Bryk and Schneider, 2002; Fullan, 2010).

Notes

1. See http://wlfs.org/accessed 10.3.16.
2. See http://school21.org.uk/accessed 10.3.16.
3. See https://www.ioe.ac.uk/study/87077.html accessed 2/11/15.

Chapter 11

Leading professional learning and development

Vivienne Porritt, Karen Spence-Thomas and Carol Taylor

Aims

In this chapter we aim to:

- explore what is meant by professional learning and development (PLD)
- consider forms of PLD, including evidence-informed approaches
- discuss the role of leading PLD and its purpose and challenges
- explore the value of evaluating the impact of PLD.

The need for shared definitions

School leaders often struggle to ensure that PLD makes a difference to teachers and students. The English Department for Education's (DfE) consultation, A *world-class teaching profession*, states 'There is currently too little robust evidence on the impact of different types of professional development for teachers' (2015: 10). To ensure that PLD improves teachers' practice and has an impact on students' learning, we need to establish a shared understanding of what effective PLD looks like, how to achieve it and how to evidence its impact. The language is used and understood in different ways by practitioners and throughout the literature. The OECD Teaching and Learning International Survey (TALIS) refers to continuing professional development (CPD) which suggests that this term is in use internationally. Some schools in England refer to In-service Training or Inset; universities often refer to Teacher Education. Helen Timperley from New Zealand promotes a focus on professional learning (PL) because 'much professional development has little meaning for teachers' (2011: 2). Cordingley et al. (2015) offer CPDL – continuing professional development and learning. This variation reflects some of the tensions in thinking that exist in this field. If we do not yet have a sharply defined and agreed language, it is no surprise that we are still working towards an understanding of what quality looks like, how best to lead this and how to evaluate the impact of PLD.

What is professional learning and development?

It is worth exploring what we mean by the related terms professional learning and professional development. In working with leaders of professional development (PD) in schools, both nationally and internationally, we have found that reconceptualizing these words can lead to better design, strategic leadership and, fundamentally, more effective learning and impact for teachers, leaders and learners. We argue that the design and implementation of learning and development may have greater impact, and so improve learning and impact, by being seen as two distinct and yet interconnected processes.

Professional learning encompasses all the *opportunities* offered for teachers and leaders to learn something new, update skills, be informed of new developments, explore new techniques or resources and refresh subject-specific knowledge. Such opportunities can be offered in a wide range of ways; courses, seminars, reading articles, visits to other organizations, lesson study, enquiry and action research, masters qualifications, peer observation. Such opportunities can be facilitated in-house by colleagues in the same or another school, a university, commercial organization or an independent consultant.

Professional development then becomes the *process* that builds on what has been learnt to effect a change 'in the thinking and practice of our colleagues so that such change improves the experience and learning for pupils' (Earley and Porritt, 2009: 139). This improved practice needs to become embedded in a teacher's everyday interactions with learners before we can say there has been professional development. While agreeing with the importance of PL as the process for 'solving entrenched educational problems' (Timperley, 2011: 5), we argue there has to be another stage after learning something valuable. It takes time to test out new understanding, skills, techniques and strategies and takes longer for improved practice to become habitual and embedded. We see PD not as the opportunity or learning activity being offered but as the embedded practice leaders look for as a result of PL. As O'Brien notes 'there is clearly a need to follow-up and follow-through CPD interventions so that clear links are established between CPD provision for teachers leading to enhanced teacher quality and the attainment and achievement of students' (2011: 106). This is where innovation is needed in PLD and its leadership. While learning and development are clearly integral to each other, by reconceptualizing the two stages schools are more able to put in place the organizational processes and systems by which this learning is converted into developed practice and raised standards.

Evidence-informed professional learning and development

Drawing on evidence from research will improve the quality of all PL opportunities and supports the potential for impact on teacher practice and students' learning. Significant convergence in the literature offers school leaders clarity over the elements that can support the design and development of high-quality PD (e.g. Timperly, 2007; Earley and Porritt, 2009, 2013; Stoll et al., 2010; Nelson, Spence-Thomas and Taylor, 2015a; Cordingley et al., 2015; Jenson et al., 2016). These studies emphasize active and collaborative PL sustained over time, follow up opportunities to apply learning in practice, focus on student learning and outcomes, external support and expertise and the importance of evaluation. A failure to apply these principles to the design of PL means many learning opportunities offered to teachers still consist of traditional designs such as a conference or a short course (OECD, 2014).

The EPPI-Centre reviews (e.g. Cordingley et al., 2007) and Earley and Porritt (2009) argue that individual design principles are more likely to be effective when they are linked in combination, and rooted in the teacher's classroom practice. Both Hargreaves (2011) and Sebba (2012) make the case that the dominant approaches to CPD, characterized as professionals passively receiving information or knowledge from a perceived expert, rarely result in lasting improvements either in teacher practice or pupil learning. Hargreaves (2011: 10) argues that PD needs to focus on 'improving what teachers do, not merely what they know'.

The first imperative is, therefore, for leaders and teachers to draw on research and engage in PL that has the potential to improve practice. We have collated the approaches for high-quality PLD as suggested by four studies in the Annex. They offer a source for educational leaders looking to maximize the impact of professional development. Does the PL offered in your school start from, and always include, these factors?

Effective approaches to professional learning and development

The studies cited suggest schools need to design PLD which shifts from a model based on knowledge transmission to a model where knowledge gained is applied and tested in classrooms and where subsequent new knowledge leads to improved practice which is embedded over time. This notion of joint practice development (JPD) is defined by Fielding et al. as 'learning new ways of working through mutual engagement that opens up and shares practices with others' (2005: 1). It encompasses a range of collaborative, mutually beneficial, school-based forms of PD such as peer-to-peer observation and coaching; within-school and cross-school PL communities; research-informed approaches such as collaborative enquiry and lesson study. In England, these forms of PLD formed the focus of enquiry for partnerships of schools designated as teaching school alliances (TSAs) which were involved in the National College for Teaching and Leadership's (NCTL) research and development (R&D) network. Thirty alliances of schools worked on theme 2: 'What makes great professional development which leads to consistently great pedagogy?' The findings of the literature review are included within the Annex (Stoll, Harris and Handscomb, 2012). Some alliances considered forms of JPD such as peer observation while others investigated coaching. Nearly half of the theme 2 alliances explored two approaches that have significant potential to apply the research evidence to design high-quality PLD which makes a difference to teacher and student learning, namely lesson study and collaborative enquiry.

Lesson Study originated in Japan where it has been long established as a method for initial teacher training and career-long PD (Fernandez and Yoshida, 2004). Following analysis of data, teachers work together to identify a research theme and explore current research in relation to their theme, a process known as *kyozai kenkyu*. Once they have an enhanced understanding of what is known about their issue, teachers engage in repeated cycles of planning and teaching, closely observing the impact of a co-designed research lesson on student learning. Observations are followed by focused post-lesson discussions and a summary of learning before the cycle begins again. A group of six primary schools participating in the NCTL Research Themes project found that the collaborative discussion that occurs within lesson study provided a 'rare chance to really unpick the most tricky or difficult concepts to teach' (Nelson, Spence-Thomas and Taylor, 2015a: 7).

The British Education Research Association/Royal Society of Arts Inquiry highlights that teachers' experience of PD in most parts of the UK is 'fragmented, occasional and insufficiently informed by research' (2014: 12): the final report stresses that 'the development of a research-rich culture is vital if schools and colleges are to develop and sustain the capacity for self-improvement' (ibid.: 27). As well as applying research into what makes effective PLD, a growing body of evidence suggests that PD which draws on high-quality research and evidence results in positive improvements in teacher practice and student learning (Greany, 2015). Nelson and O'Beirne (2014) argue that teaching practice and learner outcomes can potentially be enhanced by identification and application of the evidence around the most effective approaches to teaching and learning. How and where such evidence is sourced, as well as how it is shared and applied, remains a challenge for schools and practitioners. Debate about the accessibility and relevance of academic educational research for school practitioners has spurred the Education Endowment Foundation (EEF) in the UK and researchers such as John Hattie in Australia to bridge the gap (see Chapters 1 and 12).

Furthermore, movements such as ResearchED in the UK and internationally are seeking to address the issue by establishing a 'grass-roots, teacher-led organization aimed at improving research literacy in educational communities' (www.workingoutwhatworks.com/). Though research into the effectiveness of such fora is limited, increasing participant numbers at ResearchED events and practitioner-initiated TeachMeets speak of a growing enthusiasm for engaging in classroom-focused, research-informed PD (see Chapter 19). Also contested is the relationship between practitioner enquiry and academic educational research. Nelson and O'Beirne (2014: 27) cite Geest (2010) who asks 'when does trying out new ideas in the classroom and reflecting on the effects of the changes become research? What are the boundaries between reflective practice and "doing research"?' For Geest, enquiry involves engagement with a variety of different sources of evidence, information and expertise, and does not necessarily involve primary research (although it sometimes does).

Enthoven and de Bruijn (2010) contend that part of the answer lies in the extent to which schools and individual teachers engage with the external evidence base when trying out new ideas and reflecting on their practice: this is where a description of the process as enquiry rather than research becomes helpful. The national research themes project enabled schools to relate their investigations to robust literature reviews and provided a structure for collaborative enquiry (Harris and Jones, 2012). Summary case studies and impact reports from this project provide powerful testament that enquiries centred on the difference teachers wanted to make for students in their classrooms were highly motivating, helping to ensure that changes in practice were closely evaluated and sustained over time (Nelson, Spence-Thomas and Taylor, 2015b).

Strategic leadership of professional learning and development

The landscape in which leaders of PLD work is continually evolving; while some work exclusively within one school, others lead within and across multiple organizations. In some schools, one senior leader has strategic oversight for PLD, others distribute this leadership role across middle leaders, offering opportunities for career development and for the school to build capacity. The role of the PLD leader has also shifted from being mostly a management one to a role focused on strategic improvement and the alignment of PLD with internal school improvement priorities, as well as the demands of external policy changes. Cordingley et al. (2015: 10) describe the role as 'promoting a challenging learning culture, ... knowing what content and learning activities were likely to be of benefit and promoting evidence-informed, self-regulated learning'.

To be successful, the strategic leader of PLD needs to be aware of the external research base outlined above. The leader of PLD also has a responsibility to ensure senior leaders see PLD as a significant improvement process so it is not vulnerable to the challenges of reduced budgets and external pressures. PLD needs to be 'underpinned by senior leaders who recognise the potential of professional development for enhancing pupil outcomes, give it a central role in school improvement planning and reflect it in their policies' (Stoll, Harris and Handscomb, 2012: 8). This means PLD is embedded within a culture of learning and an unswerving commitment to promoting and participating in teachers' development (Robinson, 2011) based on a clear understanding that school improvement happens in classrooms with high-quality teachers. To make the right decisions about what PLD opportunities will be supported, the PLD leader needs to have a deep understanding and rich evidence base about the improvement needs of the school, its groups and individual learners (Earley and Porritt, 2013). By this, we mean an ability to be clear about:

- the difference we need to make for our student learners and how to achieve this
- the change/difference we therefore need our teachers/support staff to bring about
- what staff need to learn to bring about this change and effective ways to do this
- what support will be needed and from whom, both internal and external

- implications for line managers and middle leaders
- systems, processes and resources which need to be in place in order for change to be successful, evidenced and sustained over time.

There are clearly implications for understanding the adult learner's baseline in terms of existing skills, knowledge and practice and the next steps in their development. Those who have responsibility for the leadership of PLD need to be able to map the personalized needs of teachers/support staff onto the school's priorities.

Thus, the challenges for the strategic leader of PLD are considerable and grow when the school begins to distribute the leadership of PLD across phases, teams, faculties or departments. It is clear that middle leaders (e.g. heads of department and subject coordinators who are also teachers) and other informal teacher leaders do have an increasingly important role (Stoll, et al., 2015). Middle leaders are a vital link between teachers and a school's senior leaders and are perfectly positioned to support the learning of their colleagues. However, Stoll et al. (2015) make it clear that if middle leaders are to take such a leading role, they need ongoing development to enhance their skills in working alongside others to investigate their practice, articulate and share their knowledge, ask the right questions about evidence, trial new strategies and evaluate impact. They also have to 'be able to understand and facilitate PL, access, critique and share the "external" knowledge base … practice coaching skills, and develop trust with colleagues' (Stoll et al., 2015: 87). This requires a shift from a middle leader role that emphasizes improving student achievement through intensive intervention strategies designed to bring about immediate results, to one that supports deeper learning over time, leading to greater student independence. Jenson et al. (2016: 13) offer three dimensions to developing strategic leadership as seen in high-performing systems:

- 'Professional learning leaders at the school
- System leaders of professional learning, and
- School principals developing school improvement plans around professional learning.'

A key consideration in the role of the PLD leader is to ensure that there is alignment of school improvement objectives, appraisal/teacher evaluation/performance management, and PLD. The PLD leader should have strategic oversight of the leadership and management of appraisal and PLD. In our view, appraisal/teacher evaluation/performance management should not be seen as judgemental or bureaucratic: 'It was done to you. … It was a series of numbers really, percentage this and percentage that. … It was always about what you'd done and never about how we were going to move forward' (Spence-Thomas, 2010: 31). Rather appraisal should be rigorous, developmental PL focused on 'the desired changes in professional practice that have been identified and which need to occur to have an impact on pupil achievement' (Spence-Thomas, 2010: 32). In some schools, appraisal is indeed called something that better reflects its purpose, such as 'Learning and Development Review' or 'Professional Review'; titles that assert why significant amounts of time are being invested. It is about learning and development which makes an explicit difference to teaching practice so that they have an impact on pupil learning.

It remains a challenge for leaders of PLD to find the time and resources to support effective teacher learning and development and Bubb and Earley's (2013) findings outline the variety of creative approaches that school leaders have taken to address this. *A world-class teaching profession: Government consultation response* (2015) also notes that time and workload were identified as the biggest barriers to effective PD with English schools increasingly reluctant to release staff for PLD. The leader of PLD therefore needs to be creative in finding every opportunity for colleagues to work, plan, enquire, share, collaborate and evaluate in ways that are stimulating and enable teachers to engage in critical thinking about lessons and learning.

Evaluating impact of PLD

The PLD lead must also have the ability to evaluate the impact of PLD on teacher practices and outcomes for learners, without which the commitment of senior leaders to PLD will be threatened. Ofsted (2010) note that school managers often relied on anecdotal evidence and subjective impressions to judge the impact of PLD, even in schools where PLD was good. Research has consistently shown (e.g. Ofsted, 2010; Earley and Porritt, 2009) that schools lack experience, skills and tools to evaluate the impact of PLD. Earley and Porritt (2013) offer a thorough outline of the literature for PLD impact evaluation and note that 'a range of impact evaluation models, theories and frameworks therefore exist yet research and inspection evidence consistently shows that schools and PD leaders are still to employ such tools effectively' (ibid.: 115).

School leaders often shy away from rigorous impact evaluation possibly because they believe it will take several years to be able to see the results of PLD. This expectation is based on a traditional view of impact evaluation. The approach to impact evaluation that Earley and Porritt (2009) developed is a very practical one that is simple in concept yet rigorous in the difference it can make. The work undertaken with over 600 schools and colleges in the *Effective Practices in CPD* project explored Guskey's key concept that evaluation issues should be 'an integral part of discussions during the earliest stages of professional development planning when … goals are defined and activities specified' (2000: 250). Impact evaluation in schools tends to be at the end of a development activity yet 'all initial planning as to the potential impact of CPD should be undertaken *before* CPD activity starts' (Porritt, 2009: 8). This is a simple concept to agree yet requires a significant change in the PLD practice of many schools. The key is to plan the expected specific intended impact, which involves having a clear picture of what practice is like, before engaging in any PLD activity so that there is a baseline against which to evaluate progress. This difference can best be expressed as impact: the difference in staff behaviours, attitudes, skills and practice as a result of the PLD in which staff have engaged. Ultimately, impact must be the difference in the learning and experience of the children as a result of the change in staff practice and the latter becomes possible once there has been impact from PLD. Bringing about an improved outcome in the learning and experience of students is what enables a strategic leader to say that PLD has been effect-ive, which then supports the mobilization of such knowledge across the school.

A PLD project (see Vignette 1) set out to test whether a model of lesson study in mathematics, supported by external expertise from a university and combined with the approach described above to evaluate impact, could improve teacher subject know-ledge and have a consequent impact on student attainment. The Impact Frame designed by the UCL Institute of Education project leaders supported the schools to see impact evaluation as 'a learning tool that improves the quality of both the CPD activity and the outcomes achieved' (Earley and Porritt, 2009: 147) and 'provided compelling evidence of positive impact on pupils' attainment in mathematics' (Godfrey and Rowland, 2015).

When applied at the outset of the PL opportunity, this approach to impact evaluation enabled schools to design more effective improvement processes that had greater potential to ensure impact was achieved. Qualitative and quantitative data collected revealed that improvements in teacher confidence and skills contributed to statistically significant improved attainment for their students. Evaluating the impact of PLD in this way is a powerful method to raise the quality of teaching, learning and standards. School improvement happens in classrooms and the PLD of both teachers and support staff in schools must be of the highest priority for school leaders.

Vignette 1

Connecting knowledge

Project: Connecting knowledge

Participants: Twenty primary schools in Lambeth, S London, 38 teachers, 2520 students

Duration: Two years

Funder: London Schools Excellence Fund

Professional learning model: Lesson Study, evidence-informed, external expertise, focus on subject knowledge and classroom practice, impact frame

Impact:

- Teachers particularly valued the focus on teaching and learning and the supportive and collaborative nature of Lesson Study
- Teachers reported significant improvement (measured by large and medium effect sizes) in 8/9 pedagogical areas including longer term planning, assessment and inclusivity, consideration of pupil voice and building on pupils' prior experience
- Teachers increased their subject knowledge, awareness of effective teaching methods, confidence to lead lesson study
- Teachers reported that 94 per cent of desired changes in students' learning (as described in teachers' baseline data) had been achieved
- Student data showed that around 56 per cent of target students met aspirational targets for accelerated improvement with 100 per cent making expected progress

- Students' achievements included:
  - Specific numeracy strategies
  - Confidence, resilience and perseverance
  - Evidence of solving higher-level problems
  - Ability to articulate the learning process or collaborate.

Implications

Schools and their leaders need to develop:

- An understanding of the design principles that lead to effective PLD and how to apply these principles
- A culture that promotes and supports time for evidence-informed PLD and enables new practice to be trialled, tested, improved, refined and then embedded
- Processes for supporting PL and then the developed practice that emerges over time to enable teachers to embed the practices in their own classroom settings
- An understanding of the value, purpose and processes involved in evaluating the impact of PLD.

Annex Design principles for effective PLD

Hawley and Valli (1999) (adapted)	Stoll, Harris and Handscomb (2012)
Professional development should:	**Effective professional development:**
1 Focus on what students are to learn and the different problems students may have in learning the material	1 Starts with the end in mind
2 Be based on analyses of the differences between actual student performance and standards for student learning	2 Challenges thinking as part of changing practice
3 Involve teachers in identifying what they need to learn and the development of the learning experiences in which they will be involved	3 Is based on the assessment of individual and school needs
4 Be primarily school-based and built into the day-to-day work of teaching.	4 Involves connecting work-based learning and external expertise
5 Be organized around collaborative problem-solving	5 Learning opportunities are varied, rich and sustainable
6 Be continuous and ongoing, involving follow-up and support for further learning, including support from sources external to the school	6 Uses action research and enquiry as key tools
7 Incorporate evaluation of multiple sources of information on learning outcomes for students and other processes involved in implementing lessons learnt through professional development	7 Is strongly enhanced through collaborative learning and JPD
8 Provide opportunities to gain an understanding of the theory underlying the knowledge and skills being learnt	8 Is enhanced by creating PL communities within and between schools
9 Be connected to a comprehensive change process focused on improving student learning.	9 Requires leadership to create the necessary conditions

Earley and Porritt (2009 and 2013)	Cordingley et al. (2015)
• Participants' ownership of PD activity • Engagement with a variety of PD opportunities • Time for reflection and feedback • Collaborative approaches to PD • Establishing clarity of purpose at the outset in PD activity • Include a focus on pupil outcomes in PD activity • Specify a focus and goal for PD activity aligned to clear timescales • Understand how to evaluate the impact of PD • Develop strategic leadership of PD.	• The duration and rhythm of effective support • The consideration of participants' needs • Alignment of PD processes, content and activities • The content of effective professional development • Activities associated with effective professional development • The role of external providers and specialists • Collaboration and peer learning • Leadership around professional development.

Chapter 12

Leading for innovation and evidence-informed improvement

Chris Brown, Louise Stoll and David Godfrey

Aims

This chapter explores leadership in the context of evidence-informed practice (EIP). In it, we aim to:

- engage with the idea of EIP and the factors driving its uptake in many school systems worldwide

- outline the challenges facing the uptake of EIP in schools and by teachers

- argue that the challenges facing EIP can only be met if school leadership is effective in both its transformational and learner-centred aspects

- suggest that, to harness the power of EIP, school leaders must find the strength to be bold in the face of accountability.

The 'self-improving school-led system' in England

The development, seeking out, use and sharing of effective pedagogic practice is something now viewed as vital to school improvement and as a necessary response to the structural changes facing many school systems worldwide (Brown, 2015). This is perhaps most apparent in England, where the current direction of education policy is providing impetus for teachers and schools to generate their own improvements in teaching and learning. England's move from a centralized to localized approach to school improvement is perhaps best highlighted by contrasting current government policy with that of previous administrations. As Greany (2015: 15–16) notes, the 1997 to 2010 New Labour government's approach to school improvement and system reform was predominantly top-down, albeit with a significant role for local authorities in both challenging and supporting schools.

While the UK's recent (2010–15) Conservative/Liberal Democrat Coalition and newly elected Conservative governments have chosen to build on some of New Labour's foundations, their principal focus has been to develop a 'self-improving school-led school system'. In this system, schools are positioned as autonomous and account-able, with increased diversity and choice for parents through 'free schools' (akin to US Charter Schools) and with a radical reduction in central and local oversight (Greany, 2015; Godfrey, 2016). An analysis of the Department for Education's 2010 White Paper (*The Importance of Teaching*) and other related documents, which heralded this change in tack, suggests that there exist four core criteria for self-improvement. These comprise

1 teachers and schools being responsible for their own improvement

2 teachers and schools innovating (i.e. developing effective practice) by learning from existing good practice and also from research

3 the best schools and leaders extending their reach across other schools so that all schools improve through the spread of best practice

4 government support, and intervention is continuously minimized.
   (Greany, 2014)

Evidence-informed practice

Simultaneous to the notion of self-improvement, the use of research and evidence is now positioned as providing validity to teachers and learning (Brown, 2015; Stoll, 2015a), lead-ing to the coining of the term, 'evidence-informed practice' (Saunders, 2015). Although a number of definitions of EIP abound, for the purposes of this chapter we adopt that provided by England's Department for Education, who suggest such practice may be thought of as: 'A combination of practitioner expertise and knowledge of the best external research, and evaluation based evidence' (www.education.gov.uk, 2014). Our definition of evidence encompasses three forms:

1 use of formal research produced by researchers

2 evidence produced by practitioner enquiry such as action research

3 interpretation of data routinely collected by schools.

The terms 'research' and 'evidence' are used interchangeably and we treat them as synonymous throughout.

There are numerous reported benefits to practitioners engaging in EIP – for example, Supovitz (2015) observes that a common characteristic of high-performing school systems is that they facilitate the collaborative examination of research and data evid-ence in order to identify both likely problem areas (in relation to teaching and learning) and potential solutions to these problems. Likewise, Mincu (2013) and Cordingley (2013) report evidence suggesting that where research and data are used as part of high-quality initial teacher education and ongoing professional development, they make a positive difference in terms of teacher, school and system performance (similar relationships are reported in Godfrey, 2016). Furthermore, the experience of 'research-engaged' schools that take a strategic and concerted approach in this area is generally positive, with studies suggesting that research engagement can shift a school from an instrumental 'top tips' model of improvement to a learning culture in which staff work together to understand what appears to work, when and why (Greany, 2015).

Given the emphasis on self-improvement, it is not surprising that the use of evidence, research and data as drivers for innovation has also become an intentional feature of recent government education policy. Teaching Schools, outstanding schools with a designated role to, among other things, coordinate research and development (R&D) across an alliance of partner schools, have played a prominent part of the educational landscape in England since 2010. To be eligible for Teaching School designation, schools need to demonstrate clear evidence of strong engagement in school-based practitioner-led research and support for teachers gaining academic and professional awards. Those successful in achieving designation are expected to:

1 build on existing research as they contribute to alliance and wider priorities

2 base new initiatives on existing evidence and measure the impact of these initiatives

3 ensure that staff use existing evidence

4 provide necessary time and support for staff to participate in R&D activities.
(Stoll, 2015b: 7)

Becoming evidence-informed

At the same time, little has been written in terms of how teachers might actually become evidence-informed (Godfrey 2016; Brown, 2015). An innovative approach to achieving EIP is provided by Brown and Rogers (2014). Drawing on the definition of EIP set out above, they argue that any joining of research and evidence with practitioner best practice must have at its centre the notion of the 'expert' practitioner. Taking Flybjerg's (2001: 14) notion of an expert as someone who '[exhibits] thinking and behaviour that is rapid, intuitive, holistic [and] interpretive', Brown and Rogers argue that expertise of this type can only be achieved via a process of knowledge 'creation' that encourages both formal and practical learning. More specifically, it can only be reached in situations that have been engineered and are facilitated so that the producers and users of formal knowledge are able to come together to create 'new' knowledge (ways and approaches for doing so can be found in Brown and Rogers, 2014; and Brown, 2015). Such knowledge should then be internalized through practical use and as teachers continually draw upon and appraise its applicability to different situations/cases (Nonaka and Takeuchi, 1995). In relation to the nature of the activities required to achieve this, Brown and Rogers (2014) also argue that acts of knowledge creation are best achieved within the auspices of professional learning communities (for detailed analysis for how these operate most effectively, see Stoll et al., 2006).

Challenges to self-improvement

While there appear to be benefits to facilitating evidence-informed, school-led self-improvement (EISI) – particularly when it derives from the development of practitioner expertise – as the level of more centralized support for schools is rolled back to enable EISI, a number of challenges face English schools and the school system in relation to this area. Perhaps the most significant is that Teaching Schools face the removal of their Teaching School designation if they lose their 'outstanding' inspection grade. Given that educators are frequently risk-averse when it comes to trying out new practices, this can hamper the extent to which schools wish to take risks in experimenting with innovative- and evidence-led practice. It also acts as a disincentive for school leaders to allow their best teachers to do anything other than teaching (and, in particular, dissuades them from allowing teachers to spend time out of school on inter-school activity).

Similarly, as Godfrey (2016: 4: our emphasis) argues, in England, the focus on accountability (and the power afforded to external inspection) has led to a dispropor-tionate pressure on school leaders to 'account for their pupils' academic achievements and to find *quick fixes* where standards are lower than national benchmarks'. Related is the pressure on schools to adopt externally driven improvement strategies preferred by accountability bodies. Likewise, external accountability can also lead to headteach-ers gearing their schools' structures, procedures and practices towards addressing accountability requirements in an instrumental way; for example, performance manage-ment systems that align teacher 'success' to pupil attainment or to where teaching and learning practices are designed to ensure they produce exactly the outcomes required by Ofsted (Supovitz, 2015; see also Chapter 4). In both situations, the resulting approaches are unlikely to deliver EIP in the ways we have envisaged above.

Leading organizational learning

We argue that the challenges facing EISI can only be met if school leadership is effect-ive (e.g. Earley, 2013). This is because it is the role of school leaders to create the most conducive conditions within and across their school for teaching and learning to flourish. School leaders' ability to do so stems from the myriad of ways they are able formally to influence the operation and performance of schools. In themselves these qualities can be divided into the 'transformational' aspects of school leadership and 'pedagogic' or learner-centred leadership (Day and Sammons, 2013). The former is described as a process based on increasing the commitment of those in a school to organizational goals, vision and direction and has been shown to have positive impact in relation to the introduction of new initiatives or the remodelling or restructuring of school activity (e.g. Leithwood, 1994). The latter is seen to relate to the efforts of principals in improving teaching in their school and their focus on the relationships between teachers, as well as the behaviour of teachers vis-à-vis their work with students (e.g. Timperley and Robertson, 2011).

Effective development of, engaging in and sharing of, evidence-informed effective practice within and across schools is thus likely to require school leaders to address both the 'transformational' and 'learning-centred' aspects of self-improvement, and we argue that to do so requires school leaders to focus on and address four distinct but overlapping and interdependent 'organizational learning' factors. These are:

1 Ensuring school cultures are attuned to seeking out and using evidence and evidence-informed effective practice. For example, school leaders promoting the benefits of considering innovative new ideas and normalizing the notion of experimenting with new ways of working (Leithwood et al., 2006). One way to do this is suggested by Stoll (2015a) who argues that senior leaders themselves should model the characteristic of an 'enquiry habit of mind'. That is, senior leaders should actively look for a range of perspectives to help them address given issues, purposefully seek relevant information from numerous and diverse sources and continually explore new ways to tackle perennial problems.

2 Ensuring there is teacher capacity (i.e. ability) to identify, engage in and adopt effective practice, including the ability to engage in and with research activity. This involves ensuring there are processes for upskilling teachers so that they are able to engage critically with research, data and evidence as well as other sources of new practice ideas. Capacity building activity should thus include opportunities for postgraduate training (Goldacre, 2013).

3 School leaders facilitating an effective formal learning environment within which new practice can be developed, trialled, evaluated and shared, leading to the development of expertise (Stoll et al., 2006; Datnow, Park and Lewis, 2013). In addition, that development of practice includes the use of theories of action (Argyris and Schön, 1974), cycles of enquiry and approaches to measuring impact (Taylor and Spence-Thomas, 2015). These ensure that assumptions underpinning proposed new practices are made explicit and so can be challenged and improved, also that the embedding of practice is not treated as a one-off event; instead the introduction of new approaches to teaching and learning take place within the context of a wider iterative 'cycle' of investigation, innovation and improvement (Halbert, Kaser and Koehn, 2011).

4 The existence of effective structures, systems and resource that facilitate engagement with evidence and in EIP. In other words, that school leaders make available and coordinate time and the space and budget required for teachers to engage in the capacity and development outlined above. For instance, they must: free up periods

within the school day to enable teachers to spend quality time engaging with new approaches to practice; ensure the school timetable facilitates collaboration between teachers (and importantly between subgroups of teachers, such as those within subject departments); ensure experienced facilitation and appropriate protocols exist to enable meaningful discussion in relation to new practice. (Datnow, Park and Lewis, 2013). Also important is that research and evidence (including that in academic journals) is made available (Goldacre, 2013); for example, UCL IOE's R&D network offers its members access to the UCL IOE library and other resource.

The importance of relationships

In addition to the formal organizational learning factors above, however, is the role of school leaders in understanding and fostering the informal relationships within and across their schools. Historically, efforts at self-improvement, including more general approaches to encouraging practitioners to become 'evidence-informed' in Ontario, Canada, the United States and a number of other jurisdictions, have tended to result in mixed outcomes (Saunders, 2015). It is argued that, in part, this is because such initiatives often fail to take into account the informal social aspects of change as part of their implementation strategies (Daly, 2010). Patterns of social interactions within and between schools are a vital component of successful school improvement and need to be fully considered (e.g. Daly, 2010). This perspective is nicely set out by Mohrman, Tenkasi and Mohrman (2003: 321) who contend that, because change is moderated through interpersonal relationships, 'lasting change does not result from plans, blueprints, and events. Rather change occurs through the interaction of participants'. More generally, Hubbard, Mehen and Stein (2006) argue that any given reform is, ultimately, socially constructed, and so it is the interdependence of action that moderates the influence of planned change. This notion is also reflected by Spillane, Healey and Kim (2010) who argue that implementation of new initiatives must attend to the informal aspects of an organization; that is, the organization as lived by organizational members in their day-to-day work life.

Given the importance of social relations to the ultimate outcome of any attempts at self-improvement, it is vital to understand what might lead to optimal relationships between practitioners within schools. Empirical evidence suggests that where social relations are steeped in high levels of trust, they are likely to improve outcomes for pupils. In part, this is because the nature, pattern and quality of ties among teachers determine whether an individual can access resources and correspondingly whether they are able to maximize their pedagogic effectiveness. In essence, it is trust that improves the nature, pattern and quality of relations (Finnigan and Daly, 2012). In particular, high levels of trust are associated with a variety of reciprocal efforts, including where collaboration, learning, complex information sharing and problem-solving, shared decision-making, and coordinated action are required (Tschannen-Moran, 2004).

The ability of trust to produce more effective ties/interactions between teachers is further enhanced when linked to efforts at organizational learning. This is because, where there is also trust in relation to organizational learning efforts (which will be guided by aspects of transformational leadership such as vision), staff will 'buy-in' to these more wholeheartedly; thus, reciprocity, when undertaken within the direction and structure of a given organizational learning effort, is likely to lead to more consistent communication and interaction, greater inter-school coherence and so greater goal attainment (Agullard and Goughnour, 2006). When combined with more collaborative efforts centred on developing new approaches to improving teaching and learning, there is greater willingness by teachers to engage with complex information, which will be more conducive to EIP. This is likely to be the case even when organizational learning is not evenly distributed within a school. Finnigan and Daly (2012), for instance, recognizing that effective evidence-use is dependent on capacity (ability) to use evidence, illustrate how trust mediates between those with and without such capacity. In other words, where teachers feel they do not have the knowledge or skills to challenge a research-informed position, trust enables a given position is to be widely adopted.

Vitally, Finnigan and Daly (2012) also argue that reciprocal relations underpinned by trust can form a bulwark against a key challenge facing self-improvement – high-stakes accountability. So, rather than respond to such accountability by playing safe and sticking to 'tried and tested' methods – with low-trust environments serving to dampen innovation – in high-trust schools, individuals feel supported to engage in risk-taking and innovative behaviours associated with efforts at developing or trialling effective practice in a 'safe' learning environment (also Stoll et al., 2006; Mintrop and Trujillo, 2007). Similarly, when individuals feel confident in taking risks with one another and being able to expose vulnerabilities, they are generally better equipped to identify and voice problems, seek support and feedback, innovate and connect to others across the organization.

The role of school leaders in facilitating a culture of trust is highlighted by Tschannen-Moran and Hoy (2000: 573) who note that 'creating an organizational culture of cooperation rather than competition is likely to have a significant impact on the trusting and trustworthy behavior of participants'. Conversely, Daly and Finnigan (2011) caution against school leaders ratcheting up the number of improvement initiatives they are engaged in so as to improve their performance – for example, by attempting to improve their Ofsted grading. This is because the resulting intensification for schools to improve can negatively impact on staff morale and make these schools less attractive places to work. In turn, staff turnover often increases, meaning both that teachers do not have enough time together to normalize a trusting culture and that school leaders can also over-regulate the working environment to compensate for the low morale/high turnover situation (in turn exacerbating it). As a result, within such schools, there tend to be diminished levels of collaboration and professional interchange and exchange (Daly and Finnigan, 2011).

Summary

The concept of EIP is grounded in the idea that teaching practice (and so outcomes for pupils) can be drastically improved if aided by high-quality, pertinent knowledge. At the same time, as school systems move away from positions of top-down command and control, it is also believed that they will only be in a position to 'self-improve' if research-informed effective practice is helped to flow within and between teachers and schools (Goldacre, 2013). Despite these potential benefits, connecting research to practice is notoriously difficult, with the failure of research to make a widespread and sustained impact on the practices of teachers recognized as an international phenomenon.

To help alleviate this situation we argue that realizing the benefits associated with EIP will require schools to address and build the capacity of practitioners to engage with research and evidence, which we argue derives from aspects of formal organizational learning, to ensure the existence of effective, quality relationships that are steeped in high levels of trust. At the same time, we have already highlighted some of the challenges facing school and system self-improvement; for example, the impact of high-stakes accountability and the potential threat facing Teaching Schools in England should they lose their 'outstanding' rating. We argue therefore that to harness the power of EIP within their schools, school leaders must find the strength to be bold in the face of accountability and create for their teachers a safe environment that encourages and rewards effective practice. Simultaneously, school leaders must develop EIP and EISI in ways steeped in the best practices of organizational learning; for instance, employing cycles of investigation, innovation and improvement (such approaches, thus, leave open the possibilities of maximal gain while reducing the risk of testing out new practices, since new approaches will begin at a small scale and will be refined, scaled up or dropped depending on their success). These approaches thus require school leaders to be cognizant of the formal and informal requirements of their organization; that is, the need for them to put in place the most facilitative structures and to establish the most supportive cultures possible while ensuring that meaningful relationships thrive.

Implications

1 How might accountability systems be altered in order to encourage EIP and the sharing of effective practice within and across schools?

2 How might we measure the 'success' of efforts to embed EIP both in terms of teacher and pupil outcomes?

3 How might we identify and learn from those schools where EIP has been effectively and successfully embedded? In particular, how do the leaders within these schools best develop high levels of trust in the context of high-stakes accountability?

Chapter 13

Community collaboration and partnership in volatile times

Kathryn Riley

Aims

This chapter explores policy shifts in expectations about the role of schools in building community cohesion and examines the implications for school leaders. In a period of global volatility and changing social and political contexts, the author aims to address three key questions:

- How should school leaders respond to these policy requirements?
- What are the competing demands and expectations on them as leaders?
- How can they respond to their obligation to help prevent terrorism or extremism, while at the same time build relationships with communities, and make 'belonging' work for children and young people from many different backgrounds?

Background

Many of the women I contacted sought affection and praise in the arms of the Isis sisterhood. More than anything else, 'Umm Raeesa' craved human connection. She had a deep yearning to belong.

Nabeelah Jaffer, 6 June 2015

An implicit policy assumption in the UK over many decades has been that schools should build tolerance within communities (Riley, 2013a). In an uncertain and fast-moving policy environment, implicit expectations about what schools should do have now become more explicit. In 2007, schools were given a brief by government to promote community cohesion. This required them to move from 'building' tolerance to 'challenging' 'intolerance' (DCSF, 2007). The year 2015 witnessed a further shift in expectations. Schools and colleges were directed 'to have due regard' to the need to prevent people from being drawn into terrorism or extremism (HM Government, 2015).

Across the world, school leaders share a global context of uncertainty and mobility – half the world's fifty million refugees are children (UNHCR, 2015) – and while the policy features outlined in this chapter are distinctive to the UK, wherever schools are located, they face competing policy pressures and demands. Increasingly, school leaders find themselves on the front line: working to build partnerships with communities and trying to satisfy national policy imperatives in a policy arena which is highly contentious.

How do they manage issues about diversity, or threats of extremism when the impact of polices is so uncertain? Has, for example, the French response to an increasingly diverse society been more or less successful than the British one? Broadly speaking, successive French governments have sought to build a common set of values in French society through assimilationist policies which largely ignore cultural differences in the public arena; a stance which has been criticized for marginalizing and ignoring, and ultimately alienating many communities, particular those of African and Muslim origin (Malik, 2015: 35). By way of contrast, British 'multicultural' approaches to diversity have welcomed cultural pluralism. However, it has been argued that this, in its turn, has reinforced differences, encouraging people to put themselves in separate ethnic and cultural boxes, and defining and treating the individuals by those definitions: a process which has led to fragmentation and a degree of tribalism (ibid.).

Both approaches, no doubt, have their strengths and weaknesses. Nevertheless, in the context of this chapter, two salient points remain. First, both France and the UK have experienced terrorist attacks from what have been described as 'home grown jihadists' (ibid.: 36). Secondly, schools remain one of the few shared social institutions where values and beliefs are played out on a daily basis; and school leaders are the mediators of those values.

Contextual challenges

The policy environment

National policy agendas, and what has been described as the policy discourse (Ball, 1997), are shaped by political beliefs and values, as well as by the ways in which policymakers interpret and respond to national and global events. In 2007, the policy focus on community cohesion emerged in the UK in the wake of race riots which had earlier taken place in a number of towns in the north of England. The Commission of Inquiry set up in 2001 to examine the causes of those disturbances concluded that the largely white and Asian communities were highly segregated, typically living 'parallel' but separate lives and rarely, if ever, meeting (Riley, 2013a). Trust had broken down, and there were pressing issues about citizenship, diversity and opportunity which needed to be addressed (Cantell, 2001).

The political aspirations for community cohesion stemmed from a wish to create a society in which different cultures and beliefs would be valued and appreciated. Launching the policy on behalf of the then Labour government, Secretary of State for Education Alan

Johnson, speaking in Parliament on 2 November 2006, described these aspirations in the following terms:

> By community cohesion, we mean working towards a society in which there is a common vision and sense of belonging by all communities; a society in which the diversity of people's backgrounds and circumstances is appreciated and valued; a society in which similar life opportunities are available to all; and a society in which strong and positive relationships exist and continue to be developed in the workplace, in schools and in the wider community.

The schools' role in contributing to the community cohesion agenda was to ensure that 'all pupils understood and appreciated' other pupils from different backgrounds, and that all young people had the opportunity to fulfil their potential and feel 'part of a community, at a local, national and international level'(DCSF, 2007: 2). Schools were encouraged to promote 'equality of opportunity and inclusion for different groups of pupils within a school and ... shared values' (ibid.: 6). Their brief was explicit: to confront 'the corrosive effects of intolerance and harassment ... build ... mutual civility among different groups ... [and] ensure respect for diversity alongside a commitment to common and shared bonds' (ibid.: 3). Ofsted, the English schools inspectorate, was given the remit to report on schools' performance in this arena.

While the policy emphasis was on building a climate of tolerance and mutuality, the community cohesion agenda also had a second arm, the Preventing Violent Extremism Policy, also known as 'Prevent'. The Prevent strategy grew out of political concerns about divisions in society heightened by a number of extreme events, most notably the July 2005 London bombings, also known as 7/7: a series of suicide attacks in opposition to Britain's involvement in the war in Iraq.

'Prevent' sought to encourage local and national bodies to work together to prevent violent extremism. Resources were targeted at local authorities with the largest Muslim populations. The strategy generated a number of tensions for those responsible for managing its implementation. How could they on the one hand build trust, and on the other hand, identify potential sources of disaffection (Dodd, 2009)? Civil liberties leader Shami Chakrabarti condemned the gathering of sensitive data around 'Prevent' as the biggest spying programme in Britain in modern times (Dodd, 2009).

In 2015, the newly elected Conservative government introduced the Counter-Terrorism and Security Act, as part of its counter-terrorism strategy, CONTEST. The national and global context for the act was the rise of extremism, defined within the act as 'vocal or active opposition to fundamental British values, including democracy, the rule of law, individual liberty and mutual respect and tolerance of different faiths and beliefs' (HM Government, 2015: section 7). The main terrorist threats were identified as coming from organizations in Syria and Iraq and al-Qaeda-associated groups (ibid.: section 8).

The 2015 Act introduced a second phase of the Prevent strategy, extending its legal status to include schools and colleges. Along with other public sector institutions, schools were given a new statutory duty, linked to their child protection and safeguarding responsibilities, which was to prevent extremism. The extremist narrative was described within the act as a 'them' and 'us' ideology which encompassed 'the uncompromising belief that people' could not 'be both Muslim and British' (ibid.: section 10). The 'white supremacist ideology of extreme right-wing groups' was also recognized as providing 'both the inspiration and justification for people' to commit 'extreme right-wing terrorist acts' (ibid.: section 11).

The act spelt out the implications for leaders. Those in leadership positions in schools, colleges and other public sector organizations were required to:

- establish or use existing mechanisms for understanding the risk of radicalization
- ensure staff understand the risk and build the capabilities to deal with it
- communicate and promote the importance of the duty
- ensure staff implement the duty effectively.
  (HM Government, 2015)

The media climate

The act was introduced in the context of heightened concerns about external influences on young people. In February 2015, three British-born Muslim school students from a school in the East End of London took a flight to Turkey, later crossing the border into an area in Syria held by ISIL (the self-designated Islamic State of Iraq and the Levant, known as Islamic State). Their departure from the UK led to a national outcry, with attention focused on the power and reach of social media. Research on foreign fighters in Syria contributed to the debate, identifying how a network of radical preachers had been able to harness social media to 'inspire' British jihadists in Syria (Carter, Maher and Neumann, 2014). Press attention focused on the influence of tweets, Facebook and blogs on the views of young people and on the role of schools. How could young women born and educated in the UK have come to accept attitudes and beliefs which appeared to be so at variance with so-called 'British' values (Daily Telegraph, 20 February 2015)? Did they not feel that they belonged in the UK?

Concerns about belonging became central political and journalistic themes. Emma Barnett, for example, in the *Daily Telegraph* reported on the views of a young British-born Muslim woman who explained her own reactions to terrorism in the following terms: 'Feeling marginalized does not of course justify acts of terrorism. But what I do understand is the desperate search to find a place where you belong – the human desire to be listened to is incredibly strong' (Barnet, 2015: 5).

In an extended piece in the *Guardian* in June 2015, Nabeelah Jaffer explored the world of young women who had been drawn to ISIS. She concluded that many of the young women she had been in contact with, such as 'Umm Raeesa' (see opening quotation) craved a sense of connection and belonging. Prime Minister David Cameron also identified belonging as a key issue: deterring radicalism, he argued, was also about creating a sense of belonging (Coughlan, 2015).

Caught between

In this highly febrile media environment, and in the context of the requirement on schools and colleges to have 'due regard' to the need to 'prevent' young people from being drawn into terrorism or extremism (HM Government, 2015), the schools' ability to create that sense of belonging has now become a matter for public debate. School leaders find themselves under pressure. Quite rightly, they want to protect the young people in their charge from malign influences. Safeguarding is a critical responsibility for all school leaders. Feeling safe and secure in schools is a prerequisite to having a sense of belonging and being open to learning.

Nevertheless, there are tensions for school leaders in carrying out their various responsibilities. The introduction of the new statutory guidance linked to the Counter-Terrorism and Security Act 2015 has led to a proliferation of courses and programmes on how to identify inappropriate use of the internet. Schools have begun to use specialist software to filter, monitor and identify suspicious activities online. A number of software packages are now available (such as Securus, Future Digital and Impero Education Pro). For some school leaders, the new legislation has generated a sense of nervousness on their part about whether, and how, to discuss controversial issues with their students or communities. For others, in the context of the emergence of a new Islamic identity which attempts to build the 'umma' – the Islamic community (Castells, 2010: 23) – and a feeling from within the Muslim community that they are under the spotlight, there is a concern that those on the margins of society may become further alienated.

Stepping into the space

Understanding the importance of belonging

We live in a world of unprecedented change and uncertainty. For young people, this re-enforces the importance of finding a place where they can feel rooted and that they belong. 'Belonging' is that sense of being somewhere where you can be confident that you will fit in and where you feel safe in your identity. In this transient and turbulent world, the importance of young people finding a place where they feel rooted and that they can belong cannot be underestimated (Riley, 2017).

A sense of belonging is a complex and highly personalized experience. In *Leadership of Place,* I explored the lives and experiences of young people growing up in disadvantaged communities and the role of schools in creating place and belonging. For many youngsters, their experience of place was marked by living in divided communities: areas which were safe and welcoming and others which were 'no-go' areas. Within school, life could be full of contradictions and contrasts. Some young people were on the 'insider' track, experiencing school as a safe and welcoming place. Others were the 'outsiders' who did not fit in, did not belong (Riley, 2013b).

School leaders have a critical role to play in helping schools to become places of belonging for young people, and of acceptance for their families. They need, as Keith Ajegbo (a successful London headteacher) and colleagues have argued in a review of citizenship and diversity, to find ways of tackling disparities and recognizing commonalties: 'All pupils, regardless of their background need to be helped to develop a sense of belonging and a cultural understanding and critical literacy skills within their neighbourhoods, however, disparate' (Ajegbo, Kiwan and Sharma, 2007: 12).

Undoubtedly, school leaders need to take into account national policy agendas, as well as the impact of those policies on the day-to-day practices of schools (Bangs, MacBeath and Galton, 2010). This is a critical element of taking stock of their social and political realities: the social and political climate, the policies and practices which they, and their schools, will be judged or assessed on (Riley, 2013b). They would be foolish to do otherwise. However, in this complex global climate, school leaders also need to recognize that there are some core elements of what they need to do as leaders that transcend the immediacy of policy requirements. These include 'place-making'.

The art of place-making

Leaders who are place-makers work to make schools places of belonging for young people and staff, and acceptance and appreciation for diverse communities (Riley, 2016). Place-making, as a key component of leadership, offers a way of closing the gap between schools and communities, particularly when values and beliefs are at variance and communities feel that they are under the spotlight. Place-making is about working to bridge different worlds and realities. It involves schools in taking systematic steps to know and understand their communities (Riley, 2008), working to harness the spirit of those communities (Etzioni, 1991) and bringing communities and schools together in stronger, mutually supportive alliances.

However, this is far from being an easy task. In 2013, I suggested that school leaders, particularly those in highly disadvantaged urban communities, walked a tightrope, caught between the needs of communities and the requirements of national policies (Riley, 2013a). That tightrope has now become more precarious and the balancing pole more fragile. Nevertheless, the act of place-making provides school leaders with a possible safety net should they fall; a supportive community in which values and beliefs have been discussed and understood, and accommodations reached about the educational experiences on offer to young people.

An essential part of place-making is knowing and understanding the lives of young people, making meaningful connections to families, and locating the school within the wider archipelago of surrounding communities (Riley, 2013b). I want to offer one practical illustration of how this can be done by drawing briefly on *School a Place where I Belong?*, a research project undertaken in collaboration with London schools.

The project involved teacher-researchers (newly qualified teachers) and student-researchers aged 8 to 16 in a process of collaborative research inquiry around the theme of place and belonging (Riley, 2017).[1] The vignette below provides two examples of the ways in which engagement in the research process has contributed to young people's sense of wellbeing and belonging.

Vignette

School a place where I belong?

Young researchers from one of the participating schools, Mulberry School for Girls in Tower Hamlets, began their research by looking at the pattern of immigration to this east London borough. They wanted to know how they, as young Muslim women, had come to be born and to live in that neighbourhood. This process of research inquiry and reflection not only enabled them to locate themselves within the community but also encouraged them to think about themselves within the school. As one of the student-researchers from Mulberry concluded, this research 'has helped me be myself. I really feel I belong here in London and in my school.'

Young student-researchers from Corelli Cooperative College set themselves the research task of examining how successful their school was in creating a sense of belonging for other new arrivals to the UK. The research team members were themselves all recent arrivals, the majority learning English as a second or third language. They understood only too well what it meant to be a newcomer. Through their research, they came to understand the experience of others and made recommendations to their school about how to help create that sense of belonging in school. They also wrote a booklet for all new arrivals to the school which they translated into ten languages.

Place-making is also about creating spaces and opportunities within school which are safe and inspirational and which provide young people with the opportunity to speak out about what troubles them and what is important to them. In this sense it is also about criticality; equipping young people to be critical thinkers who can make sense of competing truths and realities. This is, as Paulo Freire put it, the recognition that 'literacy involves not just the reading of the word but also the reading of the world' (1993: 55).

For these students from Mulberry and Corelli, as well as for the students from the other participating schools, involvement in the research of *School a place where I belong?* strengthened their sense of belonging in their schools and communities. It developed their criticality. It also gave them a sense of wellbeing and agency. Belonging and agency go hand in hand. When schools involve young people in research that is so directly about their sense of identity and belonging, it sends a strong message to young people and communities that they are not only welcomed but also valued. It is a profound act of place-making on the part of school leaders.

Rethinking the school–community relationship

School leaders need to know and understand their responsibilities in relation to 'Prevent' but not be so fearful that they close down discussions about controversial issues. Schools are communities, 'political entities' in which young people learn how to become part of society (Alexander, 2013). If young people cannot discuss controversial issues within school, where else can they have those discussions? Creating dialogue with communities and opening the minds of young people to critical thinking re-enforces the centrality of the role of school leaders as place-makers.

The dilemmas and tensions for school leaders raised in this chapter are tough and evolving. There are important issues about ethics (Sergiovanni, 1992), values and trust (Byrk and Schneider, 2002; Louis, 2007) and about the very nature of moral leadership – the principles upon which leaders walk their leadership (West-Burnham, 2015).

In 2013, I developed a model for building and strengthening relationships between schools and communities. It was based on fostering trust, as the lubricant to link communities together, and building social capital, as a way of harnessing the 'social energy' of communities for positive good (Riley, 2013a). These issues of trust and social capital apply as much to schools' internal communities – the staff and young people – as to external communities. The model was underpinned by a theory of action which had three component parts: Bridging, Challenging and Building.

Creating a sense of shared community

Bridging is based on recognition of differences in values, beliefs and expectations between communities and the role of schools in creating a way for groups to talk to each other. Bridging is about reaching out to make links and develop relationships.

Challenging is about setting the boundaries in schools' relationships with communities which can include confronting a range of ingrained attitudes and perceptions in order to tackle prejudice and reduce ethnic or racial tension.

Building is about capacity building (recognizing the knowledge and skills within communities) and partner building (which embraces the notion of the school as a partner in re-generating communities through a range of social networks). It is also about trust building, the connector which brings together capacity building and partner building.

On the basis of the arguments put forward in this chapter, I want to add a fourth dimension to this framework: the notion of place-making.

Place-making is the recognition of the significance of schools in creating a 'sense of place' for children, young people and adults (Glasman and Crowson, 2001; Riley, 2013a). It is an approach which emphasizes the importance of social capital (Hargreaves, 2003) and recognizes – and draws on – the potential and possibilities: the knowledge and skills within school communities (from staff and students) and those within local communities.

This addition to the model or framework of school–community relationships reflects the ways in which schools and their leaders need to be less reactive to events and circumstances and more proactive. Leaders need to focus on creating a sense of agency in their young people: a belief that what they do and say can make a difference.

Final reflection

The policy and contextual challenges presented in this chapter put school leaders to the test, pushing them to revisit their core beliefs and values and reflect on what they can do to appreciate differences and welcome communities. They strengthen the importance of working even more closely with communities to manage and maintain dialogue. If the channels of communication are closed down, then school leaders cannot make the interventions that may be needed to protect children and young people. And they cannot build the sense of agency which is critical to their wellbeing. Through place-making, school leaders can begin to negotiate a new way of belonging. As one of the headteachers in the project reflected:

> For many of our children home and community are not fixed. ... This raises identity issues because belonging is about the meaning we attach to a place and our relationship to a place and the way that this changes. School is about negotiating a new way of belonging.

Note

1. The UCL, Institute of Education Project Team was Professor Kathryn Riley, Dr Dina Mehmedbegovic, Dr Max Coates and Rhoda Furniss.

Chapter 14

Working with the community, parents and students

Trevor Male and Ioanna Palaiologou

Aims

In this chapter we aim to:

- explore how the community, parents and schools can work productively in partnership to support students
- discover the key elements of successful and mutually beneficial partnerships
- identify the implications for school leaders.

This chapter is based on our research in schools into the ecology of the community where school leaders are concerned as much with the relationships with families and a number of other services such as health and social work as with national policies, reforms and global issues. Effective education settings, we argue, are those which 'have developed productive and synergistic relationships between learners, families, the team and the community, because the context, the locality and the culture in which the learners live are vitally important' (Male and Palaiologou, 2012: 112). Our views thus correspond to those of Mongon and Leadbetter (2012) who similarly argue that effective learning by all students occurs when the school, parents and learners are all actively engaged with the community, the school is not culturally separate and there is broad ownership of the purposes of school.

In this chapter, we explore issues relevant to the concept of the community, parents, students and schools working together, and examine a range of consequences in the context of England. The key characteristics of working together effectively are illustrated through examples drawn from the English school system and, in particular, through our research case study, a secondary school located in an area of urban poverty. The investigation and subsequent conclusions are of wider significance, however, and are applicable to other education systems across the world.

Definitions

'Community' refers to the immediate local environment, rather than the national or global setting which also have an impact on educational expectations. The features of that local community environment are formative in terms of desired outcomes, but can be harnessed and changed through intervention by a school.

'Parent' is used here as a description of the adult(s) responsible for the welfare of each student.

The child as learner is referred to here as a 'student'.

'School' is a descriptive term for any educational setting which takes formal responsibility for children's learning.

'Partnerships' describes relationships between the community, parents, students and school.

In the early part of this century the traditional dualistic relationship of student and school has been superseded as a consequence of examining the relationships between the community, parents and school that shape students. Relationships based on respect, listening to each other, co-operation and active participation between prospective partners have been emphasized as having positive benefits in students' development, education and wellbeing (Epstein and Sheldon, 2006; Feiler, 2010; Fan et al., 2011; Goodall and Montgomery, 2014). In 2008 the central government highlighted the importance of partnerships with families as a key element for educational achievement (DCFS, 2008), accompanied by expectations contained within the statutory framework of inspection for schools to work closely in partnership with other providers and the community (Ofsted, 2015). Schools in England thus carry a central responsibility for leading, managing and promoting student learning, attainment and achievement and are accountable to all to ensure every effort is made to align their own actions with those from outside the immediacy of the educational setting. Consequently, school leaders are expected to maximize every possibility to enhance the learning environment for their students and be able to demonstrate the ways in which this objective is achieved. In England this is now not only a moral and professional commitment, but is also a particular aspect of education provision for which school leaders are accountable.

The centrality of effective working relationships

In the school system there is an obvious need for effective working relationships between schools and the community, parents and students. Parents are a key partner in this prospective relationship, although the community cannot be ignored either. Schools that seek to operate in a microcosm without parent or community engagement and concentrate only on the relationship they have with students consequently may set themselves at a disadvantage in terms of maximizing outcomes.

The concept of student outcomes needs clarification if the greatest impact is to be achieved. In keeping with most other nations the English government is concerned with student attainment and invest heavily in the continuing improvement on national tests and examinations. At the institutional level these are often seen as being the driving force behind actions that need to be taken. One reason for seeking enhanced working relationships with other key aspects of the learning community, therefore, is to maximize academic attainment by the student body. There is the possibility of recognizing distinctiveness between attainment and achievement, however, with the latter concept embracing wider measures of success. Achievement relates as much to self-regard as it does to examination success and is how students can come to terms with who they are and what they might become, which is now being recognized as an essential part of the school curriculum, with life skills and character education becoming part of government policy (Gurney-Read, 2015). Aspirations in this regard often exceed the basic key to advancement of attainment and embrace success in other ways. Most parents wish to achieve the dream of their children having a better life than their own and thus are willing to invest in their development emotionally and practically wherever possible. With those parameters, therefore, it is incumbent on schools to seek to promote student achievement as well as attainment and to have clarity of how this is to be reached through partnership.

Case study school Part 1: Winning trust

Over a period of three years we interviewed senior leaders, governors, other staff, students, local officers and parents together with a review of documentation such as inspection reports, internal documentation, press cuttings and relevant correspondence.

The story of this school's improvement began in 1997 with the school in virtual terminal decline with low achievement, student disruption and appalling behaviour being common. The appointment of a new headteacher familiar with the social context and the locality (having served as Head of Faculty within the school for the previous seven years) saw changes that led to dramatic improvement being recognized by Ofsted within two years. This continued to the point where the school became one of the schools achieving success 'against the odds' just a few years later (Ofsted, 2009). The bedrock of this process was the establishment of a school ethos where all students could be successful and underpinned by a remorseless concentration on behaviour and achievement. The first step was to regain adult control of the school and convince the local community, especially parents, that this zero tolerance policy was real and would be sustained. Large numbers of disruptive students were excluded in the first couple of weeks after appointment of the new headteacher, with the justification that it gave the school the opportunity to talk directly with the parents. An exhaustive set of subsequent meetings resulted in ten permanent exclusions and a set of behavioural norms that have remained in place ever since. Once control was re-established within the school, huge efforts were made to convince the local community that this was not cosmetic and would be sustained. Senior leaders became highly visible outside the school premises and confronted aberrant student behaviour wherever it occurred. Trust was quickly established, with parents and the local community feeling empowered to talk directly to school staff and students aware that they were, as one senior member of staff commented, 'walking adverts for the school'.

While schools in isolation can be successful with developing and enhancing student life chances, they are more likely to be successful with the support and engagement of the community and parents in addition to the relationship they have with individual students. School leaders are advised, therefore, to invest time and energy into establishing synergistic working relationships with the other potential partners if they are to maximize student outcomes and be judged as successful.

Parental engagement

All research and commentary on the involvement of parents in their child's education shows it is a fundamental requirement for successful outcomes. There is lack of clarity on the specific actions that contribute to success, however, as much of the research has not been conducted in such a manner as to demonstrate causality (Gorard and Huat See, 2013). There is a need to recognize a difference between 'parental involvement' and 'parental engagement', however, as both may be understood in a very narrow sense of 'parental involvement with children's schooling' rather than the more useful concept of 'parental engagement with children's learning' (Goodall, 2013: 134). Parental involvement, Goodall suggests, is related to school-initiated activities, which have as their focus parental interaction with the school rather than with the learning of the child and is measured by parental presence rather than by student outcome or effect. Such activities may form part of the entire process of parental involvement in children's learning, but they are only a small section, rather than the whole of the concept. Research has made clear that the greatest lever for children's achievement is parental engagement in their learning in the home, and the atmosphere towards learning in the home (Desforges and Abouchaar, 2003; Goodall and Vorhaus, 2011). What we know, therefore, is that parental engagement with their children's learning is central when seeking to enhance attainment and achievement at all levels of their development.

Parents are the most influential figure for young children, although the influence of parents typically seems to become less direct as children grow. A meta-review of relevant research and published literature conducted by Desforges and Abouchaar (2003) on parental involvement, support and family education on pupil achievement showed that the key actions underpinning their children's success as learners were manifested in three ways:

- showing interest in the child
- holding secure values and educational aspirations
- demonstrating enthusiasm, engagement and encouragement for student learning (a positive parenting style).

Parents are largely responsible for the education of their children in the preschool phase with most learning taking place in an incidental rather than planned manner. The evidence from research is clear, however, that it is in this phase that intervention from beyond the home is most effective (e.g. Sylva et al., 1999; Siraj-Blatchford et al., 2002). Such interventions 'are most likely to succeed when they are aimed at young children, and involve parents and staff meeting regularly in an institution, with parental training, on-going support, and co-operative working with teachers' (Gorard and Huat See, 2013: 4). At all ages what matters is 'the overall attitude towards parenting and children, and the actions that then flow from that attitude, in combination with each other' (Goodall, 2013: 137). Parental interest in terms of expectations, encouragement and support are vital, therefore, and this holds good regardless of race, ethnicity or socio-economic status throughout schooling (Catsambis, 2001).

The influence of the community

Just as the socio-economic status and academic level of parents largely determine student life chances, so to a similar extent does the community. The values, beliefs and expectations of local society often have a significant influence on student behaviour and engagement as, increasingly, does the peer group as the student grows older. The social setting in which the student develops needs to reflect values and expectations that encourage students to achieve beyond any inherent assumptions and limitations of previous generations. That should not be a one-way relationship, however, with schools also having a responsibility to exhibit respect for the value that aspects of the community can bring to the learning environment, which could have implications for curriculum as well as learning experiences. Many schools in England seek to impart what is a largely a white, middle-class curriculum to other socio-economic or ethnic groupings without making essential adjustments, alterations or adaptations to take account of what those parts of the community can bring to the enhancement of student learning, attainment and achievement (Sleeter, 2001; House of Commons Education Committee, 2014). Greater success can therefore be achieved through the school reaching out to and equally drawing in the local community. Both Epstein and Sheldon (2006) and Mongon and Leadbetter (2012) suggest this leads to the concept of home, school and community partnerships being a better term than 'parental engagement' or 'involvement' as it captures the value of community in relation to young people's learning.

Case study Part 2 Respecting the community

The population of the school underwent rapid transformation with changes to the local population during the first decade of the new millennium that dramatically changed the ethnic balance of the community. The development of the area had initially been the consequence of building a huge council estate in the early 1920s in order to relocate skilled workers from the slums of the nearby major city after the First World War. This almost exclusively white working-class community was extended a decade later when a major industrial company relocated their production to the area. The consequence was that by the end of the twentieth century the student body was almost exclusively white working class. Changes to government policy on council house ownership in the late 1980s saw many of the by-now-ageing population initially purchase and then sell their property which opened the market for buy-to-rent entrepreneurs. With rental rates low (in comparison to other nearby areas) there was an influx of socio-economic immigrants which significantly diversified the ethnic balance of the community. This pattern was exacerbated with the arrival of refugees from many conflict situations in both mainland Europe and Africa, supplemented by further economic migrants from other European Union countries. By 2015 the school had a multi-ethnic population drawn from over 100 countries. The school's response was to continue the pattern of celebrating every success, but to ensure that all aspects of their community were recognized, respected and represented appropriately in both the formal and informal parts of their operation. This response moved beyond tokenism and included reviews of pedagogical practice and curricula provision. In this way the school can be considered to have engaged and involved all members of their diverse community in their continuing success.

We argue that the partnerships need to be extended further to also include the community in order to form effective multi-modal relationships and conclude that partnerships between communities, parents, students and schools need to be approached as a holistic dynamic where relationships are shaped as much by the local culture, values and ethos as well as external influences such as government agendas or policies.

Changing times, changing schools

Schools are therefore a reflection of the community, and, as demonstrated in our case study school, communities across Europe are becoming multi-ethnic and diverse due to sociopolitical and economic factors. Such change brings with it the potential for conflict.

Case study Part 3 Dealing with radical views

Like most schools in English urban settings our case study school has not only to recognize and respect the social diversity of the local community, but also to confront the potential for social divisions which also carry the potential for radicalization of vulnerable members of the student body (see also Chapter 13). Having moved from an almost universal white working-class society to one that is multicultural, yet still prone to poverty, the risk of disaffection caused by aberrant elements was a distinct possibility. As was previously shown, the school had sought to celebrate each and every aspect of that diverse community in a manner that went far beyond superficial actions. Nevertheless, there were occasions when it was considered necessary to show intolerance of some individuals, groups or actions that could influence students to behave in ways that affected social equity. One of the earliest challenges in this respect was to confront gang-related behaviour (which in major cities in England is typically associated with Black youths). There was a deliberate policy to isolate such students, take them out of the normal programme (especially if they were exhibiting visible evidence of their gang membership, including hairstyles) and require them to study with a key member of staff (in this case a parent governor and school employee who was himself Black British) until such time as their influence was removed. It was a response that was recognized by the school leadership team as extreme, but one considered necessary to avoid the imbalance to individual rights for all members of the school community. This was evidence of the school taking a proactive stance to enhancing the institutional and community ethos in support of their overarching aim to provide a pedagogy of care. At the time our research was conducted this was the only example of an interventionist approach designed to negate the influence of one aspect of the community, yet there was great awareness within the school of the need to monitor the potential for other influencing local factors that could disaffect, alienate or radicalize their students.

What we are suggesting here, therefore, is that community participation should be a tool for reducing prejudice, encouraging desegregation among the different culture groups in the community and creating partnerships based on relevant reciprocity where complementary needs and cultural components are utilized in the creation of effective learning environments.

The formation, development and sustenance of partnerships

Epstein (1995) described six types of family–school-community relationships:

- parenting partnerships where the focus is on support for families to create home environments which support children as students

- forms of communication for school to home and home to school
- volunteering
- information exchange between home and school so students can be supported in learning at home with homework
- school decision-making partnerships where parents are included
- partnerships with the community where resources and services are integrated in the school to support student learning and development.

Georgiou (1997) cautions, however, that only relationships that are meaningful to the students are positively correlated with achievement. Desforges and Abouchaar demonstrate, for example, there is virtually no impact on student attainment and achievement from in-school parental involvement, whereas 'at-home parental involvement clearly and consistently has significant effects on pupil achievement and adjustment which far outweigh other forms of involvement' (2003: 30–1). Such involvement should be in the form of interest in the child, they conclude, and manifested in the home as parent–child discussions. Engagement with parents, and supporting their engagement with children's learning thus 'needs to permeate the ethos of the school; it needs to be a core value alongside, indeed, as part of, the value given to teaching and learning' (Goodall, 2015: 174).

What this means for school leaders

Establishing a core ethos that is extended to and embraced by the community, parents and students is thus the responsibility of the school and embodied within the leadership team, particularly the headteacher. As Barr and Saltmarsh show, 'Recent research has reaffirmed that parents tend to see the headteacher as embodying the authority of the school and setting its vision' (2014: 175). School leadership is the key force, therefore, in the formation of effective partnerships and the main motivating force for changing behaviours. Given the nature of social organizations and systems, leaders hold power which can be used to impact on partnerships, for which Collins and Raven (1969) identified six forms:

1 Reward: offering or withholding various rewards
2 Coercive: decision-making on whether to punish (or not)
3 Reference: others desire to identify themselves with this person
4 Expert: holding appropriate and relevant knowledge
5 Legitimate: that comes from the role the person holds in the group
6 Informational: holding important pieces of information.

We argue that within leadership all forms of power are interconnected and tend to be found together in the formation or deformation of partnerships, but the balance of use is dependent on circumstances. In that sense leadership behaviour can vary considerably in the forms of social power and in relation to context and circumstance. In the early days of our case study school we can see examples of coercive, legitimate and expert power being exhibited. As student behaviour improved, however, we saw more in the way of reward, reference and informational power being used, although the senior leadership team also demonstrated the willingness to revert to coercive power when circumstances demanded, as was the case when confronting gang-style behaviour. It is important, therefore, for leaders to reflect on the social power they hold, to see the centrality of their role as the nucleus for formation or deformation of partnerships and to be prepared to take action that is appropriate to the situation. Schools leaders also need to acknowledge, however, that other potential stakeholders of the partnership can exhibit influence within the relationship with the dynamics of power having a decisive effect on the partnership. Silencing of the students, for example, in an attempt to take on board parents and community's views on what is best, could lead to students feeling undermined which will have negative effects on the formation of partnerships.

To conclude, therefore, we argue that school leaders hold the influential role in the formation of partnerships and need to adopt a proactive approach that appreciates the elements of power that are available to them. As explained earlier shared values and beliefs, willingness to engage, aspirations and trust are important in the formation of partnerships that empower the community, parents and students. School leaders should thus seek to form partnerships where all stakeholders' attributes and legacies are explored and understood in order to create collective ownership of desired outcomes while being prepared to adopt leadership behaviours that are 'contingent on context and circumstance' (Male, 2006: 3).

Summary

In our research we found that effective working partnerships between the community, parents, students and schools are based on the formation of relationships for which there are required elements:

- All partners need to have shared values and beliefs so they can engage and participate in the creation and sustenance of effective learning environments
- Partners need to show willingness to engage, share responsibility and exhibit trust, commitment and resilience in support of agreed objectives
- The partnership must be aspirational, inclusive and celebrate both achievement and attainment

- A common ethos must be established which enhances positive contributions from all partners, but avoids a blame culture and minimizes or removes aberrant influences

- There is a continuing need for partners to be in close proximity so they come together physically as often as possible to share information and exchange ideas

- Partnership success should be judged by the way in which reciprocity is exhibited and there is evidence of complementarity of stakeholder needs.

Implications

As a consequence of our investigation and this discussion we propose that in working effectively with the community, parents and students, school leaders should undertake the following actions:

- Explore the socio-economic, ethnic and religious constitution of their local community so the school has a clear understanding of the expectations of the local community

- Be fully aware of statutory responsibilities and accountabilities and ensure these are not neglected

- Establish an organizational ethos with agreed values and beliefs based on reciprocity of needs

- Maintain a close operational focus on the ethos and demonstrate intolerance of factors and behaviours that do not support agreed expectations

- Create and sustain effective working partnerships with all stakeholders to reflect on practice, share information and exchange ideas to ensure continued commitment and engagement

- Be adaptable with leadership behaviour according to context.

Chapter 15

The role of school business leaders

Elizabeth Wood

Aims

This chapter draws on a longitudinal study of the introduction of a new group of staff into schools (originally bursars and now generally called school business managers or leaders), as a result of significant and ongoing change in government policy since the late 1980s. The chapter aims to discuss:

- how and why the role of the school business leader has evolved
- the skills and qualities required by effective school business leaders
- the implications for practice.

Background

On 2 July 2004, the *Times Educational Supplement* featured a two-page article entitled 'Will every school be independent?' exploring the pledges of the UK Labour and Conservative parties, both of which were proposing an expansion in the number of autonomous state schools, thus bypassing local education authorities (LEAs)/school districts. This move towards increased site-based management was part of a trend that first begun in 1988 with the introduction of local management of schools and continued through a dual system of locally managed and grant-maintained schools begun in 1992, the fair funding initiative providing greater school autonomy begun in 1999, and then a programme of introducing and then increasing the number of academies and free schools (charitable companies funded by central government): an initiative begun in 2000 and extended in 2002, 2006, 2010. Figure 15.1 depicts how, as a result of the introduction of site-based management, support for schools had changed over time, demonstrating how the locus of strategic decision-making and expertise has shifted from top-down (1985, centralized power) to bottom-up (2005, school autonomy). At the same time, where appropriate, schools began to share expertise and chains or federations of schools became increasingly commonplace (see Figure 15.1; 2010, systems leadership and left-hand triangle,

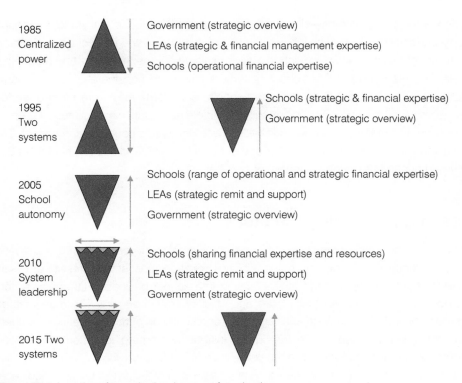

Figure 15.1 Location of organizational support for schools.

2015), although those operating independently, for example, free schools, use their own strategic and financial expertise (e.g. right-hand triangle, 1995 and 2015).

Over the thirty-year period between 1985 and 2015, in order to support schools to raise standards and provide a more comprehensive service, increasing investment has been required. Successive governments promoted a wider choice of school types often achievable through bidding for grants and providing matched funding. A programme of school building modernization was also implemented that included refurbishment, modernization and new build. Funding for these developments could be derived from a range of central government and external funding sources, but private funding initiatives were also being encouraged.

Additionally, in 2003, workforce remodelling was introduced in England by the Department for Education and Skills to reduce teacher workload, raise standards, increase job satisfaction and improve the status of the teaching profession. This initiative was implemented by restructuring the teaching profession and reforming the school work-force and resulted in a re-evaluation of the staffing complement and teaching methods in schools in order to redefine roles and reflect changes in the use of information commu-nication technology (ICT). In particular, the numbers of support staff were increased along with responsibility for their career prospects and training requirements (DfE, 2002).

The expansion of site-based management responsibilities and stakeholder account-ability, currently manifested by the proliferation of academies and free schools, inevitably led to an increase in activity in schools at administration, management and leadership levels. The responsibilities of school governors increased considerably, senior teams (SLTs) were formed, initially to manage schools, but latterly they were termed leader-ship teams (Earley, 2013). The importance of middle managers was also recognized as leadership and management responsibilities were devolved throughout the school. The role of the school business leader was one of many teaching and support staff roles that emerged during this period of significant change.

Research informing the study

The data for this chapter are derived from a longitudinal study, begun in 1996, exploring the emergence of the identity, responsibilities, relationships and professional devel-opment of school bursars and their evolution into school business managers, school business directors, heads of resources and chief operating officers. The multi-method approach provided a complete and balanced representation of multiple realities (Cohen, et al., 2000) and the research design built on insights and emerging patterns developed through prolonged engagement in the field (Lincoln and Guba, 1985).

The tools and instruments used to gather data combined previous well-tried tech-niques that had evolved as a result of understanding derived from previous research in the field. These included: a literature review to build understanding of the emerging data (started in 1998), case studies of school business leaders in their schools, docu-mentary analysis and analysis of projects carried out by school business leaders during academic/professional development programmes (started in 1998), focus groups (star-ted in 1999), three national surveys exploring the schools in which they worked, careers, relationships and roles and responsibilities (conducted in 1999/2000, 2003/2004 and 2006/2007), and observation and analysis of training provision (started in 2003). Through sampling procedures, data have been drawn from a wide range of stakeholders including experts in the field of school leadership and management, government agencies, LEAs, school staff, school business leaders and their representative associations.

External research into school business managers corroborates most of the findings, and where there are anomalies, these can be interpreted in the light of developing models and theory. Hence, as each new national survey built on the one preceding it, there was a clear progression that mapped the evolution of the profession contributing new under-standing of the role, while additional qualitative data added to the themes and issues by enhancing and contributing to phenomenological meaning that school business lead-ership has within the field of education leadership as well as the understanding of the ethnographic context of school business leaders in their workplace. There has, therefore, been a commonality across the data sets over the years of study.

The role of school business leaders

The role began by principally taking on finance management responsibilities to relieve headteachers from a duty that had previously been carried out by local authorities. At this time, most incumbents were called bursars.

> After some years as Head of a voluntary aided school, with distinct financial responsibilities and a helpful and willing local authority to fall back on, and many more as Head of an independent school, I sometimes wonder how local management and grant maintained status are going to work unless a Bursar is appointed to take the financial strain. Financial control not only needs accounting skills which play no part in the Head's training (or certainly have not done so up to date), but also daily attention to cash flow and fund management. Even if the Head has the training or natural acumen to master such tasks, how will he or she ever find time? (Smith, 1993: 21)

As a result, bursars were employed to provide a financial administration service and more comprehensive financial information as well as to support management of the budgetary cycle and negotiate contracts for the benefit of the school.

The role then evolved to include human resource management (HRM), particularly, in response to the increased numbers of support staff in schools. It then expanded into a complex role incorporating wide-ranging responsibilities, including financial management, HRM, marketing, administration management, risk management, management information services, facilities management, support services management and ICT

Table 15.1 Trends in percentage of activity in responsibility areas from 2000 to 2007

Responsibility	2000 (%)	2004 (%)	2007 (%)
Finance	27	24	20
Human resource management	19	16	16
Administration	11	11	12
Facilities	9	9	9
Marketing	8	10	13
Information and communication technology	7	6	5
Risk	6	10	10
Management information systems	6	6	8
Support services	4	6	4
Learning and teaching	3	2	3
Total	100	100	100

management. The three national surveys, carried out between 2000 and 2007 demonstrate the widening of responsibilities and the significant increase in the number and type of business management activities (Table 15.1).

While financial management is still the main activity, the shifts indicated in Table 15.1 demonstrate a refocusing of principal activities from finance and human resources to include marketing, administration management and risk management. The role, in most schools, became very similar to that of a business manager in small-to-medium enterprises with a requirement for a generalist with knowledge of a spectrum of business management responsibility areas and including a wide range of activities requiring their own specialist knowledge (Table 15.2). As a result, schools began to favour a new title for the role: school business manager, although there were arguments over the appropriateness of the term and each element of the title was contested (Woods, Woods and Gunter, 2007). Due to the breadth of the role, school business managers began to specialize in at least one of the responsibility areas listed in Table 15.2, according to the school's needs, but could not become experts in all areas at the same time.

Table 15.2 Activities carried out within responsibility areas

Responsibility	Activities
Finance management activities	Keeping accounts, managing the budget and income and developing financial systems and strategies
Human resource management	Managing contracts, remuneration and supply cover. All aspects of support staff management and development and record-keeping
Administration management	Keeping, analysing and reporting on records and managing legal, public and statutory matters. PA to the headteacher and monitoring educational trends
Marketing	Maintaining and developing positive relationships with stakeholders
Information management	Managing and developing information systems, record keeping and legal compliance. Participation in strategic management. Servicing SLTS and governing bodies
Facilities	Planning and building, grounds and equipment maintenance
Support services management	Managing and developing school transport and catering
ICT management	Managing and developing computerized systems
Risk management	The safe and secure operation of all site aspects and disaster recovery planning
Learning and teaching	Activities are related to learning resources, but include articulating the curriculum philosophy and some specialized teaching

Over time, a flexible approach to school leadership, management and administration was required in order to operate within the changing world of new public management where site-based decision-making operated alongside increasing accountability within a quality, child-focused environment. For school business leaders to contribute positively to school development their mode of operation within the school had to evolve. Focusing on administration did not help support the school's core purpose, nor did building inflexible management systems enable schools to respond to the environment in which they operated. In my research, school business leaders stated that, where possible, they would like to delegate administration or clerical activities to make space for new management and leadership activities, but this development was unlikely to happen if they were unable to meet the requirements of core clerical activities, such as record keeping, that was expected of many of them. The problem was greatest in smaller schools where it was difficult to find alternative solutions to the need to cover reception duties and manage the increase in routine administrative workload that was impacting their effectiveness.

Nevertheless, results of the three national surveys indicated that there was a decrease in administration activity and increase in management between 2000 and 2004 and 2007 (Table 15.3). The most significant decrease in administration level activity occurred between 2000 and 2004 with a significant increase in management and leadership activities consolidated in 2007.

There were three possible causes for this apparent consolidation of levels of operation:

1 School business managers had developed their role to the point where the balance of their level of operation met the requirements of their schools.

2 Increased recruitment to primary schools was weighting the sample, especially as these school business managers were usually employed at a clerical/administrative level, thus impacting levels of operation, that is, the ratio of levels of operation would remain static until the role had become more established in primary schools and the new appointees had completed national training programmes that provided them with the knowledge to work at management and leadership levels.

Table 15.3 School business leaders' levels of operation from 2000 to 2007

Level of Operation	2000 (%)	2004 (%)	2007 (%)
Administration Functional operator, reactive	60	33	31
Management (systems) Systems specialist, active	27	27	29
Management (HR) Interpersonal facilitator, active		19	19
Leadership Leading direction and development, proactive	13	21	21

3 Further changes would remain incremental without further interventions, such as the development of a consultant leader programme and the progression of more school business managers to masters- and doctoral-level qualifications that might generate informed discussion about the development of the role.

It has also been clear, since bursars were first researched, that there are many different approaches to addressing the role successfully (O'Sullivan, Thody and Wood, 2000). This view is supported by research in the United States, into chief operating officers, whose similar role working as the second in command to company chief executive officers 'is structurally, strategically, socially, and politically unique – and extraordinarily situational' (Bennett and Miles, 2006: 72). Hence, an aggregation of responses to the questionnaire may have provided an overall indication of levels of operation, but it did not illustrate how different school business leaders operate in their own schools.

Deeper analysis of the quantitative data indicated that there were nine approaches to school business leadership, but four preferential types emerged, each distinguishable in their style of operation in the school. They were:

- Type 1: Finance, administration officer or bursar (20 per cent). These 35- to 55-year-old females had the least amount of professional experience, the lowest qualifications and the worst employment terms. They focused on administration activities because they had limited or no clerical support. Nevertheless, they had begun to widen their management and leadership activities, principally to budgeting and project management. These business managers were divided into those who worked with the SLT and governing body and those who had no formal contact with either.

- Type 2: Finance, administration officer, manager or bursar (29 per cent) working in smaller primary and secondary schools. In primary schools, they were often the only member of office support staff. At secondary level and in some primary schools, they were responsible for a limited support staff team. They were directly responsible for all administration and clerical activity, as well as working with the headteacher and chair of governors at a strategic level. Although this role incorporated a flip-flop between administration and leadership, they succeeded in widening their management activities by overseeing projects, organizing contracts and widening their risk management expertise. As a result, this type should feature less widely, as time progresses, as they learn to balance their administration, management and leadership activities.

- Type 3: School business managers (16 per cent). This management/leadership approach to the role appeared in medium-to-large secondary schools. Most were female but a significant number were male. They featured the widest age range of between 36 and 55 years and had been in post an average of four years. Although they were quite well paid and were highly qualified and experienced, they were not all paid full-time nor for the full year. These school business leaders actively addressed government reform initiatives that impacted their area of influence and they took part in leadership activities, managed information systems and managed school projects.

- Type 4: Directors and heads of resources (14 per cent). Occurring more often over time, this role focused on leadership activities. These directors or heads of resources were usually found in secondary-phase schools of between 500 and 1000 pupils. They led large support teams that included middle managers, were full members of the SLT and advised, or clerked, for the governing body. With an average of eight years' experience, they earned more than the other types. They were usually highly qualified and had held senior positions in their previous posts.

Resourcing change

School business leaders have become accustomed to assisting with the implementation and resourcing of a wide range of government initiatives that directly impact their schools. These policy changes require expertise in new knowledge areas and the development of a new set of skills that include: networking, information gathering, project management, data management and contract management (Table 15.4).

It is also apparent that, since the turn of the century, the management of resources in an educational context has become increasingly professionalized (Woods, Woods and Gunter, 2007; Woods, Husbands and Brown, 2013; Southworth, 2010) while the recent identification and updating of their body of skills by National Association of School Business Managers (NASBM), the Association of School and College Leaders (ASCL) and the National College for Teaching and Learning (NCTL) supports the development of understanding of the resource management role in schools (National College, 2009; NCTL, 2014), such that in 2016, there is evidence of a growing maturity of both, the profession of school business management and the professionalism of school business leaders themselves.

A school's control over resource use is dependent upon the context within which it exists, the availability of resources to support its activities and the nature of the competition for support. Consequently, educational institutions have to demonstrate, to their stakeholders, that they are able to use resources both efficiently and effectively. As more and more school business leaders complete their national training and can draw on their professionalism to operate at a more strategic level, schools are provided with the capacity to make better use of this valuable resource. Table 15.5 indicates how schools can move from requiring a basic administrative role to developing a professional role where the school business leader provides useful management information, develops a professional support staff resource and ensures the school environment is operating at an optimal level. Such a school business leader is able to demonstrate sensitivity to the educational environment enabling them to adapt their approach to resource management and effectively support the learning environment.

Table 15.4 Impact of policy on school business leaders

Every Child Matters	• Working with wider public services and agencies • Development of systems leadership skills
Building Schools for the Future	• Project management skills required • Contract management skills required
Sustainable schools	• Knowledge of energy efficiency strategies • Understanding of the school's culture
Financial Management Standards in Schools	• Improved financial management systems • Closer working with governors and leadership teams
14–19 agenda	• Increased inter-school communication • Further data management responsibilities
Lighter touch Ofsted inspections	• Improved reporting of data • Closer working with governors and leadership teams
Personalized learning	• Further data management responsibilities
Teacher Training Agency became the Training and Development Agency	• Consideration of the school business management role within the wider workforce of teaching and support staff
Academies (New Labour)	• Reduced resource management responsibilities • Increased requirement for accountancy qualifications • Deeper relationships with sponsors and board members
Specialist schools	• Expertise in writing bids
Healthy schools	• Greater understanding of healthy diets • Sourcing of local providers
Extended school days	• Managing longer working days and an increase of staff in the school
Academies and free Schools (Coalition and Conservative government)	• Increased financial, human resource and facilities management • Expertise in writing bids and procurement
Teaching schools	• Coaching and mentoring support staff and middle leaders • Development of networking skills • Increased financial and human resource management • Further data management responsibilities
Admissions	• Development of good communication skills • Knowledge of relevant legal implications • Further data management responsibilities

Table 15.5 Making use of school business leaders, shifting from administration to management and leadership activities

Role	Administration level	Management and leadership level
Finance management	Keeping financial records	Detailed and specific financial reporting to inform budgeting decisions and contribute to strategic planning
Human resource management	Keeper of staff records and payroll	Leader of the support staff, mentor and advocate for professional development
Administration and information management	Input of school data and secretary to the headteacher	Detailed and specific reporting to contribute to strategic planning and understanding of teaching and learning strategies. Member of leadership team
Marketing	Provide a polite and friendly front of school service	Maintaining and developing positive relationships with stakeholders and ensuring support staff reflect the ethos of the school
Facilities and support services management	Grounds and equipment maintenance. Provide school transport	Planning building development, project management and informed oversight of transport and catering
ICT management	Manage maintenance of school computers	Oversight of and development of computerized systems
Risk management	Ensure compliance with health and safety requirements	The safe and secure operation of all site aspects and management of disaster recovery planning

Given the idiosyncratic nature of the school business leader's role, however, it is unsurprising that inside the school, awareness of the contribution and potential of school business leaders is variable. In many schools, their contribution is recognized and they have satisfying and productive roles; however, there is also unmistakeable frustration among a significant number who have not been deployed in a manner that makes good use of their skills and training, as the following quote illustrates: 'I feel that my skills and considerable experience are underutilized as they could be so useful if I were allowed to use them' (SBM's comments, national survey, 2007). This disappointment may be the result of the headteacher's disinclination to share responsibilities: 'I think that in more primary schools the head is the business manager. We have a finance clerk but in no way does she have the responsibility of a bursar or BM [business manager]. ... Those decisions are with me' (headteacher, 2007 national survey). Alternatively, it may be due to limited understanding of how effectively to deploy school business leaders and the skills fundamental to their role.

> We have a relatively new headteacher who completed the NPQH [National Professional Qualification for Headteachers] and when I asked her if there was any real mention of School Business Managers, Bursars etc. she said that there was not. I asked the same question recently at the start of my DSBM [Diploma in School Business Management] and was once again told that our role was not promoted. This actually quite shocked me as this would seem to be the ideal forum to promote our role in schools and yet it is not used. (Online focus group discussion, 2007)

Summary

In 2016 there is evidence that the constant introduction of government initiatives within the education sector continues to be the norm (Gibton, 2013) and the proliferation of academies and academy chains is having an effect on the role, responsibilities, skills and training requirements of school business leaders. At the centre is the headteacher struggling to focus on learning and teaching while addressing site-based management responsibilities and adapting to systems leadership and entrepreneurial approaches (PWC, 2007). School business leaders have been identified as a means of providing operational support for headteachers and their leadership teams and it is clear that they have been evolving to respond to initiatives designed to refocus teachers' activities away from administration and onto learning. After almost thirty years of development of the role, however, awareness of their role and contribution is still variable. They may no longer be a 'secret group', but their potential is yet to be fully recognized and, as Woods, Husbands and Brown (2013: 762) suggest, 'competing understandings of what "business management" means, and what "business managers" do, could limit the broader educational benefits that they could provide'.

The role of school business leaders has become increasingly complex. It has evolved in a paradoxical turbulent environment in which schools are addressing innovative policy requirements and struggling to reconcile the learning needs of the individual child with bureaucratic requirements to measure and report on many of the school's activities. Consequently, business leaders have accepted a widening remit and increased their core responsibilities to share the increased workload of the headteacher. Resource management is no longer a responsibility characterized by maintenance of systems, processes and facilities. Increasingly, there is a requirement for effective school business leaders who adopt a developmental approach linked to an understanding of policy changes and their impact on the learning environment.

Implications

Does your school have the capacity to:

- Derive projects from strategy reviews and align resources to those with highest priorities?
- Identify and eliminate activities that add little or no value (except for strategic reasons)?
- Match capacity to demand: use rolling forecasts to take early action?
- Respond effectively, using meaningful data, when new choices are presented?
- Keep the time between planning and execution short?
- Communicate effectively and productively with other educational establishments?

Part 3

New challenges, opportunities and perspectives on leadership

Chapter 16

Leadership for wellbeing

Domini Bingham and Sara Bubb

Aims

This chapter considers wellbeing among school workforces and the key role leadership can play. It explores challenges faced by school leaders, analysing workload, wellbeing, stress; the role of leadership in leading healthy organizations, resilience and motivation and the link between wellbeing and learning. It recognizes having a human resource strategy is essential for schools, playing a critical role in organizational viability and relative performance (Boxall and Purcell, 2011). More specifically, it:

- emphasizes the links between workload and wellbeing
- indicates the negative effects of work overload and poor wellbeing
- shows how workload, wellbeing and resilience for the school workforce can be improved
- emphasizes the role of, and styles of, leadership in healthy or non-toxic organizations.

Operating in a high-stakes accountability landscape, increasingly seen across many educational systems worldwide, leaders are asking how to act with integrity. There are schools that do this effectively with positive impact and where lessons can be learnt (see Vignette).

Issues of workload and wellbeing

Not only is work–life balance desirable, but it is increasingly clear that working long hours can damage health. In a meta-review analysis of twenty-five studies in Europe, the United States and Australia involving over half a million participants, those spending 55+ hours working per week were at greater risk of strokes than those working a standard week of 35–40 hours (Kivimaki, 2015).

While a feature of healthy dynamic organizations is a degree of staff turnover, too much is detrimental to staff performance and results in increased financial cost in recruitment and use of interim and supply staff (Conley and You, 2009). The pressures from increased emphasis on school and staff performance and accountability across many educational systems are seen in increasing levels of individual stress and stress-related illnesses. School leaders are required to not only meet performance expectations but also attract, retain and motivate staff when increasing numbers are leaving the profession (Education Support Network, 2015a). Senior leaders, feeling the pressure to deliver the best possible outcomes, can cause additional pressures on teachers (see Chapter 17 on toxic leadership).

Managing staff turnover is a key leadership responsibility and a hallmark of a well-managed, sustainable organization. Education systems are facing a daunting challenge in both recruiting high-quality graduates as teachers, particularly in shortage areas, and retaining them once they are hired (Schleicher, 2012).

A large-scale study of 3,500 Dutch workers comparing burnout rates between those in social professions (such as education and social work) found emotional exhaustion was strongly linked to both low time control and work overload. It concluded that teachers face a higher risk of burnout, compared with other social professions (De Heus and Diekstra, 1999).

Smithers and Robinson (2003) cite a number of reasons for teachers leaving the profession, including heavy workload, stress, poor behaviour, feeling undervalued and a desire for change or new challenges. The quality of leadership and management was also a factor. From research conducted in 2014 in the UK with a sample of teachers across all levels of experience, one-third (34 per cent) stated they planned to leave the profession in one to five years' time (Education Support Network, 2015b). Factors included excessive workloads (40 per cent), unreasonable demands from line managers (24 per cent), rapid pace of organizational change (18 per cent) and student behaviour (13 per cent). A Finnish survey of 2,310 secondary teachers indicates exhaustion and bullying are significant in teacher turnover (Pyhältö, Pietarinen and Soini, 2015).

England's school leaders have had to implement many policy changes in the last decade or so, the result of which has been increased pressure and workload. In October 2014, the Department for Education launched a workload challenge survey (DfE, 2015a) to which more than 44,000 teachers shared experiences, ideas and solutions on their 'unnecessary and unproductive' workload. Following this, a series of commitments were published (DfE, 2015b), including the setting up of three review groups exploring improving work–life balance and wellbeing around issues of marking, planning and resources and data management.

Wellbeing

Wellbeing is a subjective term but an occupational definition relevant to the entire school workforce states 'Well-being expresses a positive emotional state, which is the result of harmony between the sum of specific environmental factors on the one hand and the personal needs and expectations of teachers on the other hand' (Aelterman et al., 2007, cited in Day and Gu, 2014: 31).

Wellbeing for some is about quality of life; for others it is a symptom of work–life balance, for others a measure of stress is desirable to be high performing (Bingham 2013a). Wellbeing is important in its own right in obviating negative functioning of individuals, shown in such indicators as levels of stress. It is diminished through bullying and harassment, and it is important for organizational performance, in what can be termed 'high reliability organisations' (Lekka, 2011).

Wellbeing is both personal and societal. The first relates to a satisfying life and positive functioning, with positive feelings, while the second relates to supportive relationships, trust and belonging (Day and Gu, 2014). Subjective wellbeing that promotes a reported satisfying life and psychological wellbeing influences longevity, extending it between four to ten years (DoH, 2014).

Stress

Reliable and objective definitions of stress are elusive as stress affects individuals in different ways (Bingham, 2013b). It includes mental health and is created through external and internal factors. A distinction can be made between good stress (eustress) and bad stress (distress). The latter being 'the adverse reaction people have to excessive pressures or other types of demands placed on them' (HSE, 2008: 1). As stress is felt individually, what is stressful to one person may reflect in a positive reaction from another, making it difficult for leaders to implement one-size-fits-all school wellbeing policies.

Wellbeing, or lack of it, is strongly related to work (dis)stress – a key characteristic in employee absence. However, although connected, stress and wellbeing are different. As humans, we search for patterns to predict the future, posing a challenge in educational environments subject to political intervention and constant change. Individually, stress will present itself through emotional and mental symptoms and changes in normal behaviour (HSE, 2014a). Other stress arises from internal factors including emotional demands made on teachers and other school staff throughout the working day.

In schools, stress may arise from external factors, such as changing demands and numerous government initiatives. However, by far the most important internal factor is having control over the working environment. While having personal control over your life is critical for positive mental health, having a degree of control over decision-making, and being able to control the environment is also positively associated with psychological wellbeing and eustress. De Heus and Diekstra (1999) reveal teachers have less time control, lower participation in decision-making and less collegial support than in other social professions. Teaching can be a lonely experience. Signs of a (dis)stress problem can be seen in an organization experiencing higher levels of sickness, absence, disputes and disaffection, complaints and grievances, reports of stress, poor performance and difficulties in attracting new staff (HSE, 2014).

Leading for healthy schools

We turn now to what leaders can do to reduce feelings of stress and promote a sense of wellbeing. Leaders play an undoubted role in avoiding schools and cultures becoming toxic. School principals exert an indirect but measurable influence on pupil outcomes through their key role in shaping teachers' working lives (OECD, 2013). Leaders play a significant role in defining and sustaining a school's culture, and teachers' perceptions of their working conditions are important factors in retention, motivation levels and well-being. A good leader will align the values of the organization so they can be visible and seen to run through the school as a thread (see also Chapter 8 on vision and values).

School leaders and governors play a role in overseeing wellbeing and workload issues. Leaders should provide governors with management information required by the governing body to monitor different aspects of life in the school throughout the year. This typically includes staff absence, recruitment, retention, morale and performance. In some countries, legal requirements and responsibilities are in place safeguarding the health and safety of workers, such as the Health and Safety at Work Act (1974) in the UK. Therefore, part of the role of the governors is to keep abreast of legislation. In some countries, national support networks exist to advocate for teachers and support staff. In the UK, unions are both advocates and policy drivers for improved working conditions for the school workforce. The charity, the Education Support Partnership (previously the Teacher Support Network), champions and undertakes research across the education sector. The Health and Safety Executive (HSE), a governmental body, plays a role in regulating workplace safety and conditions and minimizing risks of stress-related illness or injury to employees (HSE, 2014).

Poor workplace conditions can cause stress and exacerbate poor mental health, thus, limiting the benefits of working. For organizations, securing employee wellbeing is an important contributor to quality, performance and productivity, and key to redu-cing sickness absence and high staff turnover. It can act positively or negatively on related concepts such as morale and motivation. Some solutions to work–life balance and wellbeing lie in coping strategies, both individual and organizational. The Foresight report (2008) contains recommendations for employers to help foster work environments conducive to good mental wellbeing and enhancement of 'mental capital'. A strategic approach starts with recognition and commitment on the part of the senior leadership: effective leaders understand the short and long term, think systemically but act practic-ally. They are able to manage change effectively; also, they thrive on change as long as it is seen as leading to improvement (Bubb and Earley, 2004).

At its essence, leaders need to place their actions in the context of promoting greater sustainability, to include the wellbeing of their workforce. Robertson and Cooper (2011) propose a framework to support leading organizational wellbeing and workplace wellness. Divided between organizational outcomes, individual outcomes, psychological wellbeing and six other elements of job conditions (work relationships, job security and change, balanced workload, control and resources and communication), it offers a targeted approach to improving psychological workplace wellbeing.

Too often teachers and schools are caught in an acceleration trap; having to exert the same amount of effort all-year round in perpetual loading and no chance to rejuvenate and recover until the summer vacation. Frequently, there appears to be no strategic focus over what the priorities are other than 'to raise standards'. To combat the problem, some governments are responding to the challenge. As noted earlier, as part of the national teaching workload challenge (DfE, 2015b), the DfE in England is consulting on three main pinch points seen in teaching, in an effort to reduce workload. Part of the response is through changing culture, in understanding innovation and the emotional effect of change. Supportive ways to deal with change include building in time and planning for reflection, alternating high energy and long hours with low energy to produce sustainable high performance.

The key aspect in leading healthy schools is related to culture and how an educational organization is led and managed. The influence of school culture on wellbeing is very important. Culture is derived from norms, values and behaviours that constitute an organization, often referred to 'as the way we do things round here'. Signs of unhealthy schools or toxic organizations include:

- excessive working time and workload
- internal politics
- excessive bureaucracy
- poor communication
- low morale
- resistance to change or excessive change
- a blame culture.

In contrast, healthy organizations manage toxicity and minimize human and financial losses.

Dunham states 'there is often an inverse relationship between management skills and staff stress; good management brings less stress but poor management results in more stress' (1995: 141). The HSE proposes six Management Standards which should be embedded into everyday custom and practice:

- Demands: workload, work patterns and the work environment
- Control: how much say the person has in the way they do their work
- Support: encouragement, sponsorship and resources provided by the organization, line management and colleagues

- Relationships: promoting positive working to avoid conflict and dealing with unacceptable behaviour

- Role: whether people understand their role within the organization and whether the organization ensures that they do not have conflicting roles

- Change: how organizational change (large or small) is managed and communicated in the organization.

These represent a set of conditions that, if present, reflect a high level of health, wellbeing and organizational performance and cover the primary sources of workplace stress (http://www.hse.gov.uk/stress/standard).

Skills need to be constantly updated and developed, so what happens in the workplace is critical. Leadership plays a key role in giving control and affording participation in decision-making. Research suggests effective and supportive leadership is the major contributor to reducing education job strain in helping individuals and organizations to cope with the increased responsibilities and external pressures. Initial research findings from the UK's Education Support Partnership and Birkbeck, University of London (2016a), using data collected across the entire UK school workforce between 2007 and 2013, from 27,000 responses (including 10,000 teachers and 667 schools), show a link between job strain and effect on job performance. Although difficult to infer causality, the research suggests professional growth, control and autonomy, meaningful communication and decision-making opportunities and having meaning in the work undertaken are all important in wellbeing, but only when combined with effective leadership support. The findings are similar for headteachers in the support that they require from governing bodies, local authorities or academy chains.

Leadership promoting wellbeing

Leaders of healthy schools pay attention to the type of leadership promoting wellbeing. In a Danish study of 274 elderly care employees in the healthcare sector, transformational or 'inspiring' leadership was found to be associated with both job satisfaction and wellbeing (Nielsen et al., 2009). Phillips and Sen (2011: 188) consider there is a need for a large national study (similar to Cooper and Kelly, 1993) to assess the current situation and in particular identify 'whether particular leadership styles, training and qualifications make a difference to stress and satisfaction' and further suggest a comparison with independent schools. The limited research available suggests supporting school leaders and managers to adopt a transformational style, that is, in establishing shared vision through which leaders provide a meaningful and creative basis from which change is brought about and should be encouraged.

Where learning-centred leadership can help to promote wellbeing is through its emphasis on modelling (see Chapter 9). Modelling is about the power of example but if leaders do not 'walk the talk' in a consistent manner, then there is little possibility of others following. Leaders should act as good role models to model improved behaviours, including managing workload and work–life balance, showing you can achieve high performance with recovery time given. Seeing leadership, especially headship as a rewarding but essentially doable job, will also have positive implications for recruitment (Future Leaders Trust, 2016).

Leaders should adopt a whole school approach to stress reduction through appropriate strategies and to involve wide decision-making and consultation. Physical surroundings impact on stress levels and so leaders should take this into account. In Norway, for instance, all teachers have their own desk in a study room so that they do not have to work at children's tables in classrooms, as many UK primary teachers do. Effort is spent on making the staffroom a pleasant place to be as working conditions are important.

Vignette

School-led improvement in New Zealand

Shocked by the number of colleagues suffering from stress, Ian Vickers, the assistant principal at Sancta Maria College in Auckland, New Zealand, launched a teacher wellbeing programme at his school in 2012. To help focus on wellbeing, he designed a 'Good New Habits Book' which contains a theme for each working week such as 'Drink Water', 'Stop for Lunch', 'No E-mails', 'Go Home Early'. It had a clear impact with a reduction in sickness rates, better exam results and reduced staff turnover. Word spread of this wellbeing programme across New Zealand and the world with many schools using the latest edition of *'The Good New Habits Book'*, and the *'Teacher Wellbeing NZ'* Facebook group and YouTube channel have ideas and videos. The first Wellbeing in Schools conference was held in October 2015 and illustrates the power of school-led system-wide improvement.

Resilience and motivation

The term 'resilience' has come to the fore in planning for workforce wellbeing and stress. Definitions of resilience are contested. One definition is the 'the level of inner grit you have to handle situations that require drive, focus and resolution and it is linked to achieving goals, getting things done and achieving personal potential' (Pryce-Jones, 2010: 74). Resilience can be learnt and having high levels is linked to wellbeing (Mowbray, 2013). A resilient attitude is heavily influenced by the environment in which people work, especially the style, approach and behaviours of leaders and managers, which brings in the role of leaders and managers in the resilience of others.

There are links between motivation and job efficacy, and related to this, morale (Bubb and Earley, 2004). Wellbeing is important for the concept of perceived self-efficacy; that is, a person's belief in being able to perform a task successfully. Self-efficacy beliefs 'determine how people feel, think, motivate themselves and behave' (Bandura, 1994: 71).

Leaders can boost self-efficacy through professional development and coaching, goal setting, reward for improvement and supportive leadership (Lunenburg, 2011).

There is a strong association between wellbeing and motivation at work. It is claimed those who are most happy at work are in the region of 50 per cent more motivated and 47 per cent more productive than their colleagues. Data collected between 1984 and 2010 on happiness over the long term, from seventy-nine countries, indicates happiness is linked to productivity. Through statistical modelling, asking people what percentage of time was focused on their work tasks and linking answers to ratings of happiness, provided a happiness-productivity link which when tested showed that in the workplace, the happier you are the more productive you tend to be (Pryce-Jones, 2010).

'Flow' too is linked to motivation. Key attributes of flow are in clear goals, continuous and unambiguous feedback about progress and opportunities to use fully personal capacity. Thus 'being in the flow' results in intense concentration and focus, a sense of time passing swiftly, and seeing that activity as rewarding in and of itself, and is experienced in a loss of self-consciousness (Csikszentmihalyi, 2003), supporting productivity and a sense of wellbeing in the workplace. However, as motivation is individual, and in the long term, intrinsic, motivating whole schools – or at least preventing demotivation – is a challenge. One way to do this is in the provision of opportunities for development and career progression, emphasizing the role of learning organizations.

Employers increasingly recognize the need to provide employees with good work–life balance and opportunities to combine work with family responsibilities and other activities. Some countries allow part-time and flexible teaching, job shares, extended unpaid leave or sabbaticals, or job exchanges for increasing skills and experience. Such costs need to be set against lower staff turnover, improved motivation and morale and the introduction of new knowledge into schools. A work-time audit can be a valuable tool in checking efficiency and effectiveness, with a follow-up action plan to help change practice and enhance resilience, motivation and wellbeing (Bubb and Earley, 2004).

Being a learning organization

It is known that teacher effectiveness is the single most important within-school factor in determining student outcomes (see Chapter 9). A widespread review of the literature on the health and wellbeing of teachers and student outcomes suggests a linkage between teachers' health and wellbeing and exam results, but so far there is little direct evidence suggesting a causal relationship (Bajorek and Gulliford, 2014). Briner and Dewberry (2007) present significant positive associations for how teachers feel about their work (expressed through satisfaction, stress and attitudes towards their jobs) and pupil performance, but are unable to prove a causal link. There is a need for large-scale studies to be conducted. This relationship is important as one of the key drivers of educational achievement and staff satisfaction and overall wellbeing is an input to school functioning (Dinham, 2008).

Although the link between wellbeing and professional learning and development is hard to establish directly, having good mental and physical health is a prerequisite to learning and acts as a barrier if absent. Professional learning is key to improving student outcomes and it improves the quality of teachers (Barber and Mourshed, 2007). Workplace stress can be mitigated by developing a supportive learning culture where learning creates positively valued outcomes (Huysman, 1999). So making time for learning will enhance wellbeing for staff. Leaders have a role to play where effective learning-centred leadership can contribute significantly to student outcomes through establishing goals and expectations; strategic resourcing; planning; teacher and curriculum evaluation; promoting professional development and offering a supportive and well-managed environment (Timperley and Robertson, 2011).

Summary

Having a work–life balance for staff is critical in maintaining motivation, developing resilience and in managing workload. Well-run healthy schools pay attention to, and strategically plan for, wellbeing. Through their culture and styles of leadership, they avoid the worst excesses of toxic organizations, recognizing the key to sustainability is in a thriving school workplace for all staff. Indeed, some schools have appointed staff and student wellbeing coordinators. We need a greater appreciation of the impact of how people feel, such as their confidence levels and their self-belief, in order to have an impact on pupil progress and outcomes.

Toxic leadership

Ian Craig

Aims

This chapter aims to address four inter-related questions:

- What is meant by toxic leadership?
- How and why is toxic leadership arising more often in schools?
- What are its consequences?
- How can it be avoided, enabling school leaders to concentrate on desirable leadership styles that are more likely to promote organizational health?

There have always been examples of toxic or destructive leaders in schools. However, this chapter argues that many of the examples we are now seeing in schools are a result of recent governments' attempts to 'modernize' school systems, particularly in England, which is providing a slide towards leadership styles that are not conducive to good professional working, and thus impact on morale. Before addressing the key issues, it is important to set a context by exploring how and why implications of New Public Management (NPM) are being experienced in schools, and to discuss what is meant by the concept of 'toxic leadership'.

Neoliberalism and NPM

The past twenty-five years or so has seen a major movement, particularly within the United States and United Kingdom, to restructure public services. This movement, sometimes referred to as neoliberalism, and at other times as NPM, promotes minimal state involvement in the delivery of public services and an extension of market rules and principles to public sector organizations and institutions, in theory to make them subject to the efficiencies, entrepreneurialism and other benefits that it is claimed operate in the private sector.

As far as education is concerned NPM has probably been developed further in England than anywhere else in the world.

We have seen this within the education system, first with the outsourcing of support services, and now effectively the wholesale outsourcing of the running of schools themselves, to non-democratic (sometimes commercially based) organizations and charities working within a competitive 'quasi-market' (see Chapters 2, 3 and 5). Central to this movement, as Whitty (2002: 80) tells us, is 'the belief that competition produces improvements in the quality of services which in turn enhances the wealth producing potential of the economy, thereby bringing about gains for the least well-off as well as for the socially advantaged'.

This policy model, which is described by some (not totally correctly) as 'Americanisation', is now being pursued to a greater or lesser extent across most developed and developing countries, especially in those developing countries heavily reliant on the West. As Ball (2008: 32) tells us, international NGOs, and 'the World Bank and the International Monetary Fund in particular are firmly committed to the Americanisation of the world economy – a vigorous privatisation of education as a response to declining public budgets, especially in Africa'.

It is clear, as Bell and Stevenson (2006: 161) remind us, that 'governments increasingly view education as an important adjunct to economic development and national competitiveness. The result has been to elevate economic values into the prominent position when policy is developed'. There has been a major shift since the 1980s in the management of all public services, including education, away from a focus on the professional discipline to a focus on business, economic effectiveness and value for money. This chapter is less focused on the educational rights and wrongs of NPM in education than its effects. It suggests that the changes are putting ever-greater pressures on school leaders to act in particular ways, which they believe will ensure that their schools conform to what is being required of them by governments and their agencies.

What is toxic leadership?

Toxic leadership is where those having responsibility and control, over a group of people or an organization, abuse the leader–follower relationship in some way and move the group or organization into a worse condition than it was before – long-term organizational health being sacrificed for short-term gains. Walton (2007: 20) defines it as 'behaviour which is exploitative, abusive, destructive and psychologically corrupt and poisonous'. It is directive and coercive leadership that fails to recognize – or develop – individual worth, experience and the professionalism of staff.

There is a subtle difference between 'toxic' and 'destructive' leadership and cultures, even though they are closely related. A destructive culture (as described by Krasikova, Green and LeBreton, 2013) totally destroys the organization – it is easily recognizable as it damages the organization quickly, as it is impossible to work within it. A toxic culture has a slower influence, and it can be appealing to some members who will willingly adapt their own patterns of behaviour to accept it. It may not totally destroy an organization immediately; indeed, there may be some perceived improvements to the organization in the short term, but in the longer term the poison within the system begins to have its influence. A 'toxic' culture is sometimes difficult to detect from outside the organization, and for that reason often more difficult to deal with. Toxic leadership is a poison which works slowly to destroy the organization, by damaging relationships, processes and ethos over time.

The term 'toxic leadership' was first widely used to describe a particular, serious and specific issue in the US military, and is now widely studied in military staff colleges across the world. Williams (2005: 1), herself a senior US Army officer, quotes Lipman-Blumen (2005) to help explain why it is so important to deal with it: 'Toxic leaders have poisonous effects that cause serious harm to their organizations and their followers.' She goes on to say (ibid.: 18) that 'to count as toxic, these behaviors and qualities of character must inflict some reasonably serious and enduring harm on their followers and their organisations'.

Wilson-Starks (2003: 2) considers that 'it is a leadership approach that harms people – and, eventually the company as well – through the poisoning of enthusiasm, creativity, autonomy and innovative expression'. She believes that some toxic leaders have had poor role models. Having been mentored by toxic leaders, they operate under a faulty definition of leadership and are often vocal advocates of 'strong leadership'. She notes:

> In addition to diminished commitment on the part of employees, toxic leadership can produce systematic damage throughout an organisation. Under toxic leaders, employees have basically two options: conform or leave. … Others, however, may come to see toxic leadership as normal, and conform willingly. These will be groomed to be the next generation of toxic leaders. (ibid.: 4)

Toxic leadership is related to the culture of the organization and not intended to be damaging by leaders who inflict it. They may well think that the style that they are using is necessary for the delivery of targets passed down to them and the more anxious they become about the achievements of targets, the more they will adopt this style. Walton (2007: 19) observes that 'we may do well to consider workplace dysfunction and toxicity as normal – rather than abnormal – phenomena of modern organisational life'.

The effects of neoliberalism and NPM on leadership

Many writers have pointed out the impact of neoliberalism and NPM for schools, some citing what they consider to be positive effects, and others negative ones. Few would disagree that for many years the professional autonomy of teachers has been undermined and slowly eroded. Olssen, Codd and O'Neill (2004: 185) talk about 'the wearing-away of professional-ethical regimes in schools to be replaced by entrepreneurial-competitive regimes – a process of de-professionalisation'. Most people who become teachers do so because they wish to change the lives of children and young people. They see teaching as a profession where they can use their knowledge and skills to their fullest extent. They want to work within a supportive professional environment where they can see that they are making a difference.

Finland boasts of having some of the most educated and respected teachers in the world. When Sahlberg (2011: 75) asked Finnish teachers what would prompt them to leave teaching, many pointed out that if they were to lose their professional autonomy, their career would be called into question. This would suggest that in countries where the education system is heavily influenced by NPM, the consequent de-professionalization of teaching may lead many of the brightest young people to turn away from teaching as a long-term career – either before they begin it, or once they have truly found out what it means in practice in schools.

Over the past twenty-five years or so the government in England has promoted almost a 'cult of leadership' in schools – the leader being seen as the key driver of school quality. Headteachers are now almost a separate 'tribe' within the education service, lauded by politicians at the expense of classroom teachers who clearly do have a direct impact and make a significant difference to pupils' lives. By definition, if we have 'leaders' we have to have 'followers' – the rest of the school staff. However, the emphasis of this differentiation is breaking down the professional standing of classroom teachers, turning them away from teaching. Gunter (2005: 175) asks us whether true 'professionals' can *just* be followers – or to turn her question around, can 'followers' ever be true professionals, and if not, what implications does this have for the professionalism of teachers? The reforms of recent years have now led to a stratified workforce in schools with three distinct tiers: at the top school leaders, followed by teachers, and, at the base, support staff.

Under NPM reforms, governments clearly steer or direct at a distance what takes place in schools, and the delivery of government targets and policies is now seen by many as the prime function of school leaders, not the exercise of their professional judgement in relation to individual pupil needs. It is arguably now more difficult for heads to work primus inter pares within a team of professionals within schools. They are expected to be 'managers' leading within clear government frameworks, not the professional leaders of education that most would wish to be. Stoten (2015: 3) tells us that 'the imposition of NPM over the public sector during the past two decades … has led to changing work relationships between managers and teachers', and Bottery (2000: 21) says that under this new structural regime 'a school principal becomes a strategist for implementing external directives – a professional manager rather than a senior teacher'. Wright (2001) refers to this as 'bastard leadership'. The part that principals play or do not play in implementing their own or their school's vision rather than that of the government has led to an interesting and ongoing debate (see, e.g. Rayner, 2014; Hammersley-Fletcher, 2015).

Although some pressure can be a good thing, the current excessive pressure that is focused on both teachers, and, especially, headteachers, is particularly damaging. The removal in England by Ofsted in 2012 of the 'satisfactory' inspection judgement to replace it with 'requires improvement' has put further pressure of heads to achieve at least 'good' or 'outstanding' in inspections, as nothing else is acceptable. In theory, a laudable aim, but the pressure this places on school leaders, who are in danger of losing their livelihoods if their schools do not perform well, is immense. Many headteachers, particularly those in more difficult schools, are now working in an environment of fear. It may be that we now expect too much from our leaders, and that we have loaded onto them unrealistic expectations. Ball (2008: 45) warns us that 'schools are being inducted into a culture of self-interest, manifested as survivalism – a concentration on the well-being of the institution and its members rather than a concern with the more general social and educational issues within the community'. Headship has always been a lonely task, but now in many schools the fragmentation of headship from the teaching force may have led to a further isolation of headteachers from their erstwhile colleagues.

The consequences of these pressures and the vulnerability of the school leader within the current culture therefore encourage a leadership style that is directive and authoritarian. This is the opposite of what most education professionals and researchers would agree is productive – an open, inclusive, participative, collaborative, distributed leadership style which is proved to be more effective (see Chapter 7). Furthermore, the fragmentation of the school system into thousands of parts is taking away any controls that were previously in place. Fragmentation of control leads to it being easier for authoritarian leadership and leaders to flourish.

In terms of the long-term consequences of this style, Williams (2005: 15) reminds us that potential leaders are

> taught at an early age to find leaders to emulate. (They) are advised to observe and emulate older, senior, successful (leaders) to determine what they have done to be successful... . Since there are toxic leaders, it is inevitable that toxic leadership will be replicated. It will be seen by some to be a pathway to success.

Ball (2008: 47) suggests that 'the manager/leader is the cultural hero of the new public services paradigm', and it is clear that in order to have status in the teaching profession, particularly in England, you must now strive to be a headteacher, and if you want to 'get on' in schools it is inevitable that many will copy a toxic model of leadership.

The consequences of toxic leadership in schools

The current ongoing fragmentation of control of schools makes it easier for authoritarian leadership and leaders to flourish. All those who work within education believe that it is their duty to deliver the best-quality teaching and learning for students. However, current demands being made by many governments on schools, and the way in which they are 'policed' (by Ofsted and others) are creating a toxic atmosphere within which leaders have to conform or risk being removed from their posts. Governors (and local authorities and management boards) also interpret and pass on these pressures to school leaders, and they in turn transmit their pressures on to staff, placing unrealistic demands on them.

My view, like Walton's mentioned earlier, is that in the current free enterprise, quasi-market and targets culture in education toxic management of schools is widespread and inevitable. Walton also comments (2007: 19) that 'a relentless drive to achieve more and more can be expected to result in increasingly difficult and toxic working environments'.

The current 'toxic' culture within education generally, where headteachers are publicly vilified and 'punished' when targets are not met (a little like the medieval village stocks!) does one of a number of things to them. There are many 'heroic' heads who revel in this pressure and can manage to maintain both their own and their staff's morale while still achieving external targets. These school leaders should be, and are, celebrated – yet not at the expense of other equally hard-working but less 'heroic' colleagues.

A second group of heads find that the pressure on them, the stress, the lack of time for 'people skills' (often the reason they came into teaching), the loss of morale and the lack of job satisfaction, often leads them to illness, long periods of time away from school, and eventually to retirement, or a complete change of job – usually outside of schools (see also Chapter 16).

A third group sit somewhere between the first two – these heads are determined to achieve government targets and be 'effective' school leaders, but for many reasons they find this hard to achieve, sometimes because they do not have the appropriate skills, at other times not the appropriate staff – and at other times are not working in easy environments. It is this group who often make undue demands, and put undue pressure on their staffs, leading to a toxic leadership culture in their schools.

We all know that some pressure, both on leaders and on their staffs, is not always a bad thing – quite the opposite, but it needs to be delivered with consideration. What we must not lose sight of is the close relationship between heroic management and toxic management: 'My toxic leader may be your heroic saviour' (Lipman-Blumen, 2005).

Teachers also suffer from similar pressures relating to job satisfaction, professionalism, stress and morale. In a 'toxic' or unhealthy school this leads to a high absence rate for staff through illness, a high level of staff loss, and the inability to recruit (see Chapter 16). The 'grapevine' among teachers should never be underestimated – teachers will not apply for schools with a 'toxic' reputation. If such schools are lucky, they will recruit significant numbers of new teachers from outside the area, who may not be aware of the school's reputation – but this is unlikely to be a good or sustainable way forward in the long term.

Although knowledge of the schools where heads have resigned early may well be providing the reasons why fewer and fewer candidates are putting themselves forward for headship, a bigger worry is that 'toxic' schools, where pressures on teachers are unreasonable and not well handled, may well provide the poor view of teaching that is dissuading new entrants into the teaching profession, particularly at a time when teacher training is making more and more use of in-school placements and where prospective teachers can 'experience' what it is like to be in such environments day by day.

The 'toxic' style of hard, autocratic leadership may drive up some focused and limited standards, but this may be to the long-term detriment and damage of other parts of pupils' learning more generally. As Walton (2007: 20) says: 'Toxic leaders will "make it happen" and "get things done," but how they go about this can be profoundly damaging to those around them and, potentially, to the business itself.'

Toxic leadership is therefore corrosive to organizational health and this has knock-on effects to performance. It should be discouraged wherever it is encountered. This means challenging many of the views of what might be the best ways for encouraging enhanced performance of a school. Stoten (2015: 3) quotes Padilla, Hogan and Kaiser (2007) who say that it is 'the interaction between abusive leaders, vulnerable followers and their environment that leads to dysfunctional organisational culture and corporate underperformance'. Although toxic leadership and management may improve test scores, and drive short-term measurable gains for pupils, these are not sustained, and will almost certainly be extremely damaging in the longer term. It may be the case that in many schools teachers are being deterred from remaining in the profession, and only those who are prepared to act in a certain way, complying with a preferred style, are putting themselves forward for headship.

How can toxic leadership be dealt with?

Walton (2007: 25) suggests that

> with such forces threatening an organisation's success it remains surprising that a fuller exposition and exploration of the darker side of leadership, and the misuse of institutional power, is not at the top of the curricula for organisational and professional studies... .
> It may well be that most, if not all working environments are toxic to some degree. If so, the key question is how we prepare and constructively engage with such a reality. If indeed leadership toxicity is an inevitable affliction of organisational life, the sooner it occupies a place of prominence in the preparation and training for leadership, the better.

The current pressures being placed on school leaders, teachers and other staff are not likely to go away in the foreseeable future, so what can be done to challenge toxic cultures? First, we need to recognize that it does exist and it is then essential that it is recognized in the training of our current and future school leaders. Bubb and Earley (2005: 1) have said that 'much has been written about the "bright" side of leadership, about best practice and effective leadership for example, but in the meantime, the "dark" side has been largely ignored'. Understandably, training is currently focused on positive leadership practices, and dysfunctional leadership and its consequences are often not considered.

Leadership trainers must also recognize that all headteachers are working within a potentially toxic environment. Trainers need to highlight the dangers of accepting, supporting and replicating such leadership within their schools. Mehta and Maheshwari (2014: 23), like Watson (2007), conclude their own discussion of toxic leadership by saying that 'if leadership toxicity is an inevitable disease of organisational life, the sooner it is recognised in the development of leaders, the better it is'.

Uhl-Bien and Carsten (2010: 367) suggest that toxicity is inherently linked to the traditional top-down transactional model of leadership – an issue inherent in the delivery of the NPM outcomes-based model. If this is the case, it is essential that we challenge this style of management, and promote the involvement of more staff in leadership and decision-making processes which has many benefits.

Bubb and Earley (2004: 38) and others maintain that 'the development of a collegiate culture, or a culture of collaboration, consultation and shared decision-making is the most important factor for successful change'. Section 2 of this book contains various chapters that explore aspects of this model of leadership, with the articulation of a clear, shared set of values and beliefs about children's learning and the development of a high-trust but robust professional learning culture perhaps being the key elements. Perhaps this should be prefaced with 'in the long-term', as other methods are often seen to have more immediate observable outcomes in the shorter term, and are often more attractive to headteachers under pressure to be seen to be making a difference and removing their schools from an Ofsted category.

Is distributed leadership the answer? There is now a considerable literature suggesting that a distributed leadership model is helpful in achieving results in schools, but several writers urge caution. Lumby (2015: 587) suggests that 'the mirage-like form of leadership within the distributive leadership narrative is evident', and Hartley (2010: 279) suggests that 'distributed leadership is little more than emancipatory rhetoric'. If it is to be employed, it needs to be more than the tokenism often reported by teachers in their schools.

Summary and conclusions

With the advent of NPM, neoliberalism and the demise of local authorities in England and many other countries to 'mediate' between schools and central governments and their agencies, we are seeing more directive and punitive management, pressure to conform to targets and penalties for not doing so. These pressures are encouraging school leaders to become more directive, leading to a reduction in the professional autonomy of teachers who have over recent years become more and more qualified, and wishing to make their own judgements in exercising their professional expertise. The move towards academies and multi-academy trusts may well exacerbate this trend.

Some headteachers, feeling vulnerable in such situations, pass on their anxieties to their staff in the form of more directive and coercive leadership, which presents itself as a role model for ambitious teachers who wish to become school leaders. The added problem is that such headteachers who run 'tight ships' are often regarded as 'heroic' leaders themselves, and lauded for their directiveness. This may be short-sighted.

Such leadership is likely to be 'toxic', for although it may deliver short, or even medium, term gains in certain measurable outcomes, there is clear evidence that there are often considerable and greater penalties for the organization in the longer term. This in turn is resulting in a crisis of recruitment and retention for all staff, particularly in schools in more demanding areas. This is a particular issue for recruitment to headship.

For high-performing schools, 'leadership' is now considered by many to be more, or at least equally, important to the quality of the teacher in the classroom. Government promoted preparation and continuing professional development programmes on leadership are plentiful. This chapter suggests that the issue of 'toxic leadership' should be highlighted in such programmes, counselled against, and attention drawn to its consequences.

Finally, it is important to make the point that in drawing attention to the 'dark side' of leadership we can sometimes forget the 'bright side'. Toxic leadership is still only an issue in a minority of schools, albeit possibly a growing number. Even with all the pressures they have on them, the majority of education leaders continue to retain a broad education vision, and deliver this within collaborative school cultures. Long may it be so.

Implications

- Within a changing education environment, how can the morale of both teachers and school leaders be improved to ensure that we maintain, and hopefully enhance, an effective profession?
- How can we eradicate toxic leadership practices in schools?
- How can we educate and ensure that future leaders understand the dangers in toxic leadership?

Chapter 18

Leadership, technology and learning

Mark Quinn

Aims

The aims of this chapter are to provide:

- an overview of the landscape: use of technology in schools
- a summary of the debate: the impact of technology use in schools
- where we are heading: the possible future direction of technology use in schools
- the implications: the choices school leaders are confronted with.

Whether as enthusiastic natives or reluctant luddites, we all inhabit a digital world. A teacher will be woken by her phone. Over breakfast, a smartphone app will remind her that she is to collect homework today, to be uploaded to cloud storage. She has exchanged lesson ideas with colleagues online and jazzed up lesson 4 with video clips downloaded from the internet. Every afternoon she places her lessons on the school's learning management system, so her students can access them from home. Before she leaves for school, she updates her students' progress on the data tracking system; it informs her that her summer-born students are falling behind. At home that evening she joins a discussion on that topic on social media and finds a link to an academic paper. Before she goes to sleep, she thinks to email the link to her online research community. One hopes she has remembered to switch all her devices to flight mode.

She knows her students will not have done. The media look under the bed covers and find teenagers messaging other teenagers, sharing files and photos, trading insults and not sleeping. Before breakfast, (if he eats breakfast) he will already have played a computer game with his online friends and earned credits for the next level. The homework app on his phone pings. That is fine because the thirty-minute bus ride is long enough for him to find, cut and paste a nearly relevant article and submit it to his class's secure storage area. He will sit at the back of his classroom, shielding his eyes from the sun, unable to make out the content on the interactive whiteboard. He prefers his art teacher, who lets him listen to the music he has streamed to his personal device.

An overview of the landscape: Use of technology in schools

The above picture will not be recognized by everyone. Technology, and how teachers and students interact with it, is subject to much variability. It is a matter of space and time. There are countries, then there are jurisdictions within countries, then schools within those, and classrooms within schools, all using technology to varying extents and evolving all the while. The north London school where I work will not stand for all, but it may illustrate some of the range of choices teachers, and school leaders, have to make. These choices can be broadly categorized as follows:

1 Teaching and learning

2 Management of teaching and learning

3 Management of resources

4 Communications

5 Connecting to the wider education system

1. Teaching and learning   Every classroom is equipped with an interactive whiteboard, loaded with software, which is upgraded every three to four years. It is operated via the computer on each teacher's desk, which is internet-enabled. There are six computer suites across the school. The broadband network is supported by the London Grid for Learning (LGfL), a non-profit charitable consortium linking London local educa-tion authorities and schools. One of its services filters internet searches for unsuitable content. Several departments have purchased off-the-peg licences for interactive learn-ing schemes, some of which can be accessed by students at home, providing repeated practice and instant feedback. The school deploys a number of Learning Management Systems (LMSs). One LMS mimics a social network, secured at class level; another shares schemes of learning and other learning resources with the students; a third allows teachers to set homework, which can be accessed by students and parents remotely via an app, and can be monitored by the school leadership team; another is a careers and further education guidance package.

2. Management of teaching and learning   The management information system is a platform for timetabling, holding student and staff information, recording attendance, logging incidents and recording progress data. A separate platform translates student performance data into graphs to facilitate tracking of students individually and by cohort, offering comparisons with performance indicators set by the central government's

Department for Education. Teachers are encouraged to upload resources on the shared storage network. Professional development materials, generated from in-house professional learning programmes, are hosted on a bespoke website linked to the school internet.

3. Management of resources The school's financial information system allows it to manage its budget, tracking income from commercial lettings and expenditure on capital outlay. It is a 'cashless' school: online payments are deducted at the tills in the canteen from staff identity cards and student free travel passes. These same student passes act also as 'library cards' in the learning resources centre; the staff ID affords access around the school site through centrally locking doors.

4. Communications Internal communications are conducted largely via email. This holds also for parental contacts, although same-day messages are often sent by text. The school operates an open-source website, which celebrates achievement, shares school policies and notifies the school community of upcoming events.

5. Connecting to the wider system In England central government policy consultations and statutory guidance are often available only online (www.education.gov.uk). Likewise, the English schools' inspectorate Ofsted publishes its handbook and best practice guidance on its website, alongside a 'data dashboard' of school performance and a platform for parents to post their views of their child's school. Students and teachers have access to the websites of the exam boards, informing them of past exam papers, reports from examiners and course specifications; teachers can train using online webinars. There is a vast array of teaching resources available via the internet, many of which are subject specific. Teachers are also active on social media, engaging in discussions of pedagogy and educational policy. They have taken on Jill Berry's advice, that social networking can help them to 'develop a professional learning network which can prove a valuable source of ideas, resources, strategies and connections' (Berry, 2015: 60). These online engagements have evolved into networks such as TeachMeet (where teachers meet to exchange ideas) and ResearchEd (which seeks to bridge the gap between practitioners and academics). Indeed, teachers wanting to engage in research for themselves are better able to do so, and make use of resources such as the Educational Endowment Foundation's teaching and learning 'toolkit', and, for example, the UCL Institute of Education's Research and Development Network (www.ioe-rdnetwork.com).

Other schools have made different decisions. Often with dedicated external funding, some schools have invested heavily in hardware, software and staff training. In 2010 the UK's Home Access Grant made 270,000 grants to low-income families in England to buy laptops with internet access. In 2014, 'The Year of Code', the UK government supported the training of teachers in coding with £500,000 of match funding, to coincide with its introduction to the national curriculum, apparently the first G20 country to do so. There are online solutions for everything from recording classroom observations to awarding student incentives, from teachers' annual appraisal to staff recruitment. There is plenty available. What is in shorter supply is evidence that any of it makes much difference.

The impact of technology use in schools

Nesta, the innovation charity, reported that UK schools had spent more than £1 billion in the five years up to 2012 on digital technology. 'The education sector has invested heavily in digital technology; but this investment has not yet resulted in the radical improvements to learning experiences or educational attainment' (Luckin et al., 2012: 8). Higgins, Xiao and Katsipataki (2012) conducted their meta-analysis of forty years of research evidence for the impact of technology in the UK and internationally, saying it 'consistently identifies positive benefits' (ibid.: 3). However, studies linking 'the provision and use of technology with attainment tend to find consistent but small positive associations with educational outcomes' (ibid.: 3). And the studies do not find a causal link:

> It seems probable that more effective schools and teachers are more likely to use digital technologies effectively than other schools. We need to know more about where and how it is used to greatest effect, then investigate to see if this information can be used to help improve learning in other contexts. We do not know if it is the use of technology that is making the difference. (ibid.: 3)

Higgins et al. (2012) state that interventions using technology, aimed at improvements in student attainment, are slightly less effective than other non-technology-based approaches, such as peer tutoring and effective feedback. The authors acknowledge the difficulties in understanding and applying the research evidence, given the rapidly changing nature of the technology and the conflicting need to wait to see the evidence emerging. Nevertheless, they conclude that 'it is not whether technology is used (or not) which makes the difference, but how well the technology is used to support teaching and learning' (ibid.: 3).

It is all down to the teaching. This is a more measured response to the claims made by Bennett and colleagues that 'a sense of impending crisis pervades the debate' (Bennett, Maton and Kervin, 2008: 1). They refer to the 'digital natives' and 'digital immigrants' first encountered by Marc Prensky: 'These young people are said to have been immersed in technology all their lives, imbuing them with sophisticated technological skills and learning preferences for which traditional education is unprepared. Grand claims are being made about the nature of this generational change and about the urgent necessity for educational reform in response' (Bennett, Maton and Kervin, 2008: 1). They note that the debate – about how students may learn differently in the twenty-first century – is poorly informed by research or theory, and amounts to a 'moral panic'.

Bennett et al. (2008) could have been writing about the reporting of a study commissioned by the security software firm Kaspersky Lab. Perhaps unsurprisingly for a company engaged in cybersecurity, they maintain that 'digital technologies are not just transforming the way we live and work; they are changing the way we think, learn, behave – and remember' (2015: 4). This was translated by BBC online into 'Digital dependence "eroding human memory"' (Coughlan, 2015). The Kaspersky study – of 6,000 adults in UK, Germany, France, Italy, Spain and the Benelux countries, conducted by Opinion Matters – investigated the growing tendency among adults to search online before attempting to recall information. Adults in the UK were least likely to recall their partner's phone number, with the (presumably more romantic) Italians being most mindful. 'Moral panic' might be an apt term too for Paul Kirschner (2015). The Distinguished Professor from the Open University of the Netherlands notes the shallow information processing of those who read intensively online, how the nonlinearity of hyperlinked text requires 'extra non-productive *cognitive effort*', reducing 'the cognitive resources available to the reader for deep learning and efficient memory consolidation'. He continues:

> In other words, there might really be the case that *the result of this digital immersion is that how these children think and process information makes it difficult for them to excel academically*, but NOT because of outdated teaching methods in schools but rather due to the possible changes in their brain functioning that impede learning. (Kirschner, 2015) (Author's italics)

Kirschner blames the text-type; the OECD thinks it lies in the teaching. Their 2015 report found that countries' PISA rankings for reading, mathematics and science were impervious to heavy spending on technology for education. The digital divide will be better crossed when every child reaches a basic proficiency in reading and maths; access to high-tech equipment is not the issue. More is not better. 'Overall, students who use computers moderately at school tend to have somewhat better learning outcomes than students who use computers rarely. But students who use computers very frequently at school do much worse, even after accounting for social background and student demographics' (OECD, 2015: 3).

OECD education director Andreas Schleicher (2015) and Luckin et al. (2012) both make similar points about the continuing role of the teacher. Schleicher, offering his analysis of the OECD report cited above, says that one interpretation is that

> schools have not yet become good enough at the kind of pedagogies that make the most of technology; that adding 21st Century technologies to 20th Century teaching practices will just dilute the effectiveness of teaching. If students use smartphones to copy and paste prefabricated answers to questions, it is unlikely to help them become smarter. Educators who want to ensure that students become smarter than a smartphone need to think harder about the pedagogies they are using to teach them. (Schleicher, 2015)

Luckin and colleagues (2012) predict that the digital devices will keep flowing into schools and homes, but, after all the money that has been spent, we need to 'make better use of what we've got'. They argue:

> We need to change the mindset amongst teachers and learners: from a 'plug and play' approach where digital tools are used, often in isolation, for a single learning activity; to

one of 'think and link' where those tools are used in conjunction with other resources where appropriate, for a variety of learning activities. Teachers have always been highly creative, creating a wide range of resources for learners. As new technologies become increasingly prevalent, they will increasingly need to be able to digitally 'stick and glue'. (2012: 62)

As Higgins and colleagues remind us: 'It is … the pedagogy of the application of technology in the classroom which is important: the *how* rather than the *what*. This is the crucial lesson emerging from the research' (2012: 3).

Future directions

As Schleicher (2015) says, 'Technology is the only way to dramatically expand access to knowledge.' It seems a safe prediction that access to technology will expand, even if the concomitant improvements in knowledge remain disappointing. Not everyone is pessimistic about the prospects, however. One might expect the chief marketing officer of an LMS to espouse the joys of hypertext. Renny Monaghan claims: 'Teachers and administrators have begun to embrace the idea of creating a personalized learning experience for students. Instead of teaching a subject at one speed to an entire class, technology allows us to reach students individually at a speed and pace that's right for them, and then scale that experience as appropriate' (Monaghan, 2015). She envisages a 'real-time analytics', drawing down student data from 'the full learning ecosystem', allowing adjustments to be made at the level of the individual. This might be termed 'the small curriculum', where teaching can be truly personalized in classrooms or anywhere else the learning management system can penetrate. It consorts with 'big data': the mining of huge sets of data (such as England's National Pupil Database) for nuggets of new knowledge of 'what works' in schools. This calls to mind Higgins and colleagues' six myths:

Myth 1: New technologies are being developed all of the time, the past history of the impact of technology is irrelevant to what we have now or will be available tomorrow.

Myth 2: Today's children are digital natives and the 'net' generation – they learn differently from older people.

Myth 3: Learning has changed now that we have access to knowledge through the internet. Today's children do not need to know stuff, they just need to know where to find it.

Myth 4: Students are motivated by technology so they must learn better when they use it.

Myth 5: The Everest Fallacy: we must use technology because it is there!

Myth 6: The 'More is Better' Fallacy (2012: 20–1).

Their list is perhaps the product of a mind unencumbered by the need to market what they write about.

Alongside Higgins and colleagues' six myths might sit Luckin et al.'s 'two key errors'. These frequently occur when trying to make gains in education from technology. They note

> Collectively, they have put the *technology above teaching* and *excitement above evidence*. This means they have spent more time, effort and money looking to find the digital silver bullet that will transform learning than they have into evolving teaching practice to make the most of technology. If we are to make progress we need to clarify the nature of the goal we want to satisfy through future innovation. (2012: 64 – original emphasis)

Summary

Digital technology is all around us. It is convenient, ever-present and often designed in formats which are engaging to the point of addiction. It pervades our schools, from its security systems to its timetables. It connects every member to the school community, and it connects the school to the wider educational community beyond. It is expensive but it is making a difference, at least a little, or at least where technology is being used in moderation, there are moderate gains. There may be losses too, as young people, trying to cope with the interruptions in digital texts (and the interruptions from their other devices), fail to learn deeply or even to commit things to memory at all. So, teachers still matter. With some concerted professional development in ways to align the technology to genuine learning goals, teachers could make an even greater difference.

The implications: Choices for school leaders

- To become an early adopter of new technologies, or not. If so, education leaders need to invest not only in the technology 'kit', but also in the teachers wielding it. They also need to build sound evidence for its efficacy in terms of academic gains, improvements in 'literacy' as well as 'digital literacy'.

- To embrace 'digital nationhood', or not. The archaeology is inconclusive on the existence of a new species of digital native. There may or may not be such a thing as learning exclusive to the twenty-first century. And, if young brains have adapted, that may not be such a good thing if they intend to really learn anything. On the other hand, the potentialities of the internet and related technologies to expand what we know and what we can do with what we know are undoubtedly so great as to be impossible to ignore.

- To let in the digital giants, or not. It seems the mind is a marketplace. Into the space where learning happens come charitable non-profit makers and deep-pocketed multinationals. They can be persuasive, but they will know less about the needs of the children in a school than their teachers and school leaders. The learning as ever will still need to be designed around the needs of the children (see Chapter 10), rather than the cleverness of the technology.

Chapter 19

School networks, peer accountability and the brokerage of knowledge and expertise

George Berwick and Sue John

Aims

This chapter draws on the experiences of two former London headteachers who also held major system leadership roles. It contains:

- a brief description of the collaborative approach's origins within London Challenge (2003–8) and City Challenge (2008–11)

- a comparison between the collaborative approach and the dominant existing paradigm for school improvement in England in 2000

- one of the current manifestations of their approach, Challenge Partners

- a description of the largest hub within Challenge Partners, London West Alliance

- the lessons from their work that may assist others who wish to follow a similar path of sharing and improving best practice to achieve enhanced student performance.

The origins of the collaborative approach

In 2011 a group of experienced headteachers within the English state system came together to determine how they could work collaboratively to improve their practice. This group, including the authors, had led schools rated outstanding by Ofsted and designated as National Teaching Schools and National Support Schools by the National College for School Leadership (then later the National College for Teaching and Leadership – NCTL). They committed to developing a self-funding, sustainable and national partnership. The organization they formed was called Challenge Partners. The approach they adopted built upon the theory of action they had developed while leading the London Leadership Strategy in the London Challenge (2003–8), City Challenge (2008–11) and the development of Teaching Schools (2003–11).

The impact of London Challenge is continually open to debate (Ofsted, 2011; Hutchings et al., 2012; Rudd, Poet and Featherstone, 2011). However, what cannot be denied is that the performance of London state schools in all the measures used is now better than any other region in the country and continues to improve year on year. In addition there are a number of tangible legacies to be found both in England and internationally. These are:

- The designation of schools nationally by NCTL (informed by the developments in the London Challenge) – Teaching Schools (600+), National Support Schools, and individuals – National Leaders in Education (1,000+), Specialist Leaders of Education

- The development of a headteacher-led, state-sponsored governing body – the Teaching Schools Council

- Charities and organizations providing and developing the work nationally and internationally – including Challenge Partners, London Leadership Strategy and Olevi International.

The two different paradigms of school improvement

At the turn of the century the abiding mantra for school improvement in England was as follows:

- A school's performance was judged against examination results and Ofsted grading

- When a school was perceived to be failing, school improvement was imposed from the top-down. This improvement effort was focused on trying to eradicate failure, made limited use of best practice, and often imposed a range of competing and conflicting initiatives from outside of the school; yet the responsibility if these efforts failed was placed on the school itself – for example, through 'naming and shaming' it

- The schools received considerable additional funding to address their failings

- Those schools not falling into this category were mainly left to their own devices. (It is important to point out that this was not the case in all Local Authorities (LAs) in London – see Chapter 6)

- The limited collaboration that took place between schools mainly focused on the vested interest of schools seeking additional resources or improving student intakes, not school improvement

- In addition, given the close proximity of the schools and a highly competitive system in which schools vied for students, staff and kudos, there was little trust between schools or between schools and the system

- Finally, the approach adopted for sharing best practice was rudimentary compared to that emerging from other professions such as medicine and the knowledge management frameworks being developed by business, especially in information technology.

In contrast, the approach adopted by the Leadership Strategy came from a pragmatic understanding of how schools improved coupled with a view that this was to do with the system-wide management of knowledge. The knowledge to improve the system was within the system. However, it was not being shared effectively with those who needed it. However, if outstanding staff shared their best practice with their school colleagues then the performance gap would close. It was vital that this would not just be a strategy that set out to eradicate failure but one that increased performance overall. The outstanding teachers and leaders were also challenged to improve themselves further. In this way, over time, the gap between the best and the rest would narrow while the best would improve further. This concept is called upwards convergence and it became the mantra of the approach (see Figure 19.1).

Therefore, the initial plan was to identify schools providing best practice within a given education/social context, capture their knowledge, provide their key staff with the skills to transfer this complex knowledge to other schools and, finally, broker their work with a failing school serving a similar catchment. They also networked to give them the opportunity to share and develop their practice further. The key focus was upon schools working collaboratively to improve the quality of leadership and teaching and learning in their schools. For many this was their first involvement in this type of system-wide work.

From the outset it was clear that no single school or individual had the answer to the whole system reform required. Yet a solution framed within a theory of action based on effective knowledge management could assist in deciding how effective actions were and what to do next. As a result, within this intellectual framework decisions were made

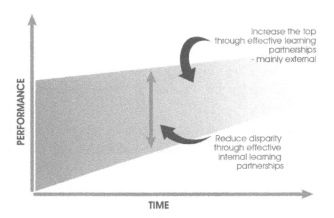

Figure 19.1 Upwards convergence.
Source: Berwick, 2011.

collaboratively based on the emerging evidence. This was easier for some colleagues to accept than others and a number left (often to lead the emerging academy chains). By making decisions collaboratively this made it easier to adopt a shared responsibility for the City's education service and it led to a pan London approach. This collective identity became a powerful force for continuing the work. In addition the process was open and evidence based, enabling the Department of Education and politicians to support it.

The headteachers who led this work across schools were referred to as consultant leaders (Earley and Weindling, 2006). They acted as 'systemic leaders' as opposed to 'system leaders'. In this definition, system leaders had direct responsibility for a group of schools, as with a LA Director of Education or the chief executive of a group of schools forming an academy trust. A systemic leader, on the other hand, only had direct responsibility for their own school, but, nevertheless, also made a consider-able commitment to help the other schools in their partnership. As such, systemic leaders were able to achieve their ambitions for their own school within those of the collaborative.

These systemic leaders worked with their colleagues to come to an open consensus, based upon evidence about:

- what they were trying to achieve
- where they were now
- what they should do (from what they knew worked) about moving from *a* to *b*.

This formed the basis for them to build a robust theory of action. The current manifesta-tion of which in Challenge Partners is now described.

Challenge Partners

Challenge Partners was formed in 2011 based on the historical context described above and upon the evolving theory of action of those involved in the challenges. It is a charity, owned and led by schools that work together to lead school improvement. The partner-ship has grown from sixty-four schools in 2011 to 350 in 2015 and from eleven hubs to twenty-eight. Most of these schools cluster around one or more Teaching Schools. The schools all come from different contexts across the country (Figure 19.2). The schools cover all governance arrangements (Figure 19.3) and all phases (Figure 19.4). They recognize that they are stronger together and that collaboration is the key to their contin-ued success.

They exist to support schools in that role by facilitating constructive collaboration and challenge between them and providing a platform for activities that would not be possible for a school to undertake on its own. Together, they aspire to become a world-class,

Figure 19.2 Distribution of hubs across the country.

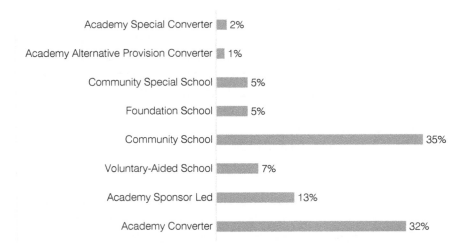

Figure 19.3 Types of governance arrangements of schools, 2014–2015.

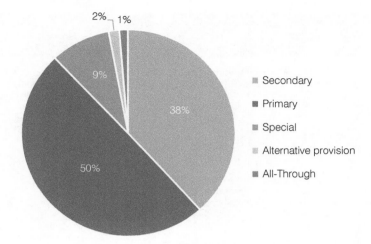

Figure 19.4 Distribution of phases of schools 2015–2016.

knowledge-sharing community, which leads the way in school improvement and raises the standards of education for all.

From the outset the partners committed themselves to four aims which impact on the young people they serve:

1 Improve examination results at a rate above the national average and accelerate the progress of the disadvantaged
2 Enable all schools to improve at a rate above the national average
3 Create more national leaders and outstanding schools that fulfil the Teaching School criteria
4 Develop a world-class, self-improving and sustainable system that contributes to national research and policymaking.

Activity is run through a hub model. These hubs are generally local or regional geographical partnerships of schools, often Teaching School Alliances, which come together to pool their knowledge and resources. The role of the central team is to help make these hubs more effective, as well as create new hubs. The aim is to reduce the disparity in performance of the schools in the hub while increasing the performance of the hub overall.

Schools pay an annual subscription based on the number of students with a minimum charge for small schools and a maximum for large ones. Over 40 per cent of the money goes towards providing central services, of which the quality-assured peer review (QAR) takes a significant amount (see Chapter 4). The rest is delegated back to hubs for them to determine how it is used based upon locally agreed priorities.

The benefits of being a Challenge Partners member are shown in Figure 19.5.

Challenge and **support** for your school	Support for your **local** partnership	Be part of a **national** partnership
QA Review • An annual peer review • Continuing Professional Development (CPD) for senior leaders to review other schools • Accreditation of areas of excellence in your school	**Funding for your local partnership** • Places on Improving and Outstanding Teacher Programmes (ITP/OTP) • Support for activities, reviews, events and projects which help develop schools	**Helping you identify & link up with best practice** • Access to our online tool which identifies subject-level expertise • Free places at all our national conferences and events
Post QA Review Support • Follow-up conversation after your Quality Assurance (QA) Review • Sign-posting to NLEs, SLEs and areas of excellent practice	**An evidence-driven approach to collaboration** • Strategic support to develop your teaching school alliance, multi-academy trusts (MAT) or local partnership • Hub reviews	**Meeting common challenges** • Collectively problem solve through phase or theme specific forums • Use your evidence & experience to contribute to research

Figure 19.5 Benefits of being a Challenge Partners member.

Challenge Partners as a manifestation of the theory of action

The theory of action used by Challenge Partners for creating an effective collaborative of schools has, at its heart, a moral purpose. It ensures that all students, especially the most disadvantaged, receive an education that represents the current wisdom of the education community, that is, the schools involved in the partnership. The charity actively seeks to support schools that serve disadvantaged students, wish to be transformed by working with others and/or feel isolated.

The ways that members challenge and support each other drives moral purpose and builds moral capital. Challenge is based on agreed progressive professional standards and is constructive and inclusive. The standards represent an amalgam of political policy, the outcome of research, emerging effective innovation and the best practice of our schools. Schools are challenged to do better. An annual QAR is central to this process (see Chapter 4). Support is provided both locally and nationally, resulting in a nation-wide brokerage service. Evidence is used to determine what support works, where, when and by whom. This takes into account the stage of teacher development and the capacity of the leadership to manage change.

Through this constantly updated knowledge audit Challenge Partners know what knowledge is needed, who owns it (within or outside of the collaborative) and how best to use it to improve learning. Knowledge transfer is not left to chance. Instead, a collaborative learning model has been created that allows for tacit knowledge to become explicit and for learning opportunities to be provided which reflect the degree of complexity of the learning to be undertaken by the learner. While developing members' social skills, organizational capital is also provided to ensure that this knowledge becomes embedded.

Staff who can act as catalysts are identified and developed, energizing the links between and within the many networks engaged with the collaborative. Leaders who can reconcile their own ambitions for the good of their peers lead the collaborative. These leaders ensure the process is quality-assured, recognize the positive contribution others make beyond their own responsibilities and ensure that the culture of collaboration is strictly adhered to. This is not a static situation. The knowledge of how to run an effective collaborative is constantly improving from research, emerging effective innovation and best practice in schools.

The collaborative is based on relationships and, as a result, the schools and groups of schools and their staff adapt to this process at varying speeds. Thus, growth tends to be organic. The greater the physical contact between members the more effective the collaboration. Therefore, hubs tend to be locally or regionally based. As well as sharing knowledge, they may also be formed to play a local political role but this is not an absolute requirement. However, initially the hubs were required to have at their centre an outstanding school with the capacity to challenge and support others. Over time the leadership and support provided has become more distributed.

The development of the collaborative is strategic. Selection and induction of both new hubs and new members is rigorous as considerable valuable energy can be lost focusing on the disaffected. Initially, the activity between schools is directed at improving the quality of teaching and learning and leadership. To obtain buy-in, interventions that are low cost/high impact are initially used. New members are developed quickly to ensure they have the capacity to provide support as well as receive it. As the collaborative develops so do the members so that in time they can:

- take responsibility for the success of all of the schools involved
- effectively induct new members and succession plan
- use shared data to provide real depth to the challenge they offer each other
- provide quality-assured support for other schools
- engage in a collaborative decision-making process with their colleagues
- rationalize their involvement in effective emerging innovation
- use their collective power to gain resources they could not access on their own
- provide resources, often on a reciprocal basis, for other members.

It is essential that at the centre there is a team that facilitates this process and which ensures that it is encapsulated in a theory of action. The central team ensures that the moral purpose is retained by monitoring the nature of the membership and its impact on student outcomes. It also ensures that the latest research findings and emerging research is made accessible by identifying and locating current best practice and mobilizing programmes which have the capacity to improve the performance of students, teachers and leaders. There is regular engagement with the major stakeholders, such as the Social Business Trust, EEF and UCL Institute of Education, in order to seek influence where necessary and also to access resources. The effectiveness of the collaborative is constantly researched and evaluated as a configuration for school improvement and the theory of action is adjusted accordingly (Matthews and Headon, 2015).

Finally, as part of the moral purpose, Challenge Partners take responsibility in using the collective power to bring a positive influence to bear at all levels of the education system. Research and reports are published regularly; members contribute to most major decision-making bodies both locally and nationally, such as the regional headteacher boards and the national teaching school council. The work of the London West Alliance is now described to illustrate how a hub works in practice.

The London West Alliance

The London West Alliance (LWA) is currently the largest alliance of schools (hub) within Challenge Partners. In 2011, when Challenge Partners was formed, the LWA comprised of seventeen schools, predominantly secondary and pan London. Over the past four years the hub has grown in size significantly and is now a complex, cross-phase network of thirty-seven schools. Only one school from the hub has opted out of Challenge Partners over that period of time (see Figure 19.6).

At the centre of the hub is Lampton School. The school is a large, mixed, comprehensive serving a disadvantaged area of West London (over 20 per cent of all students are on free school meals). It was one of the first pilot schools for Teaching Schools and as such has a long history of working with other schools to improve the education it provides for its students. It has been rated outstanding by Ofsted four times in succession and was identified by them in 2009 as an example of best practice. The headteacher, one of the

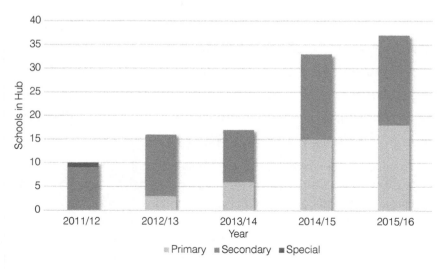

Figure 19.6 Development of London West Alliance.

authors, has held a number of major roles outside of her school, including non-executive director of the Department for Education from 2011 to 2015, director of the London Leadership Strategy from 2008 to 2011, and lead consultant headteacher, London Leadership Strategy from 2003 to 2008. She and her staff over a ten-year period have built the capacity to support other schools by deploying staff with the skills to improve the quality of teaching and learning and in specific subject areas, establish new initiatives such as the Brilliant Club, and coordinate the work of a group of schools to support each other such as the LWA.

Challenge Partners is not the only network the schools in the alliance are involved in, but it is the central one. The founding partners of the LWA were all good or outstanding schools and this was important when creating a best practice model. They made explicit their commitment to improving the quality of teaching and learning, developing outstanding leaders and challenging each other. Once the alliance was established, they sought other suitable schools, often not as successful as themselves but facing similar difficult challenges, to join them.

From the outset the schools that joined the hub pledged their support for the Challenge Partner aims, specifically wanting to make a difference to the life chances of all students across the partnership and especially the most disadvantaged, thereby demonstrating a real moral purpose and creating moral capital. Rules of engagement were established, particularly in relation to behavioural expectations of 'good partners' and protocols were agreed to establish the need for openness, honesty and trust. In terms of behaviours there were very clear expectations – during induction and through the annual pledge it was made clear that 'we do not expect a service level agreement mentality'.

A highly structured approach has been developed to induct schools into the alliance (see Figure 19.7). This includes a site visit to ensure the leaders of the joining school subscribe to working collaboratively.

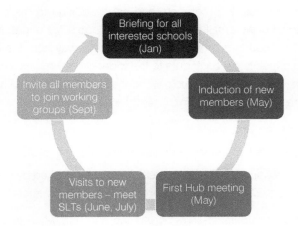

Figure 19.7 The induction cycle for new schools joining the hub.

The collaborative leadership of the hub is provided by an elected cross-phase Steering Group of six headteachers. Opportunities for other headteachers to lead on particular projects and aspects of professional development are also provided. The Steering Group focuses on the following areas:

- Applications from potential new members – on occasion these have been turned down, usually when there have been concerns over values and professional behaviours
- Dispersal of funds that are returned to the alliance from the Challenge Partner's central team
- The running of the annual LWA conference – agreeing the theme/location/key note speakers and overall format
- Finalizing hub priorities
- Bidding opportunities for the alliance.

They meet on a regular basis with the hub and Teaching School managers. The hub is run jointly by a deputy who is the Teaching School Director and a part-time experienced educational professional who acts as the Hub manager. They provide the organizational capital to ensure that data are used effectively, the QAR is tracked and the follow-up support from other schools is brokered either within the hub or across other Challenge Partner Hubs. This ensures that the collaboration between the schools has a positive outcome. The fact that the headteacher of Lampton School and the Hub manager both worked at a national level on a number of school improvement initiatives means that the hub can more effectively distinguish between what is a purely local need as opposed to a wider system need.

There is a constant need for the hub's leadership to check that partners understand the financial elements of their subscription, such as learning credits, to ensure that their involvement represents good value for money. Excellent communication is vital both for new members and existing members and so in addition to the central CP weekly email there is a local news email from the Hub manager. The engagement of partners is monitored and tracked in a proactive and supportive way and it is expected that all schools that have capacity will contribute to the wider school improvement offer.

To facilitate this approach to the hub's work, the LWA has invested heavily in its infrastructure to ensure that:

- decisions are made collaboratively
- knowledge is captured, managed and quality assured
- joint practice development is based on real need as evidenced by the auditing of best practice, use of the QAR and access to the wider subject directory.

There is a massive generosity of spirit across the hub and when a request for help is made there are often multiple offers of support.

In line with the CP philosophy of encouraging new and innovative ideas to flourish and potentially 'go to scale' across the collaborative, the LWA perceives that the role of the hub is to enable entrepreneurship to grow and develop.

This is done in a number of ways:

- Removing the barriers to implementation – these often lie around capacity issues, for example, admin, set-up and funding
- Nurturing talent and providing project management and bidding expertise to support colleagues through this time-consuming process
- Using networks and contacts to put people in touch with the relevant personnel
- Recognizing a need and then sourcing through a known provider, for example, 'Big Maths Ideas' and Hegarty Maths.

An example of the support provided to one of the LWA's SLEs is as follows. A secondary maths specialist set up a primary maths project providing both master classes for pupils and teachers focusing on Level 6 achievement in maths. This simple idea of using the SLE's expert knowledge, her coaching style and organizational abilities has enabled the project to be rolled out to other CP Hubs and has the potential to grow.

The LWA has developed a number of similar projects led by the Research Group, including an English as an Additional Language (EAL) project now being supported by the EEF, university-style teaching in schools and a Deliberate Practice programme for teachers who had graduated from the Outstanding Teacher Programme.

The LWA has also played a key role in promoting and supporting the educational charity, known as the Brilliant Club. A significant factor here was the identification of shared priorities and our joint moral purpose. The charity places PhD students into state schools to work with high-performing students, a percentage of whom must be in receipt of FSMs. It also enables the pupils to experience a university-style series of seminars, coupled with aspirational visits to select universities. The case was overwhelming in terms of disadvantaged pupils and their lack of access to the top universities in our country.

The headteacher of Lampton chose to champion the Brilliant Club and this gave the programme credibility within the LWA hub and then across the wider partnership. This could have been perceived to be a risk but the charity has gone from strength to strength – it started in London and now has a national footprint – predominantly in Challenge Partner schools but also working with some of the more successful chains of schools. In a similar way, the alliance has played a key role in setting up the Researchers in Schools initiative. The idea of providing a postdoctoral route into teaching, particularly for maths and physics teachers appeared to be a logical development of the work of the Brilliant Club.

Conclusions and implications

It can be seen from this description of Challenge Partners and the work it evolved from that moral capital, of which trust is an intrinsic part, is an essential component of building a collaborative of schools that achieves its moral purpose of providing the best education it can, especially for disadvantaged students. Moral capital is hard-earned and quickly lost. It depends for its growth on long-term constructive and professional relationships. These relationships, to be successful, have to be open, trustworthy and emphatic and allow for professional challenge and committed support based upon best practice. As with all such developments they grow organically and therefore need nurturing, are relatively unpredictable in their configuration and are threatened by insularity and lack of succession planning. The skills to lead such organizations are not to be found in all headteachers, especially those who adopt a purely directive style.

In an increasingly global, knowledge-based, competitive educational service, complex alliances of schools, such as CP, have a critical role to play in effective knowledge transfer. They contribute to ensuring that students receive an education that represents the wisdom of the global education community. The work described here is in its early stages and forms a key part of a self-managing school system.

Chapter 20

Diversity: New leaders and new leadership

Karen Edge, Sergio Galdames and Juliet Horton

Aims

Most educational leadership and diversity research focuses on gender, race and ethnicity. We believe there is merit and urgency in including age and generation as potential factors influencing leadership experience, practice and careers. This chapter aims to:

- highlight trends in diversity and educational leadership research focusing on gender and race and ethnicity

- introduce our GenX (under age forty) Global City Leaders study

- present GenX leader views on age-related advantages and disadvantages

- expand discussions of diversity and leadership to include generation and age

- suggest responsive recruitment, development and retention solutions.

The active and growing body of research and policy-related work explores diversity among educational leaders from specific vantage points including:

1 leader experience with and/or reflection on the influence of a particular attribute of diversity on their lived leadership experience (Lumby, 2014; Rodríguez and Alanís, 2011; Shah, 2008)

2 programme evaluations of leadership recruitment, development or retention initiatives for leaders from particular backgrounds (Boske, 2010; Moorosi, 2012; Ogunbawo, 2012)

3 leadership styles, approaches and possible influences of leaders from particular backgrounds (Fernandez et al., 2015; McCray and Beachum, 2010; Santamaría and Jean-Marie, 2014).

This somewhat simplified categorization offers a useful organizer for exploring how diversity is currently presented in educational leadership literature and subsequent evidentiary gaps and policy futures.

We believe that one of the most important elements of diversity in any education system is the cadre of leadership talent that is tapped to improve and inspire it. As most research and policy attention focuses squarely on gender and race and ethnicity, there is merit and urgency in expanding current educational leadership evidence beyond more traditional or visible diversity attributes. For example, beyond the small but growing body of knowledge on leadership and sexuality, there remains little, if any, research into the influence of other attributes that may shape the experience and approaches of current and future educational leaders, including age and generation.

Expanding how researchers and policymakers examine diversity could emerge by creating deliberate strategies to support and encourage the examination of a wider range of leadership attributes, including age, generation, sexuality, nationality, socio-economic status, family and relationship status. In conjunction, explicitly encouraging more intersectional research could enhance the knowledge base of how multiple diversities may influence leaders' lived experience and/or approach to leading and their influence on followers.

In this chapter, we contribute to these discussions by:

- highlighting trends and patterns within two dominant areas of educational leadership and diversity research: gender and race/ethnicity
- exploring our own research to understand more about the new, younger, generation of school leaders taking up senior roles
- offering examples of our own attempts to diversify the lenses used to examine leaders' experience, enactments and aspirations
- showing how GenX leaders in London, New York City and Toronto perceive age-related advantages and disadvantages via two vignettes from our Economic and Social Research Council-funded GenX Global City Leaders study.

With this evidence in mind, we examine potential implications for leaders, leadership developers and policymakers. Finally, we posit the potential benefits of widening how diversity is investigated and understood to support, engage and retain the incoming cohort of current and future leaders.

Trends in gender and educational leadership research

Several core themes continue to gain traction within gender-focused educational leadership research, including leader recruitment, parenthood, gender and promotion, work conditions and workload, and leadership self-perception and readiness. In this section, we provide a brief summary of these emerging themes acknowledging the wider work related to gender and educational leadership.

Leader recruitment challenges

Globally, leader recruitment remains one of the most pressing issues facing education systems. Within many academic and policy discussions of recruitment, gender-focused considerations often highlight women's will and ability to access senior school-level roles. In the UK, Coleman (2002, 2011), Fuller (2009, 2014) and Wilson (1997) underline a lack of proportional representation of women in both secondary and primary headship. Similar international trends have also been noted (Blackmore, 1999; Shakeshaft, 1993; Newcomb and Mansfield, 2014).

Recruitment challenges are often linked to strong US- and UK-based accountability frameworks which produce more hostile work environments and discourage women from leadership (Shakeshaft et al., 2007; Coleman, 2007; Smith, 2011). England and Wales provide examples of accountability systems that make leaders more vulnerable as they may be fired as a result of a negative inspection results (MacBeath, 2011). These conditions may make the role less attractive to potential candidates.

The lack of proportional representation of women leaders in English schools is also often linked to the decentralization of school leader hiring to school-level governing bodies comprised of community members. Coleman (2007) notes how women leaders perceived that governors showed a covert preference for male leadership candidates. While discrimination by governing bodies has often been cited as a barrier for women's advancement (Selvarajah, 2015), few research studies specifically examine school-level hiring bias and its relationship to gender.

Parenthood, gender, work and promotion

Women educational leaders' career patterns are often more affected by home and family (Shakeshaft et al., 2007; Coleman, 2007; Fuller, 2014). More often than not, discussions of parenthood and educational leadership centre on women and rarely include men and fatherhood. Increasing motherhood demands are often cited as reasons why more women delay or avoid pursuing headships. For example, Eagly and Carli (2007) found that working mothers in 2000, on average, spent more time with their children than stay-at-home mothers did in 1975. The additional demands of modern mothering create greater pressures on work–life balance. Women leaders also often discuss the challenge of public perception and the possibility of prevailing assumptions that women with children are less committed to their employment, less competent than women without children (Williams and Segal, 2003) and 'less productive' as a result of domestic responsibilities (Blau and DeVaro, 2007). Ely et al. (2014) link these stereotypes to women's decisions to leave jobs after having children often because they were assigned unfulfilling roles and sidelined from promotion. Williams and Segal (2003) coined the term 'maternal wall' (2003) describing the challenge facing women's career advancement when they become parents. Eagley and Carli (2007) described the loss of income associated with motherhood as a 'maternity tax'.

However, parenthood may also empower both men and women leaders through adding an additional pupil perspective; using families as a touchstone for school standards; providing empathy with parents; and engaging with a broader discussion about education. As Fuller (2014) and Lumby and Azaola (2014) demonstrate, being a parent increases women's sense of agency by refining their sense of self.

Work conditions and workload

As highlighted above, the negative influence of high-stakes accountability and high-pressure leadership roles may create disincentives for men and women to apply for school leadership posts. This role 'intensification' for school leaders encompasses the increasing pressure to do more in less time, to be responsive to a greater range of demands from external sources and to meet a greater range of targets (MacBeath, O'Brien and Gronn, 2012). Workload increases push leaders to work longer hours, putting additional pressure on life beyond work. For example, PricewaterhouseCoopers (2007) found 61 per cent of headteachers describe their work–life balance as 'poor' or 'very poor'. Leaders commonly report twelve- to fifteen-hour workdays (Brunner, 2000; MacBeath, 2011) with English headteachers working more than fifty-five hours per week. Based on research beyond education, women appear to be more strongly negatively influenced by such 'extreme work models' (Hewlett and Luce, 2006) that create extreme pressures and demand more than seventy hours a week. Hewlett and Luce (2006) found that among extreme workers, more men than women have support at home resulting in women being more significantly affected by the inability to work extreme hours due to domestic and childcare responsibilities (Hewlett and Luce, 2006; Halpern, 2008). Also, women may be more socially affected by extreme hours because they do not have time to invest in personal relationships, which takes a toll on health and wellbeing (Philipsen and Bostic, 2010). The new generation of leaders, who are known to prioritize work–life balance, worry about extreme work hours on the grounds of wanting a more balanced life. This may have a knock-on effect on those willing to step into school leadership roles (Edge, 2014).

Coleman previously found (2005, 2007) that 94 per cent of male versus 78 per cent of female headteachers were married (2005), and 90 per cent of men as opposed to 63 per cent of women had one or more children. Perhaps extreme working demands have perpetuated the challenges as English women headteachers remain more likely than men to be single and have fewer or no children (Fuller, 2014).

Leadership self-perception and readiness

There are many different reasons posited for why women leaders are often less willing to move into more senior roles. For example, unfamiliarity with leadership responsibilities has been identified over a genuine lack of belief in personal leadership abilities (Cubillo and Brown, 2003; Shakeshaft et al., 2007). Shakeshaft et al. (2007) also suggest that women education professionals often want to gain more education and experience in the classroom before seeking headship (Young and McLeod, 2001). Grogan and Brunner (2005) report that only 40 per cent of women in US-based senior district-level positions felt competent and ready to take on those roles. However, Cubillo and Brown (2003) in their small-scale study found all nine participating women leaders displayed high levels of self-confidence and self-esteem. While perceived lack of confidence has been linked to holding women back from aspiring and planning for career advancement, men more consistently demonstrate high levels of agency and willingness to engage in self-promotion (Coleman, 2007; Kaparou and Bush, 2007). Within these discussions, Gilespie and Temple (2001) found that perfectionism was the most inhibiting factor in balancing work and family, even over inflexible work places, unhelpful partners and financial pressures.

Trends in race, ethnicity and educational leadership research

A similar acceleration of research addressing issues of race and ethnicity in educational leadership has been particularly buoyant in England and the United States. This may be due to an acknowledgement of the rapid demographic changes of student, and to a lesser extent teachers and leaders, particularly in cities (Brown, 2005; Cooper, 2009). School leaders' integral role in working with diverse communities and managing the opportunities and challenges in these new, more diverse, contexts is becoming increasingly widely recognized (Blackmore, 2010; Dantley, 2005). In this section, we highlight some of the emerging themes in race and ethnicity-focused educational leadership research, including professional development, careers and gender.

Professional development

Educational leadership research has focused attention on issues related to race and ethnicity within leadership development exploring the context of the history, voice and challenges of marginalized groups (women, African Americans, Latinos, Native Americans and LBGT community members) (Alston, 2012). The dominant critique is that diverse perspectives have not been heard or acknowledged on traditional programmes characterized by male and white discourses. Campbell-Stephens (2009) has argued that not only is it important to prepare more diverse school leaders, but also that the curricula of these programmes should consistently include social justice and equity in their core. There is growing agreement that many current professional learning opportunities are most often dominated by white discourses (Blackmore, 2010; Coleman and Campbell-Stephens, 2010; Johnson and Campbell-Stephens, 2010).

Careers

Studies also focus on the challenges faced by black and minority ethnic (BME) school leaders when moving up the educational leadership career ladder. Bush, Glover and Sood (2006) found that UK school leaders encounter diverse forms of discrimination when attempting to gain headteacher positions. Shah and Shaikh (2010) describe similar examples of struggle and bias for UK-based Muslim school leaders which have been exacerbated by global events, including 9/11. In the United States, Young and Young (2010) found that white superintendents may hold negative bias when interviewing Hispanic candidates.

Intersection of gender and race

An increasing number of studies address the influence and importance of both the intersection of multiple attributes of diversity and their influence on the experience, careers and aspirations of school leaders. Much of this emerging research links gender and race or ethnicity with a specific focus on BME women leaders (Bloom and Erlandson, 2003; Lumby, 2014). For example, Reed (2012) identified that black female leaders understand leadership in a larger social, historical and political context in a way that positively influences their leadership. Horsford (2012) argues that understanding the influence of the intersection of gender and race, and specifically the role of black female school leaders, could widen policy, research and support opportunities for all leaders.

GenX leaders in big cities: expanding diversity

Recently our team recognized that school leadership shortages are becoming more common in many urban jurisdictions with links to teacher apathy about leadership roles (Gronn and Lacey, 2004) and headteacher retirements (Howson and Sprigade, 2008). A further defining characteristic and complexity of education in large cities, compounding staffing issues, is the high volume of staff turnover (McKinney et al., 2007). Challenging circumstances may make recruiting and retaining staff members problematic (Harris, 2016). The confluence of these factors is resulting in a new generation of leaders entering into leadership roles. This new cohort of leaders marks an important transition, yet there is little research exploring their working practice, experiences, careers and aspirations.

To address this knowledge gap, our ESRC-funded research has engaged cohorts of thirty or more young school leaders in each of three global cities – London, New York and Toronto (Foreign Policy, 2009). We chose three global cities to start our research as they are seen to be centres of innovation, influence, and are often indicative focal points for international trends (Sassen, 1991). Our research targeted leaders under the age of forty (GenX) as they have grown up in the most rapidly progressive technological era and tend to be more globally minded, techno-savvy, informal (Zemke et al., 2000) and collaborative (Wey Smola and Sutton, 2002). These oft-shared traits shape GenXers' desire for collaboration (Wey Smola and Sutton, 2002), mobility (Duscher and Cowin, 2004), diversity and more experimental structures in organizations (Kunreuther, 2003).

As these characteristics are markedly different from those of their predecessor baby boomer leaders, we were interested in how these attributes were influencing new leadership experience or models. To understand more about GenX leadership, we conducted between twenty and thirty individual interviews with deputy heads and headteachers each year in each city. We explored career development/aspirations, work–life issues, professional identity, organizational improvement and leadership. Our study aimed to contribute to the theory and practice of age and generation of educational leaders as a diversity attribute. Examples from young leaders across the three global cities related to how they perceive that their age creates advantages and disadvantages to their work, lives and aspirations are noted in the Vignettes.

Vignette 1

Advantages of being a younger leader in London, Toronto and New York City

As part of the ESRC-funded Global City Leaders study, sixty leaders across the three cities were asked their perceptions on the advantages of being a young leader. In all three cities, leaders shared a similar list of characteristics that they believed provided them with an advantage as a senior school leader.

Advantages
1. Innovative/open to new ideas
2. Able to relate to younger staff/students
3. Energy
4. Tech-savvy
5. More collaborative
6. Receptive to change
7. More time (no children)
8. Confidence/willing to 'rock the boat'
9. Having children (better understanding)
10. More time to build opportunities/experience

Most young leaders declared their openness and receptiveness to new ideas as the greatest advantage of being a young leader. Leaders talked of their approach as a 'mind-set' that provides them with 'the capacity to explore and try new strategies and being willing to assume risk'. As one London leader said, 'I can try new things; I'm not stuck in my ways. I don't believe things have to be done in a certain way.' Another described her openness to innovation in terms of teaching and learning, her recent experience in the classroom, which was 'not long ago', and a desire to keep up with current best practice:

> I'm also very current in terms of practice and pedagogy and curriculum knowledge, all of those things I'm still very current and up to date on. I'm not stuck in old practices or older ways of looking of things, that I have a mind-set that can't be moved so I think that the perception is that being this young makes me more open to change and someone that can relate really right across the continuum.

Leaders in New York also echoed the benefit of recent classroom experience and understanding the current reality of school improvement processes. As one leader explained:

> I think you're definitely closer to some of the classroom experiences, more familiar with the reforms coming from the research side of things, definitely more understanding why policy and reform have kind of moved in a certain way, and being able to explain it to people helps.

Being closer in age to parents and teachers can also provide significant advantages in the eyes of young leaders, who share common experience and may understand each other better, which may decrease the power distance between leaders and other stakeholders. Leaders believed their younger age made them more approachable.

Given the pace of most urban school environments, leaders suggested that they 'have more energy' to run and implement diverse activities in the school. Many suggest that their limited family commitments mean they have more time for school-level leadership and work. One leader shares: 'I've got lots of energy, but I'm not sure if I'll still have that in ten years ... maybe that's because I don't have a family yet.'

This advantage has an important consequence on their leadership practices. Having more energy in many cases means having more opportunities to explore and participate in diverse activities and to engage with the community. This creates many opportunities for developing relationships with stakeholders which is seen as beneficial because 'the stronger your relationships, the easier the job is'.

Vignette 2

Disadvantages of being a young leader in London, Toronto and New York City

1. Having to prove yourself
2. Lack of credibility
3. Negative/inaccurate perceptions
4. Lack of experience
5. Looking young/perception
6. Managing older staff
7. Managing expectations
8. Parental communication
9. Burnout
10. Wanting to start a family

Young leaders most commonly identified the greatest disadvantage of being a young leader as 'having to prove themselves to others'. The second and third most frequently highlighted disadvantages were 'lack of credibility' and 'being perceived negatively or inaccurately by others'. In many cases, leaders discussed how 'looking too young' for the job played into stakeholder perceptions or misconceptions about their experience and ability to lead their schools. To combat these challenges, most young leaders reported having to put in more effort to be seen as credible as their older peers. One London leader explained:

> You have to work harder. You have to prove your worth. You have to prove you know your stuff. You can't take anything for granted. Especially, I look young. Many people my age don't look young – but I do. You have to prove yourself more than if you were not young.

The perceived lack of credibility created a greater sense of pressure to excel in post and to put more energy into building credibility with teachers, parents and community members.

Young leaders reported being openly challenged by colleagues, especially when working on improvements in teaching and learning. One New York leader explained: 'I've run into challenges, I believe, when I am supervising older teachers that sometimes are like: "I've been teaching since you were in elementary school".'

The credibility struggle appears compounded by the assumption by stakeholders that age directly correlates to a lack of experience and skills. One leader explained: 'I need to work in those instances, work a little bit harder to prove myself and to show that I'm competent at what I do and to help people understand that I'm not in this role because somebody liked me. I'm in it because I can do the job and I'm qualified to do the job.'

There was an additional, but important, disadvantage facing young female leaders which is associated with stakeholder fear of young leaders taking maternity leave, building their own family and abandoning the school. These challenges were discussed most frequently in London and were linked to hiring and in-post work of leaders.

> There is an unfortunate 'perfect storm' for women [school leaders] in their early 30s. There is this weird scepticism that we're all going to suddenly want to have ten children, in ten consecutive years, coming back from maternity for three months at a shot, for the next ten years.

The vignettes provide insights into how GenX leaders feel about age influencing their roles within and beyond their schools. Almost all leaders in the study felt there were advantages as well as disadvantages to being a younger than average leader in the system. The main concern about age and leadership rests with a heightened sense of having to prove themselves and the amount of additional time that takes and, in turn, takes away from other important leadership tasks. Most disadvantages identified by the young school leaders related to misperceptions about their professional capacities based on their appearance and the challenges in mediating and rectifying these challenges.

These findings indicate that young leaders believe they are different than their older leader colleagues and that they bring an energy and openness to experimentation that is different and new. These findings, along with the wider evidence base generated by the study, point to some specific strategies for recruiting, developing and retaining young leaders. The importance of age and generation, in the eyes of participants, is palpable and indicates that broadening current limits of how diversity is considered could produce gains across the system and address the current crisis in recruiting and retaining school leaders.

Summary

- There is a need to build on the legacy and strength of current educational leadership research examining gender, race and ethnicity
- Gaps in educational leadership literature need to be addressed to expand conceptions of diversity that may influence leader and follower experience and actions
- The analytical and policy merit in understanding how new generations of leaders work and experience their roles can enhance recruitment, development and retention strategies.

Implications

- Comparative studies of the lives, leadership and aspirations of all school leaders need to be deeply embedded in national and local policy and practice

- The educational evidence base needs to examine and celebrate multiple views of and visions for educational leadership

- As policy and practice leaders notice differences in how generational cohorts approach their work and careers, quick, deliberate and targeted strategies for ensuring a diverse cadre of leaders joins and remains in the profession are paramount

- Policymakers, system and school leaders need to actively encourage a more diverse cadre of leaders to step up into senior leadership roles to ensure school systems are led by individuals with different experiences and perspectives.

Postscript

The future of leadership
Peter Earley and Toby Greany

One of us recently drew upon a number of research reviews to compare the leadership landscape over the last decade or so in England. We wanted to see how school leadership had changed during that time to meet the ever-growing and changing demands of policymakers and other stakeholders (Earley, 2013). The constant factor over this time period had been the need for leaders to raise standards and for schools continuously to improve in an attempt to raise the quality of teaching and learning and enhance student outcomes. This period has been described by Cranston (2013: 131) as 'an era of standards-based agendas, enhanced centralized accountability systems where improved student learning, narrowly defined, becomes the mantra for school leaders, who themselves are subject to enhanced accountabilities'. So what, if anything has changed, and how do we envisage the future of school leadership and associated educational reform in the near future?

Future trends

An ongoing theme of several contributions to this edited collection has been how the role of the headteacher or principal has changed over the last twenty-five years, in particular with regard to the extent of autonomy, the levels and patterns of accountability and the nature of leaders' responsibilities (Schleicher, 2012). We have witnessed a growing global interest in leadership and a widespread recognition that it has a significant impact on educational systems, school performance and, indirectly, student outcomes. At the school and college level, this form of leadership has increasingly been seen as learning-centred leadership or leadership for learning, a combination of transformational and student-centred leadership.

The well-known Finnish educationist, Pasi Sahlberg, has coined the acronym GERM – the Great Education Reform Movement – to describe the process of global policy borrowing and system reform, which he has identified taking place in so many education systems throughout the world, both developed and less developed (Sahlberg, 2011a, b). Although he makes no specific reference to leadership, he refers to the growth of accountability in education systems along with other common themes such as competition, testing, standardization and choice; for him they are all part of the GERM. For Sahlberg, for education systems to become high-performing ones, they need to move from 'test-based accountability' to 'trust-based responsibility' and to stress the importance of professional capital and its development. He argues that high-performing jurisdictions give teachers 'agency, moral purpose and autonomy' and have accountability systems based on trust. For him the 'Fourth Way', which depends much more on collaboration, personalization, trust-based responsibility, professional capital and equity, is the way forward for high-performing systems and the leadership of their schools.

There seems little doubt that Sahlberg would see England's policy framework as infected by the GERM, although the emphasis on networks and school-led reform do perhaps reflect elements of his Fourth Way. The question here is what it means for school leaders to lead in GERM-infected systems. To move towards high-performing systems and schools the message for school leaders is clear: give emphasis to developing teachers and other staff as professionals and promote respectful professional dialogue. Two related things are especially important and have been key messages of this book: improving the quality of staff/the workforce and enhancing the quality of teaching and learning. People development is crucial, and although a cliché, it is true that a school's greatest resource is its staff. More specifically, the key to improving educational standards is the growth of professional capital – in particular, increasing the quality, knowledge and skills of teachers and leaders in schools (Hargreaves and Fullan, 2012). As several chapters in this book have demonstrated, this can be achieved by giving priority to professional development and learning with evidence-informed practitioners working in 'research learning communities'. Leaders of the future will need to learn to focus even more on these aspects of their role – to be more learning focused or learning centred with both staff and students. Looking ahead, however, this is likely to present its own set of difficulties. Specifically, we believe these difficulties and challenges will centre around the following:

- the intensification of leadership roles
- leading the learning
- collaboration and the move towards a self-improving school system.

The intensification of leadership roles

Educational leadership is often discussed in terms of a changing and challenging environment where heads and schools are being given an even bigger job to do either on their own or, increasingly, working with others in MATs, collaboratives and alliances (Earley, 2013; Greany, 2014). The term 'work intensification' is often used to describe this state of affairs where there is 'increasing pressure to do more in less time, to be responsive to a greater range of demands from external sources and to meet a greater range of targets, accompanied by impatient deadlines to be met' (MacBeath, O'Brien and Gronn, 2012: 422).

Fink summed it up well when he said headteachers were 'overburdened, overworked and overwhelmed' (2010: 35). To help overcome or minimize this state of affairs, training and development and effective systems of support for school leaders will be essential.

The many and varied demands on school leaders in combination with the dominating image that heads have to carry all the burdens of managing a school makes it a difficult and challenging, often isolated, job (Grubb and Flessa, 2006). It is perhaps unsurprising that so many education systems throughout the world are facing difficulties in attracting and recruiting high-quality applicants for headships. It is important that the job of school leaders, especially headship, is seen as doable. The task must be seen as possible for 'ordinary mortals' if we are to ensure a continuing succession of effective leaders. Matters are unlikely to improve until we engage with Peter Drucker's question of many years ago:

> No institution can possibly survive if it needs geniuses or supermen to manage it. It must be organised in such a way as to be able to get along under a leadership composed of average human beings.

Work intensification and increased demands of the job could also be addressed by restructuring and rethinking principals' tasks. The greater sharing of job responsibilities and job-sharing or 'co-headship' with an administrative team could be a solution. We need to think of innovative and different ways of addressing the ever-increasing demands and complexity of the role.

Working in teams, sharing responsibilities and working smarter will therefore become even more important over the next decade and increasingly leaders 'must choose to spend time on the right things and spend that time effectively' (Burkhauser, et al., 2012: 37). The 'right things' have been the subject of much debate as headteachers increasingly become more like chief executives running academies as businesses or entrepreneurs and less like leading professionals running a school. Drawing on the complementary skills of school business managers and other non-teaching professionals will be key here. Schools have increasingly been recognized as autonomous businesses, yet few would deny that their core business should be 'learning'. But, as has been argued in several chapters, 'learning for what purpose?'

Leading the learning

The nature of 'learning' – learning for what? – and its 'leadership' – leadership for what? – are key questions for the future. How will leaders ensure that their focus on learning avoids schools becoming 'examination factories' (Hutchings, 2015) with a narrowly defined standards-based curriculum, where teaching is to the test and other unsavoury and unethical practices are commonplace? As Alexander says:

> What schools can and should do is to concentrate on the task for which they exist for and which their teachers, one hopes, are trained: providing a rich, fulfilling and

empowering education which secures children's basic skills while raising their sights to larger educational horizons. To achieve this, we need to move from a concept of standards as test scores in limited aspects of literacy and numeracy to one that relates to the quality of provision and achievement across the entire curriculum to which children are entitled. (2011: 280)

Leading the learning will need to take priority over other competing pressures but this may be easier said than done. The 2012 landscape study found that the nature and demands of education policy were seen as potentially disrupting the focus of schools and leaders from teaching and learning and their improvement (Earley, 2013). Additional managerial responsibilities and powers as an academy or part of a MAT or chain could disrupt a leadership focus on learning at the same time when the normal channels of support from, for example, the local authority, were likely to be missing. Leadership of learning will increasingly need to be seen as everybody's responsibility with school leaders fostering a culture of learning for all. An emphasis on organization structures, such as academization, and new forms of schooling, such as free schools or university technical colleges, could be perceived as unhelpful distractions from this key objective. The growing number of competing pressures and demands on school leaders' time will make this an increasingly difficult task and will call for even more sharing and collective responsibility. Staff in charge of teaching and learning will need to keep 'learning' as a high priority and know how to lead and effectively promulgate shared visions of teaching, learning and 'a rounded education'.

Whatever the structures they operate within, we believe that school leaders will increasingly be extolled to become leaders of learning, with headteachers appraised or evaluated in terms of 'fostering pedagogical leadership in schools' (OECD, 2013: 485). We know that school leaders play a major indirect role in improving school outcomes by influencing the motivation and capacity of staff and affecting the culture and surroundings in which they work and learn. There will be a continuing expectation that school leaders focus their efforts on 'learning matters'. The evidence does suggest however that it is becoming increasingly difficult to maintain the focus on the leadership of teaching and learning (Earley, 2013). This is likely to continue.

Another unknown is whether the growth and development of a self-improving school system will help or hinder the development of leadership for learning. What does a self-improving system mean for learning-centred leadership? How will leading learning play out in a federation or chain? Will chief executives become further removed from the 'core business' of schools which will increasingly be seen as the responsibility of senior and middle leaders? Will such leaders have even less 'autonomy' than under previous arrangements? Will chains develop standard operating procedures and approaches to pedagogy that restrict local creativity, or will they create more exciting and developmental learning communities for staff to work across schools? Will executive heads and chief executives of academies and chains be more likely to have a business rather than an education background? These are all unknowns and areas worthy of further research. It is to collaboration and the move towards a self-improving school system that we next turn.

Collaboration and the move towards a self-improving school system

In an era of growing school autonomy, academization and diminishing local authority support, the need for schools in England to work in a more collaborative manner is greater than ever, although they still must compete for pupil admissions and staff. A self-improving system involves identifying the challenges and encouraging collaborative working between schools in order to tackle them. The concept of a self-improving system 'has become synonymous in some quarters with academization and other structural solutions' (National College, 2013: 11) and school-to-school support is being encouraged through 'system leaders' who exercise leadership beyond their own schools, sharing their expertise and their school's practice with other less effective schools through school improvement partnerships. There is the very real danger that the gap between the best schools and the rest could widen. As noted by the National College:

> There is a risk of a two-tier system emerging in which some schools gain significantly from the enhanced continuing professional development, the sharing of expertise and peer evaluation and challenge that comes from working with other schools, while others find themselves increasingly isolated. (ibid.: 3)

The most recent evidence from the two-year evaluation of Teaching Schools (Gu et al., 2016: 167) suggests that while there has undoubtedly been impressive progress in many localities, this danger does remain present:

> It appears that some schools still have limited knowledge of the purpose of teaching schools. There are examples of schools that are suspicious of receiving support from a teaching school because of the fear of a 'takeover' or the feeling that the alliances are owned by and exist to serve the needs of an elite group of 'outstanding' schools that are 'the centralised machinery of government'.

At a national level, the self-improving system is still not yet fully in existence and how it develops from its current state remains to be seen and will depend on a number of educational and political factors. Many schools undoubtedly prefer the model that is emerging in which they collaborate with peers to find solutions to their improvement challenges, rather than relying on courses run by local authority staff who often lacked credibility. The challenge seems to be how uneven these developments are: one delegate at a recent conference referred to the English education 'system' as akin to the 'wild west'. An education system in which some schools are left behind, or disenfranchised, as a consequence of not feeling a part of this 'self-improving system' is a very real possibility.

One of us has pointed out the inherent contradictions within the strategies used to promote school improvement in England, for example, where the accountability framework inhibits the innovative benefits of autonomy (Greany, 2014). Similarly, the competitive nature of the school system, where high-stakes testing and meeting the demands of inspection may take precedence over longer term and, perhaps, more sustainable arrangements for groups of schools taking responsibility for their own improvement. However, it is not always clear how the potential tension between partnership and co-operation and school choice and competition can be resolved. Earley (2013) voices an element of doubt and uses the term 'co-opetition' – a neologism coined to describe co-operative competition. Professional networks and peer support offer different models 'to market- or competition-based models in which the best schools flourish solely on the basis of their own innovation and success' (Smith, 2013: 5). However, it is not always clear how the potential tension between partnership and co-operation, and school choice and competition can be resolved. There are examples where partnership and collaboration work well but are they limited to a few schools? Those examples where it is successful may be at the leading edge but in national terms, Greany's question, 'Are we nearly there yet?' could quite easily have been, 'Do we know where we are going?' The somewhat haphazard development of England's 'middle tier', in which local authorities are trying to reshape and reduce their role while Regional Schools Commissioners take up responsibility for the academies and chains, will be a key factor in how this picture plays out (Greany, 2015).

What next?

More and more educational systems are moving towards decentralization, schools are more autonomous in their decision-making, and increasingly held to account for their results which are made public and widely available. As schools have gained more autonomy, the more important the role of school leaders, especially principals and headteachers, has become. However, despite years of evolving school improvement policy, it is home background that still seems to be the key determinant of how well students do in school and life more generally. Schools do make a difference and there is still too wide a gap in performance between the best and the worst, but as Bernstein (1970) said all those years ago 'education cannot compensate for society'. More recently Alexander notes that this attainment gap 'maps closely onto indicators of inequality in other aspects of children's lives, notably income, health, housing, risk, ethnicity and social class; and it confirms that tackling inequalities in educational outcome requires action across a broad range of public policy, including much that lies outside the control of schools' (2011: 270).

We wrote in the Introduction about the paradoxes of policy and the quest for successful leadership that could help resolve those paradoxes. The chapters in this book set out some of the many challenges involved, but also the ways in which research shows that leaders are successfully enhancing the quality of schools, the professional learning of staff and the richness of children's learning. Headship has often been seen as 'a work of passion' and most of those working in education do so with a 'moral purpose'. School leaders do face challenges – the need to raise standards, rising expectations from government, inspectors, parents and students, a highly diverse school population, a changing curriculum, assessment and so on – and these challenges are unlikely to go away. But most headteachers retain their view that it is 'the best job in education' – and this has not changed very much over the years (Earley, 2013). Sustaining this optimism so that school leadership remains a challenging, but doable and rewarding, vocation, even as it continues to change and evolve throughout the twenty-first century, will be key.

References

Adams, R. (2015) Call for schools to have a more active role in teaching character and morality, http://www.theguardian.com/education/2015/feb/27/call-for-schools-to-have-a-more-active-role-in-teaching-character-and-morality.

Agullard, K. and Goughnour, D. (2006) *Central Office Inquiry: Assessing Organization, Roles, and Actions to Support School Improvement*, San Francisco: CA, WestEd.

Ainscow, M. (2015) *Towards Self-Improving School Systems: Lessons from a City Challenge*, London: Routledge.

Ajegbo, K., Kiwan, D. and Sharma, S. (2007) *Curriculum Review: Diversity and Citizenship*, London: DfES.

Alexander, R. (2011) Evidence, rhetoric and collateral damage: the problematic pursuit of 'world class' standards, *Cambridge Journal of Education*, 41 (3): 265–86.

Alexander, R. (2012) *Curriculum Freedom, Capacity and Leadership in the Primary School*, Nottingham: National College for School Leadership.

Alexander, T. (2013) *Citizenship Schools: Learning Democracy, Raising Attainment, Building Community*, Manchester, UK: Cooperative College.

Alston, J. A. (2012) Standing on the promises: a new generation of black women scholars in educational leadership and beyond, *International Journal of Qualitative Studies in Education*, 25 (1): 127–9.

Altricher, H. and Kemethofer, D. (2015) Does accountability pressure through school inspections promote school improvement? *School Effectiveness and School Improvement,* 26 (1): 32–56.

Ancona, D., Malone, T. W., Orlikowski, W. J. and Senge, P. M. (2008) In praise of the incomplete leader, *Harvard Business Review*, February: 111–21.

Argyris, C. and Schon, D. (1974) *Theory in Practice: Increasing Professional Effectiveness*, San Francisco: Jossey-Bass.

Arthur, J., Kristjansson, K., Walker, D., Sanderse, W. and Jones, C. (2015) *Character Education in UK Schools: Research Report*, London: DfE.

Audsley, J., Chitty, C., O'Connell, J., Watson, D. and Wills, J. (2013) *Citizen Schools: Learning to Rebuild Democracy*, London: IPPR.

Baars, S., Bernardes, E., Elwick, A., Malortie, A., McAleavy, T., McInerney, L., Menzies, L. and Riggall, A. (2014) *Lessons from London Schools: Investigating the Success*, Reading, UK: CfBT.

Bajorek, Z. and Gulliford, J. (2014) *Healthy Teachers, Higher Marks? – Establishing a Link Between Teacher Health and Wellbeing, and Student Outcomes*, Lancaster: The Work Foundation.

Ball, S. (1997) Policy sociology and critical social research: a personal review of recent education policy and policy research, *British Educational Research Journal*, 23 (3): 257–74.

Ball, S. (2003) The teacher's soul and the terrors of performativity, *Journal of Education Policy*, 18 (2): 215–28.

Ball, S. (2007) *Education Plc: Understanding Private Sector Participation in Public Sector Education*, London: Routledge.

Ball, S. (2008) *The Education Debate*, Bristol: Policy Press.

Ball, S. (2012) *Global Education inc: New Policy Networks and the Neo-liberal Imaginary*, London: Routledge.

Ball, S. (2012) The reluctant state and the beginning of the end of state education, *Journal of Educational Administration and History,* 44 (2): 89–103.

Bandura, A. (1994) Self-efficacy, in V. S. Ramachaudran (ed.), *Encyclopedia of Human Behavior*, Vol. 4, 71–81, New York: Academic Press. (Reprinted in H. Friedman [Ed.] *Encyclopedia of Mental Health*, San Diego: Academic Press, 1998).

Bangs, J., MacBeath, J. and Galton, M. (2010) *Reinventing Schools, Reforming Teaching: From Political Visions to Classroom Realities*, London: Routledge.

Bangs, J. and Frost, D. (2016) Non-positional teacher leadership: distributed leadership and self-efficacy, in J. Evers and R. Kneyber (eds), *Flip the System: Changing Education from the Ground up*, 91–107, London: Routledge.

Barber, M. (2007) *Three Paradigms of Public Sector Reform*, London: McKinsey&Co.

Barber, M. (2008) *Instruction to Deliver: Fighting to Transform Britain's Public Services*, London: Methuen.

Barber, M. (2015) *How to Run a Government so that Citizens Benefit and Taxpayers don't go Crazy*, London: Allen Lane.

Barber, M. and Mourshed, M. (2007) *How the World's Best Performing School Systems Come Out on Top*, London: McKinseys&Co.

Barber, M., Chijoke, C. and Mourshed, M. (2010) *How the World's Most Improved School Systems Keep Getting Better*, London: McKinseys&Co.

Barnett, E. (2015) British girls join Islamic State, *Daily Telegraph*, 22 January.

Barr, J. and Saltmarsh, S. (2014) 'It all comes down to the leadership': the role of the school principal in fostering parent–school engagement, *Educational Management, Administration and Leadership*, 42 (4): 491–505.

Bassett, D., Lyon, G., Tanner, W. and Watkin, B. (2012) *Plan A+: Unleashing the Potential of Academies*, Reform/SSAT.

BBC (2013) *Public Perceptions of the Impartiality and Trustworthiness of the BBC*, London: BBC.

Beare, H. (2001) *Creating the Future School: Student Outcomes and the Reform of Education*, London: Routledge-Falmer.

Bell, L. and Stevenson, H. (2006) *Education Policy*, London: Routledge.

Bell, L. and Stevenson, H. (2015) Towards an analysis of the policies that shape public education: setting the context for school leadership, *Management in Education*, 29 (4): 146–50.

Bendikson, L., Robinson, V. and Hattie, J. (2012) Principal instructional leadership and secondary school performance, *SET*, 1.

Bennett, N. and Miles, S. A. (2006) Second in command: the misunderstood role of the chief operating officer, *Harvard Business Review*, May 71–8.

Bennett, S., Maton, L. and Kervin, K. (2008) 'The "digital natives" debate: a critical review of the evidence', *British Journal of Educational Technology*, 39 (5): 775–86.

Ben-Porath, S. R. (2010) *Touch Choices: Structure Paternalism and the Landscape of Choice*, Princeton, NJ: Princeton University Press.

BERA (2014) *Research and the Teaching Profession: Building the Capacity for a Self-Improving Education System*. Final report of the BERA-RSA Inquiry into the role of research in teacher education, London: BERA.

Berends, M., Cannata, M. and Goldring, E. B. (2011) School choice debates, research, and context, in M. Berends, M. Cannata and E. B. Goldring (eds), *School Choice and School Improvement*, 3–16, Cambridge, MA: Harvard Education Press.

Bernstein, B. (1970) Education cannot compensate for society, *New Society*, 26 February, 344–7.

Berry, J. (2015) Using social networking for professional development, *Professional Development Today*, 17 (2): 60–4.

Berwick, G. T. (2011a) *The Approach: Engaging in Excellence*, Volume One, GTB Associates, London: Olevi.

Berwick, G. T. (2011b) *Engaging in Excellence*, London: Olevi.

Biesta, G. (2016) Good education and the teacher: reclaiming education professionalism, in J. Evers and R. Kneyber (eds), *Flip the System: Changing Education from the Ground up*, 79–90, London: Routledge.

Bifulco, R. and Bulkley, K. (2015) Charter schools, in H. Ladd and M. Goertz (eds), *Handbook of Research in Education Finance and Policy*, 423–43, New York and London: Routledge.

Bingham, D. (2013) Wellbeing in educational settings, in M. Dawe (ed.), *The School Leader's Toolkit*, 17–33, London: Sage.

Black, J. (2001) Decentring regulation: understanding the role of regulation and self regulation in a 'post- regulatory' world, *Current Legal Problems*, 54: 103–47.

Black, P. (2003) *Assessment for Learning: Putting it into Practice,* Oxford: Oxford University Press.

Blackmore, J. (1999) *Troubling Women: Feminism, Leadership and Educational Change*, Buckingham, UK: Open University Press.

Blackmore, J. (2010) 'The other within': race/gender disruptions to the professional learning of white educational leaders, *International Journal of Leadership in Education,* 13 (1): 45–61.

Blatchford, R. (2014) *The Restless School,* London: John Catt.

Blau, F. D. and DeVaro, J. (2007) New evidence on gender differences in promotion rates: an empirical analysis of a sample of new hires, *Industrial Relations: A Journal of Economy and Society,* 46 (3): 511–50.

Bloom, C. M. and Erlandson, D. A. (2003) African American women principals in urban schools: realities, (re)constructions, and resolutions, *Educational Administration Quarterly,* 39 (3): 339–69.

Bloom, N., Lemos, R., Sadun, R. and Van Reenen, J. (2014) *Does Management Matter in Schools?* Centre for Economic Performance, LSE, Discussion Paper No 1312, London.

Bolam, R. (1993) School-based management, school improvement and school effectiveness: overview and implications, in C. Dimmock (ed.), *School-Based Management and Effectiveness*, 219–34, London: Routledge.

Bolton, P. (2014) *Education Spending in the UK*. http://www.parliament.uk/briefing-papers/SN01078.pdf.

Boske, C. A. (2010) 'I wonder if they had ever seen a black man before?' Grappling with issues of race and racism in our own backyard, *Journal of Research on Leadership Education,* 5 (7): 248–75.

Bottery, M. (2000) *Education, Policy and Ethics*, London: Continuum.

Boxall, P. and Purcell, J. (2011) *Strategy and Human Resource Management*, Chichester: Palgrave Macmillan.

Boyd, W. L. (2003) Public education's crisis of performance and legitimacy: rationale and overview of the yearbook, in W. L. Boyd and D. Miretzky (eds), *American Educational Governance on Trial: Change and Challenges* – the 102nd Yearbook of the National Society for the Study of Education (NSSE), 1–19, Chicago, IL: Chicago University Press.

Brighouse, T. M. and Woods, D. C. (2014) *The A-Z of School Improvement*, London: Bloomsbury Education.

Brighouse, T. M. (2007) *How Successful Headteachers Survive and Thrive*, London: R M Publications.

Brighouse, T. M. and Woods, D. (2013) *The A-Z of School Improvement, Principles and Practice*, London: Bloomsbury.

Brighouse, T. M. and Woods, D. C. (2008) *What Makes a Good School Now?* London: Continuum.

Briner, R. and Dewberry, C. (2007) *Staff Wellbeing is Key to School Success*, Worklife Support, www.worklifesupport.com.

Brown, C. (ed.) (2015) *Leading the Use of Research and Evidence in Schools*, London: IOE Press.

Brown, C. and Rogers, S. (2014) Knowledge creation as an approach to facilitating evidence-informed practice: examining ways to measure the success of using this method with early years practitioners in Camden (London), *Journal of Educational Change*, 15 (1): early online publication.

Brown, F. (2005) African Americans and school leadership, *An Introduction, Educational Administration Quarterly,* 41 (4): 585–90.

Brundrett, M. and Duncan, D. (2014) Leading curriculum innovation in primary schools project: a final report, *Education 3-13*, 32 (1): 1–10.

Brunner, C. (2000) Unsettled moments in settled discourse: women superintendents' experiences of inequality, *Educational Administration Quarterly,* 36 (1): 76–116.

Bryk, A. S. and Schneider, B. (2002) *Trust in Schools: A Core Resource for Improvement*, New York: Russel Sage Foundation.

Bubb, S. and Earley, P. (2005) *Unprincipled Principals? Towards a Research Agenda for the Understanding of Rogue Principals and their Practices*. Paper presented to the Belmas symposium at the Educational Management Association of South Africa, 11–13 March 2005.

Bubb, S. and Earley, P. (2004) *Managing Teacher Workload: Work-life Balance and Wellbeing*, London: Sage.

Bubb, S. and Earley, P. (2010) *Helping Staff Develop in Schools*, London: Sage.

Bubb, S. and Earley, P. (2013) The use of training days: finding time for teachers' professional development, *Educational Research*, 55 (3): 235–47.

Buck, A. (2013) *What Makes a Great School?* National College and London Leadership Strategy.

Burgess, S., Wilson, D. and Worth, J. (2010) *A Natural Experiment in School Accountability: The Impact of School Performance Information on Pupil Progress and Sorting*, Bristol: CMPO Working Paper No. 10/246.

Burns, T. and Köster F. (eds) (2016) Governing education in a complex world, *Educational Research and Innovation*, Paris: OECD Publishing.

Bush, T. and Glover, D. (2003) *School Leadership: Concepts and Evidence*, Nottingham; National College for School leadership.

Bush, T. and Glover, D. (2014) School leadership models: what do we know? *School Leadership and Management,* 34 (5): 553–71.

Bush, T., Glover, D. and Sood, K. (2006) Black and minority ethnic leaders in England: a portrait, *School Leadership and Management,* 26 (3): 289–305.

Byrk, A. and Schneider, B. (2002) *Trust in Schools: A Core Resource for Improvement*, New York: Russell Sage Foundation.

Caldwell, B. (2002) Autonomy and self-management: concepts and evidence, in T. Bush and L. Bell (eds), *The Principles and Practice of Educational Management*, 34–48, London: Sage.

Caldwell, B. and Spinks, J. (2013) *The Self-transforming School*, London: Routledge.

Callaghan, J. (1976) *A Rational Ddebate Based on the Facts*, 18 October, Ruskin College, Oxford, http://www.educationengland.org.uk/documents/speeches/1976ruskin.html.

Campbell-Stephens, R. (2009) Investing in diversity: changing the face (and the heart) of educational leadership, *School Leadership and Management*, 29 (3): 321–31.

Carr, S. (2016) *Motivation, Educational Policy and Achievement: A Critical Perspective*, London: Routledge.

Carter, J. A., Maher, S. and Neumann, P. R. (2014) *Using Social Media to Track the Activities of Western Jihadi Fighters in Syria*, London: International Centre for the Study of Radicalisation and Political Violence.

Castells, M. (2010) *The Power of Identity: The Information Age: Economy, Society and Culture:* Vol II, Second edition, Chichester: Wiley-Blackwell.

Catsambis, S. (2001) Expanding knowledge of parental involvement in children's secondary education: connections with high school seniors' academic success. *Social Psychology of Education*, 5 (2): 149–77.

Chapman, C. (2013) Academy federations, chains, and teaching schools in England: reflections on leadership, policy, and practice, *Journal of School Choice*, 7 (3): 334–52.

Chapman, C. (2015) From one school to many: reflections on the impact and nature of school federations and chains in England, *Educational Management, Administration and Leadership*, 43 (1): 46–60.

Chapman, C., Muijs, D. and MacAllister, J. (2011) *A Study of the Impact of School Federation on Student Outcomes,* Nottingham: NCSL.

Chapman, C., Muijs, D., Sammons, P., Armstrong, P. and Collins, A. (2009) *The Impact of Federations on Student Outcomes,* Nottingham: National College for Leadership of Schools and Children's Services.

Christodoulou, D. (2013) *Seven Myths about Education,* London: Routledge.

Cirin, R. (2014) *Do academies Make use of their Autonomy?* DfE Research report (RR336), London: Department for Education.

Claxton, G. and Lucas, B. (2010) *New Kinds of Smart*, Maidenhead: Open University Press.

Claxton, G., Chambers, M., Powell, G. and Lucas, B. (2011) *The Learning Powered School*, Bristol: TLO Ltd.

Coates, M. (2015) The co-operative: good with schools? *Management in Education*, 29 (1): 14–19.

Coates, S. (2015) *Headstrong: 11 Lessons of School Leadership*, London: John Catt.

Coffield, F. (2012) Why the McKinsey reports will not improve school systems, *Journal of Education Policy*, 27 (1): 131–49.

Cohen, M. D. and March, J. G. (1972) A garbage can model of organizational choice. *Administrative Science Quarterly*, 17 (1): 1–25.

Coldron, J., Crawford, M., Jones, S. and Simkins, T. (2014) The restructuring of schooling in England: the responses of well-positioned headteachers, *Educational Management, Administration and Leadership*, 42 (3): 387–403.

Coleman, M. (2002) *Women as Headteachers: Striking the Balance*, London: Trentham.

Coleman, M. (2005) *Gender and Headship in the Twenty-first century*, Nottingham: NCSL.

Coleman, M. (2007) Gender and educational leadership in England: a comparison of secondary headteachers' views over time, *School Leadership and Management,* 27 (4): 383–9.

Coleman, M. (2011) *Women at the Top,* London: Palgrave Macmillan.

Coleman, M. and Campbell-Stephens, R. (2010) Perceptions of career progress: the experience of black and minority ethnic school leaders, *School Leadership and Management,* 30 (1): 35–49.

Coles, M. (ed.) (2015) *Towards the Compassionate School*, London: IOE Press.

Collins, B. and Raven, B. (1969) 'Group structure: attraction, coalitions, communication and power', in G. Lindzey and E. Aronson (eds), *The Handbook of Social Psychology,* Vol 4, 2nd ed, 102–204, Reading, MA: Addison-Wesley.

Collins, J. (2001) *Good to Great*, London: Random House Business Books.

Confederation of British Industry/Pearson (2013) *Changing the Pace: Education and Skills Survey,* London: CBI.

Conley, S. and You, S. (2009) Teacher role stress, satisfaction, commitment, and intentions to leave: a structural model, *Psychological Reports*, 105: 771–86.

Connolly, P. (2015) Keynote address, *British Educational Research Association Annual Conference*, 15–17 September, Queen's University Belfast.

Cooper, C. and Kelly, M. (1993) Occupational stress in headteachers: a national UK study, *British Journal of Educational Psychology*, 63 (1): 130–43.

Cooper, C. W. (2009) Performing cultural work in demographically changing schools: implications for expanding transformative leadership frameworks, *Educational Administration Quarterly,* 45 (5): 694–724.

Cooperrider, D., Whitney, D. and Stavros, J. (2003) *Appreciative Inquiry Handbook*, Bedford Heights: Lakeshore Publishers.

Cordingley, P., Bell, M., Isham, C., Evans, D. and Firth, A. (2007) What do specialists do in CPD programmes for which there is evidence of positive outcomes for pupils and teachers? *Research Evidence in Education Library*, London: EPPI-Centre, Social Science.

Cordingley, P. (2013) The contribution of research to teachers' professional learning and development, https://www.bera.ac.uk/wp-content/uploads/2013/12/BERA-Paper-5-Continuing-professional-development-and-learning.pdf.

Cordingley, P., Higgins, S., Greany, T., Buckler, N., Coles-Jordan, D., Crisp, B., Saunders, L. and Coe, R. (2015) *Developing Great Teaching: Lessons from the International Reviews into Effective Professional Development*, London: Teacher Development Trust.

Corelli College website (2015) www.corellicollege.org.uk/.

Coughlan, S. (2015) Digital dependence 'eroding human memory', BBC Education and Family, http://www.bbc.co.uk/news/education-34454264.

Couglan, S. (2015) Can you make schools integrate? 27th July http://www.bing.com/search?q=Couglan%2C+S.+%282015%29.+Can+you+make+schools+integrate.

Covey, S. (2006) *The Speed of Trust*, London: Simon and Schuster.

Crick, R., Haigney, D., Huang, S., Goldspink, C. and Coburn, T. (2013) Learning power in the work place: the effective Lifelong Learning Inventory (ELLI) and its reliability and validity and implications for learning and development, *International Journal of Human Resource Management*, 24 (2): 2255–72.

Croft, J. (2015) *Collaborative Overreach: Why Collaboration Probably isn't key to the Next Phase of School Reform*, London: Centre for the Study of Market Reform of Education.

Csikszentmihalyi, M. (2003) *Good Business: Leadership, Flow and the Making of Meaning*, London: Hodder and Stoughton.

Cubillo, L. and Brown, M. (2003) Women into educational leadership and management: international differences? *Journal of Educational Administration,* 41 (3): 278–91.

Daly, A. (2010) Mapping the terrain: social network theory and educational change, in A. Daly (ed.), *Social Network Theory and Educational Change*, Cambridge, MA: Harvard Education Press.

Dantley, M. E. (2005) African American spirituality and Cornel West's notions of prophetic pragmatism: restructuring educational leadership in American urban schools, *Educational Administration Quarterly,* 41(4): 651–74.

Darling-Hammond, L. (2010) *The Flat World and Education: How America's Commitment to Equity will Determine Our Future*, New York: Teachers College Press.

Datnow, A., Park, V. and Lewis, B. (2013) Affordances and constraints in the context of teacher collaboration for the purpose of data use, *Journal of Educational Administration*, 51 (3): 341–62.

Day, C. and Gu, Q. (2014) *Resilient Teachers, Resilient Schools*, London: Routledge.

Day, C. and Sammons, P. (2013) *Successful Leadership: A Review of the International Literature*, Reading: CfBT Education Trust.

Day, C., Sammons, P., Hopkins, D., Harris, A., Leithwood, K., Gu, Q., Brown, E., Ahtaridou, E. and Kington, A. (2009) *The Impact of School Leadership on Pupil Outcomes*: Final report, Nottingham: Department for Education.

Day, C., Sammons, P., Leithwood, K., Hopkins, D., Gu, Q., Brown, E. and Ahtaridou, E. (2011) *Successful School Leadership: Linking with Learning*, Maidenhead: Open University Press.

De Heus, P. and Diekstra, R. (1999) Do teachers burnout more easily? A comparison of teachers with other social professionals on work stress and burnout symptoms, in B. Vandenbergghe and A. Huberman (eds), *Understanding and Preventing Teacher* Burnout, New York: Cambridge University Press.

De Wolf, I. F. and Janssens, F. J. G. (2007) Effects and side effects of inspections and accountability in education: an overview of empirical studies, *Oxford Review of Education,* 33: 379–96.

Dean, M. (2010) *Governmentality Power and Rule in Modern Society*, 2nd edn, Thousand Oaks, CA: Sage.

Department for Children, Schools and Families (2008) *The Impact of Parental Involvement on Children's Education*, Nottingham: DCSF Publications.

Department for Children, Schools and Families (DCFS) (2007) *Guidance on the Duty to Promote Community Cohesion*, London: DCFS.

Department for Education (2010) *The Importance of Teaching: The Schools White Paper*, London: DfE.

Department for Education (2013) *Implementing Curriculum and Qualifications Reform: Proposals from the 2013 Fellowship Commission,* London: DfE.

Department for Education (2014a) *Academies Annual Report: Academic Year 2012-13*, London: DfE.

Department for Education (2014b) *Do Academies Make use of Their Autonomy? Research Report*, London: DfE.

Department for Education (2014c) *Guidance on Promoting British Values in Schools*.

Department for Education (2015d) *A World-class Teaching Profession: Government Consultation Response*, DfE Reference: DFE-00110-2015.

Department for Education (2015e) *Government Response to the Workload Challenge*, London: DfE.

Department for Education (2015f) http://www.gov.uk/government/statistics/schools-in-academy-chains-and-las-performance-measures.

Department for Education (2015g) *Workload Challenge: Analysis of Responses*, London: DfE.

Department for Education (2015h) *Reducing Teachers' Workload*, London: DfE.

Department for Education (2015i) Response to Freedom of Information request from R. Hill, https://www.whatdotheyknow.com/request/number_of_multi_academy_trusts_a?nocache=incoming-699386#incoming-699386.

Department for Education (2015j) Letter from Rt Hon Nicky Morgan MP to Sir Michael Wilshaw, 22 January, https://www.gov.uk/government/uploads/system/uploads/attachment_data/file/397810/Nicky_Morgan_letter_to_Ofsted.pdf.

Department for Education (2015k) Measuring the performance of schools within academy chains and local authorities (Statistical Working Paper) https://www.gov.uk/government/statistics/schools-in-academy-chains-and-las-performance-measures.

Department for Education (2016) *Educational Excellence Everywhere*, London: DfE.

Department of Health (2014) *Compendium of Factsheets: Wellbeing Across the Lifecourse*, London: DoH.

Department for Education and Skills (2002) Developing the role of school support staff: consultation, https://www.education.gov.uk/consultations/index.cfm?action=conResults&consultationId=1198&external=no&menu=3.

Desforges, C. with Abouchaar, A. (2003) *The Impact of Parental Involvement, Parental Support and Family Education on Pupil Achievement: A Literature Review*, London: DfES.

Di Liberto, A. Schivardi, F. and Sulis, G. (2014) *Managerial Practices and Students' Performance*, Rome: Economic Policy Sixtieth Panel Meeting.

Dimaggio, P. J. and Powell, W. W. (1983) The iron cage revisited: institutional isomorphism and collective rationality in organizational fields, *American Sociological Review*, 48: 147–60.

Dimmock, C. (2012) *Leadership, Capacity Building and School Improvement: Concepts, Themes and Impact*, London: Routledge.

Dimmock, C. (1993) School-based management and linkage with the curriculum, in C. Dimmock (ed.), *School-Based Management and Effectiveness*, 1–21, London: Routledge.

Dinham, S. (2008) *How to Get Your School Moving and Improving: An Evidence-based Approach*, Melbourne: ACER Press.

Dodd, V. (2009) MPs investigate anti-extremism programme after spying claims, http://www.guardian.co.uk/uk/2009/oct/18/prevent-extremism-muslims-information-allegations.

Duchscher, J. E. B. and Cowin, L. (2004) Multigenerational nurses in the workplace, *Journal of Nursing Administration*, 34 (11): 493–501.

Dunford, J., Hill, R., Parish, N. and Sandals, L. (2013) *Establishing and Leading New Types of School: Challenges and Opportunities for Leaders and Leadership*, Nottingham: NCSL.

Dunham, J. (1995) *Effective School Management*, London: Routledge.

Dweck, C. (2006) *Mindset: The New Psychology of Success*, London: Random House.

Dweck, C. (2006) *Mindset: How You Can Fulfil Your Potential*, New York: Random House.

Eagly, A. H. and Carli, L. L. (2007) Women and the labyrinth of leadership, *Harvard Business Review,* 85 (9): 62.

Earley, P. (2000) Monitoring, managing or meddling? Governing bodies and the evaluation of school performance, *Educational Management and Administration*, 28 (2): 199–210.

Earley, P. (2013) *Exploring the School Leadership Landscape: Changing Demands, Changing Realities*, London: Bloomsbury Academic.

Earley, P., Higham, R., Allen, R., Allen, T., Howson, J., Nelson, R., Rawar, S., Lynch, S., Morton, L., Mehta, P. and Sims, D. (2012) *Review of the School Leadership Landscape*, Nottingham: NCSL.

Earley, P. and Porritt, V. (2013) Evaluating the impact of professional development: the need for a student-focused approach, *Professional Development in Education,* 40 (1): 112–29.

Earley, P. and Porritt, V. (eds) (2009) *Effective Practices in Continuing Professional Development: Lessons from Schools*, London: IOE.

Earley, P. and Weindling, D. (2004) *Understanding School Leadership*, London: Sage.

Earley, P. and Weindling, D. (2006) Consultant leaders: a new role for headteachers? *School Leadership and Management*, 26 (1): 37–53.

Edelstein, F. S. (2015). Advocates and partners for education excellence: a 21st century role for mayors, in B. S. Cooper, J. G. Cibulka and L. D. Fusarelli (eds), *Handbook of Education Politics and Policy*, 2nd ed, 62–85, London: Routledge.

Edge, K. (2014) A review of the empirical generations at work research: implications for school leaders and future research, *School Leadership and Management,* 34 (2): 136–55.

Education Endowment Foundation (2015) *About the EEF*, https://educationendowmentfoundation. org.uk/about/.

Education Support Network (2015) *YouGov Survey Results*, www.educationsupportpartnership.org. uk/inspection-survey-0/.

Education Support Partnership (2016) New research suggests good leadership is the major contributor to reducing education job strain as charity launches formal consultation on recruitment and retention, https://www.educationsupportpartnership.org.uk/new-research-suggests-good-leadership-major-contributor-reducing-education-job-strain-charit.

Education Week (2015) *Budget cuts threaten Institute of Education Sciences*, http://blogs.edweek. org/edweek/inside-school-research/2015/09/budget_cuts_threaten_institute.html.

Ehren, M., Perryman, J. and Shackleton, N. (2014) Setting expectations for good education: how Dutch school inspections drive improvement, *School Effectiveness and School Improvement*: *An International Journal of Research, Policy and Practice*, 26 (2): 296–327.

Ehren, M. C. M. and Perryman, J. (2017, forthcoming) School inspections in a polycentric context; Ofsted and a self-improving school system, *Journal of Education Policy*.

Ehren, M. C. M., Janssens, F. J. G., Brown, M., McNamara, G., O'Hara, J. and Shevlin, P. (2017, forthcoming) Emerging models of school inspections; Shifting roles and responsibilities of Inspectorates of Education in a polycentric system, *Oxford Review of Education*.

Ehren, M. C. M. and Visscher, A. J. (2008) The Relationship between school inspections, school characteristics and school improvement, *British Journal of Educational Studies*, 56 (2): 205–27

Ely, R. J., Stone, P. and Ammerman, C. (2014) Rethink what you 'know' about high-achieving women, *Harvard Business Review*, 92 (12), 100–9.

Enthoven, M. and de Bruijn, E. (2010) Beyond locality: the creation of public practice-based knowledge through practitioner research in professional learning communities and communities of practice. A review of three books on practitioner research and professional communities, *Educational Action Research*, 18 (2): 289–98.

Epstein, J. (1995) School, family, community partnerships: caring for children, *Phi Delta Kappan*, 76: 701–12.

Epstein, J. and Sheldon, S. (2006) 'Moving forward: ideas for research on school, family, and community partnerships', in C. Conrad and R. Serlin (eds), *SAGE Handbook for Research in Education: Engaging Ideas and Enriching Inquiry*, 117–38, Thousand Oaks, CA: SAGE.

Etzioni, A. (1995) The spirit of community: a framework for intervention, *Harvard Educational Review*, 7 (4): 1–17.

Evans, B. and Reid, J. (2014) *Resilient Life: The Art of Living Dangerously*, Cambridge: Polity Press.

Evans, R. (2001) *The Human Side of School Change: Reform, Resistance and the Real-life Problems of Innovation*, San Francisco: Jossey-Bass Education.

Evers, J. and Kneyber, R. (eds) (2016) *Flip the System: Changing Education form the Ground up*, London: Routledge.

Feiler, A. (2010) *Engaging 'Hard To Reach' Parents*, Chichester: Wiley-Blackwell.

Feinstein, L. (ed.) (2015) *Social and Emotional Learning: Skills for Life and Work*, London: Routledge.

Feintuck, M. (2010) Regulatory rationales beyond the economic: in search of public interest, in R. Baldwin, M. Cave and M. Lodge (eds), *The Oxford Handbook of Regulation*, 39–63, Oxford: Oxford University Press.

Feintuck, M. and Stevens, R. (2013) *School Admissions and Accountability: Planning, Choice or Chance?* Bristol: Policy Press.

Fernandez, C. and Yoshida, M. (2004) *Lesson Study: A Japanese Approach to Improving Mathematics Teaching and Learning*, Mahwah, Lawrence Erlbaum Associates, Inc.

Fernandez, R., Bustamante, R. M., Combs, J. P. and Martinez-Garcia, C. (2015) Career experiences of Latino/a secondary principals in suburban school districts, *NCPEA International Journal of Educational Leadership Preparation,* 10 (21): 60–76.

Fielding, M., Bragg, S., Craig, J., Cunningham, I., Eraut, M., Gillinson. S., Horne. M., Robinson. C. and Thorp, J. (2005) *Factors Influencing the Transfer of Good Practice*, Nottingham: DFES Publications.

Finch, A., Haldenby, A., Thorpe, L., Watkin, B. and Zuccollo, J. (2014) *Plan A+ 2014: The Unfinished Revolution*, Reform/SSAT.

Finnigan, K. and Daly, A. (2011) The ebb and flow of social network ties between district leaders under high stakes accountability, *American Educational Research Journal*, 48 (1): 39–79.

Finnigan, K. and Daly, A. (2012) Exploring the space between social networks, trust and urban school district leaders, *Journal of School Leadership*, 22: 493–530.

Flyvbjerg, B. (2001) *Making Social Science Matter*, Cambridge: Cambridge University Press.

Foreign Policy (2009) *The 2008 Global Cities Index* (November/December 2008).

Foresight Mental Capital and Well-being Project (2008) *Making the Most of Ourselves in the 21st Century,* London: Government Office for Science.

Freire, P. (1993) *Pedagogy of the City*, New York: Continuum.

Fullan, M. (2005) 'Leadership across the system', http://www.michaelfullan.ca/media/13396061760.pdf.

Fullan, M. (2008) *The Six Secrets of Change*, San Francisco: Jossey-Bass.

Fullan, M. (2010) The big ideas behind whole system reform, *Education Canada*, 50: 3, Canadian Educational Association.

Fullan, M. (2014), *The Principal: Three Keys to Maximizing Impact*, San Francisco: Jossey-Bass.

Fullan, M., Rincón-Gallardo, S. and Hargreaves, A. (2015) Professional capital as accountability, *Education Policy Analysis Archives*, 23 (15): 1–18.

Fuller, K. (2009) Women secondary head teachers: alive and well in Birmingham at the beginning of the twenty-first century, *Management in Education,* 23 (1): 19–31.

Fuller, K. (2014) Gendered educational leadership: beneath the monoglossic façade, *Gender and Education,* 26 (4): 321–37.

Future Leaders Trust (2016) *Heads Up – Meeting the Challenge of Head Teacher Recruitment*, London: Future Leaders Trust.

Garner, R. (2015a) Quakers go to war over 'bellicose' school pack that promotes 'pro-military values', http://www.independent.co.uk/news/education/education-news/quakers-go-to-war-over-bellicose-school-pack-that-promotes-promilitary-values-10081151.html#.

Garner, R. (2015b) Ofsted must focus on how 'well rounded' pupils are and not just exam results, says CBI chief, http://www.independent.co.uk/news/education/education-news/ofsted-must-focus-on-how-well-rounded-pupils-are-and-not-just-exam-results-says-cbi-chief-10308040.html#.

Gawande, A. (2007) *Better: A Surgeon's Notes on Performance*, New York: Profile Books.

Georgiou, S. (1997) Parental involvement: Definition and outcomes. *Social Psychology of Education*, 1(3): 189–209.

Gibton, D. (2004) *Legalized Leadership: Law-based Educational Reform in England and what it does to School Leadership and Headteachers*, London: Institute of Education, University of London.

Gibton, D. (2011) Post-2000 law-based educational governance in Israel: from equality to diversity? *Education Management, Administration and Leadership*, 39 (4): 434–54.

Gibton, D. (2013) *Law, Education, Politics, Fairness: England's Extreme Legislation for Education Reform*, London: IOE Press.

Gilbert, C. (2012) *Towards a Self-improving School System: School Accountability,* Nottingham: NCSL.

Gillespie, B. B. and Temple, H. S. (2011) *Good Enough is the New Perfect: Findings Happiness and Success in Modern Motherhood*, Toronto, Canada: Harlequin.

Glasman, N. and Crowson, R. (2001) Re-examining relations and a sense of place between schools and their constituents, *Peabody Journal of Education*, 76 (2): 1–8.

Glatter, R. (2002) Governance, autonomy and accountability in education, in T. Bush and L. Bell (eds), *The Principles and Practice of Educational Management*, 225–40, London: Sage.

Glatter, R. (2006) Leadership and organization in education: time for a re-orientation? *School Leadership and Management*, 26 (1): 69–83.

Glatter, R. (2012) Persistent preoccupations: the rise and rise of school autonomy and accountability in England, *Educational Management, Administration and Leadership*, 40 (5): 559–75.

Glatter, R. Woods, P. and Bagley, C. (1997) 'Diversity, differentiation and hierarchy: school choice and parental preferences', in R. Glatter, P. Woods and C. Bagley (eds), *Choice and Diversity in Schooling: Perspectives and Prospects*, 7–28, London: Routledge.

Godfrey, D. (2016) Leadership of schools as research-led organisations in the English educational environment cultivating a research-engaged school culture, *Educational Management, Administration and Leadership*, 44 (2): 301–21.

Godfrey, D. and Rowland, M. (2015) *Lambeth Connecting Knowledge: Final Report*, London Schools Excellence Fund (unpublished).

Goldacre, B. (2013) Building evidence into education, https://www.gov.uk/government/news/building-evidence-into-education.

Goodall, J. (2013) Parental engagement to support children's learning: a six point model, *School Leadership and Management*, 33 (2): 133–50.

Goodall, J. (2015) Ofsted's judgement of parental engagement: a justification of its place in leadership and management, *Management in Education*, 29 (4): 172–7.

Goodall, J. and Montgomery, C. (2014) Parental involvement to parental engagement: a continuum, *Educational Review*, 66 (4): 399–410.

Gorard, S. (2013) Growth of academies and free schools reinforces student segregation, *The Conversation*, theconversation.com/growth-ofacademies-and-free-schools-reinforces-studentsegregation-19411.

Gorard, S. (n.d.) Education can compensate for society – a bit, http://eprints.bham.ac.uk/304/1/Gorard_2010_British_Journal_of_Educational_Studies.pdf.

Gorard, S. and Huat See, B. (2013) *Do Parental Involvement Interventions Increase Attainment? A Review of the Evidence*, London: Nuffield Foundation.

Gove, M. (2011) quoted in http://www.telegraph.co.uk/education/educationnews/8396823/Michael-Gove-pupils-should-read-50-books-a-year.html.

Gray, S. P. and Streshly, W. A. (2008) *From Good Schools to Great Schools: What Their Principals Do Well*, Thousand Oaks, CA: Corwin Press.

Greany T. (2014) *Are we Nearly there yet?: Progress, Issues and Possible Next Steps for a Self-improving School System*, London: IOE Press.

Greany, T. (2015a) 'How can evidence inform teaching and decision making across 21,000 autonomous schools?: learning from the Journey in England', in C. Brown (ed.), *Leading the Use of Research and Evidence in Schools*, 11–29, London: Institute of Education Press.

Greany, T. (2015b) More fragmented, and yet more networked: analysing the responses of two local authorities in England to the coalition's 'self-improving school-led system' reforms, *London Review of Education*, 13 (2): 125–43.

Greany, T. (2015c) *The Self-Improving System in England: A Review of Evidence and Thinking*, Leicester: Association of School and College Leaders.

Greany, T. and Cheong, Y. (eds) (2016) School autonomy and 21st century learning: special issue, *International Journal of Education Management*, 30: 7.

Greany, T. and Waterhouse, J. (2016) Rebels against the system: leadership agency and curriculum innovation in the context of school autonomy and accountability in England, in 'School autonomy and 21st century learning: special issue', *International Journal of Education Management*, 30: 7.

Greany, T. and Scott, J. (2014) *Conflicts of Interest in Academy Sponsorship Arrangements: A Report for the Education Select Committee*, London: IoE.

Greaves, G., Macmillan, L. and Sibieta, L. (2014) *Lessons from London Schools for Attainment Gaps and Social Mobility,* Social Mobility and Child Poverty Commission Research report, London: Institute for Fiscal Studies and Institute of Education.

Grogan, M. and Brunner, C. C. (2005) Women leading systems: what the latest facts and figures say about women in the superintendency today, *School Administrator,* 62 (2): 46.

Gronn, P. and Lacey, K. (2004) Positioning oneself for leadership: feelings of vulnerability among aspirant school principals, *School Leadership and Management,* 24 (4): 405–24.

Gu, Q., Rea, S., Smethem, L., Dunford, J., Varley, M. and Sammons, P. (2015) *Teaching Schools Evaluation: Final Report*, London: Department for Education.

Gunter, H. (2005) Conceptualising research in educational leadership, *Educational Management, Administration and Leadership*, 33 (2): 165–80.

Gurney-Read (2015) Nicky Morgan: being academic 'isn't enough in the modern world'. Daily Telegraph 16 March, http://www.telegraph.co.uk/education/educationnews/11475816/Nicky-Morgan-being-academic-isnt-enough-in-the-modern-world.html.

Guskey, T. (2000) *Evaluating Professional Development*, New York: Corwin.

Halbert, J., Kaser, L. and Koehn, D. (2011) Spirals of inquiry, building professional inquiry to foster student learning, paper presented at ICSEI 2011, Limassol, Cyprus.

Hallinger, P. (2005) *Instructional Leadership and the School Principal: A Passing Fancy that Refuses to go Away*, Thailand: College of Management, Mahidol University.

Hallinger, P. and Heck, R. (2003) Understanding the contribution of leadership to school improvement, in M. Wallace and L. Poulson (eds), *Learning to Read Critically in Educational Leadership and Management*, 215–35, London: Sage.

Hallinger, P. and Heck, R. (2010) Collaborative leadership and school improvement: understanding the impact on school capacity and student learning, *School Leadership and Management*, 30 (2): 95–110.

Hallinger, P. (2012) Leadership for 21st century schools: from instructional leadership to leadership for learning, Presentation to Italian Ministry of Education, December.

Halpern, D. F. (2008) Nurturing careers in psychology: combining work and family, *Educational Psychology Review,* 20 (1): 57–64.

Hammersley-Fletcher, L. (2015) Value(s)-driven decision-making. The ethics work of English headteachers within discourses of constraint, *Educational Management, Administration and Leadership*, 43 (2): 198–213.

Hansen, M. T. (1999) The search-transfer problem: the role of weak ties in sharing knowledge across organization subunits, *Administrative Science Quarterly*, 44, (1): 82–111.

Hanushek, E. A., Link, S. and Woessmann, L. (2012) Does school autonomy make sense everywhere? panel estimates from PISA, *Journal of Development Economics*, 296: 212–32.

Hargreaves, A. (2003) *Leadership for Transformation within the London Challenge*, London: Annual Lecture of the London Leadership Centre, 7 May.

Hargreaves, A. (2016) *Autonomy and Transparency: Two Good Ideas Gone Bad*, in J. Evers and R. Kneyber (eds) (2016) *Flip the System: Changing Education from the Ground up,* 120–33, London: Routledge.

Hargreaves, A. and Fullan, M. (2012) *Professional Capital: Transforming Teaching in Every School*, London: Routledge.

Hargreaves, A. and Harris, A. (2012) *Performance Beyond Expectations*, Nottingham: NCSL.

Hargreaves, A. and Shirley, D. (2009) *The Fourth Way: The Inspiring Future for Educational Change*, Thousand Oaks, CA: Corwin.

Hargreaves, D. (2008) *The Four Deeps in Action*, London: SSAT.

Hargreaves, D. (2010) *Creating a Self-improving School System*, Nottingham: NCSL.

Hargreaves, D. (2011) *Leading a Self-improving School System*, Nottingham: NCSL.

Hargreaves, D. (2012a) *A Self-improving School System in International Context*, Nottingham: NCSL.

Hargreaves, D. (2012b) *A Self-improving School System: Towards Maturity*, Nottingham: NCSL.

Harris, A. and Jones, M. (2012) *Connecting Professional Learning*, Nottingham: NCSL.

Harris, A. and Spillane, J. (2008) Distributed leadership through the looking glass, *Management in Education*, 22 (1): 31–4.

Harris, J. (1 February 2016) Long hours, endless admin and angry parents – why schools just can't get the teachers, *The Guardian*. Retrieved from http://www.theguardian.com/.

Hartley, D. (2010) Paradigms: how far does research in distributed leadership 'stretch'? *Educational Management, Administration and Leadership*, 38 (3): 271–85.

Hatcher, R. (2014) Local Authorities and the school system: the new authority-wide structures, *Educational Management, Administration and Leadership*, 42 (3): 355–71.

Hattie, J. (2008) *Visible Learning: A Synthesis of over 800 Meta-analyses Relating to Achievement*, London: Routledge.

Hattie, J. (2011a) *Visible Learning for Teachers*, London: Routledge.

Hattie, J. (2011b) *Visible Learning: Maximising Impact on Learning*, New York and London: Routledge.

Hattie, J. (2015a) *The Politics of Collective Expertise*, London: Pearson.

Hattie, J. (2015b) *What Works Best in Education: The Politics of Collaborative Expertise*, London: Pearson.

Hauerwas, S. (2001) *Virtues in Public, Christian Existence Today*, Grand Rapids: Brazos Press.

Hawley, W. and Valli, L. (1999) The essentials of professional development: a new consensus, in L. Darling-Hammond and G. Sykes (eds), *Teaching as the Learning Profession: Handbook of Policy and Practice,* 127–50, San Francisco: Jossey-Bass.

Health and Safety at Work Act (1974) http://www.legislation.gov.uk/ukpga/1974/37/contents.

Health and Safety Executive (2008) Working Together to Reduce Stress at Work, http://www.hse.gov.uk/pubns/indg424.pdf.

Health and Safety Executive (2014) Stress – Legal Requirements, http://www.hse.gov.uk/stress/furtheradvice/legalresponsibility.htm.

Health and Safety Executive (HSE) The Management Standards, http://www.hse.gov.uk/stress/standards.

Heifetz, R. A. (2002) *Leadership on the Line: Staying Alive through the Dangers of Leading*, Boston, MA: Harvard Business School.

Hewlett, S. A. and Luce, C. B. (2006) Extreme jobs – the dangerous allure of the 70-hour workweek, *Harvard Business Review,* 84 (12): 49–59.

Higgins, S., Katsipataki, M. and Coleman, R. (2014) *Reading at the Transition: Interim Evidence Brief*, https://educationendowmentfoundation.org.uk/uploads/pdf/EEF_Interim_Evidence_Brief_-_Reading_at_the_Transition.pdf.

Higgins, S., Katsipataki, M., Coleman, R., Henderson, P., Major, L. E. and Coe, R. (2015) *The Sutton Trust-Education Endowment Foundation Teaching and Learning Toolkit*, London: Education Endowment Foundation.

Higgins, S., Xiao, Z. and Katsipataki, M. (2012) *The Impact of Digital Technology on Learning: A Summary for the Educational Endowment Foundation*, Durham University, https://educationendowmentfoundation.org.uk/uploads/pdf/The_Impact_of_Digital_Technologies_on_Learning_(2012).pdf.

Higham, R. (2013) School autonomy, government control and a changing policy landscape, in P. Earley, *Exploring the School Leadership Landscape: Changing Demands, Changing Realities*, 11–32, London: Bloomsbury Academic.

Higham, R. (2014) 'Who owns our schools?': an analysis of the governance of free schools in England, *Educational Management, Administration and Leadership*, 42 (3): 404–22.

Higham, R. Hopkins, D. and Matthews, P. (2009) *System Leadership in Practice,* Maidenhead: Open University Press.

Hill, R. (2015a) Written evidence to the parliamentary Education Committee (RSC0001) http://data.parliament.uk/writtenevidence/committeeevidence.svc/evidencedocument/education-committee/therole-of-regional-schools-commissioners/written/18836.pdf.

Hill, R. (2015b) The rise and rise of Multi-Academy Trusts, blog http://roberthilleducationblog.com/ posted on 31 August 2015.

Hill, R., Dunford, J., Parish, N., Rea, S. and Sandals, L. (2012) *The Growth of Academy Chains: Implications for Leaders and Leadership*, Nottingham: NCSL.

Hirsch, E. D. (1999) *The Schools We Need: And Why We Don't Have Them*, New York: Anchor Books.

Hopkins, D. (2005) *A Short Primer on System Leadership*, Keynote address given to the Congress of the Swiss Society for Research in Education on 'Educational Leadership and the Changing School', Lugano, Switzerland – Thursday, 22 September.

Hopkins, D., Stringfield, S., Harris, A., Stoll, L. and Mackay, T. (2014) School and system improvement: a state of the art review, *School Effectiveness and School Improvement*, 25 (2): 257–81.

Horsford, S. D. (2012) This bridge called my leadership: an essay on Black women as bridge leaders in education, *International Journal of Qualitative Studies in Education,* 25 (1): 11–22.

House of Commons Education Committee (2013) *School Partnerships and Cooperation*: Fourth Report of Session 2013–14, Volume I.

House of Commons Education Committee (2014) *Underachievement in Education by White Working Class Children*, London: The Stationery Office.

House of Commons Education Committee (2015) *Academies and Free Schools*, London: The Stationery Office.

House of Commons Education Select Committee (2015) *Academies and Free Schools*, London: Fourth report of session 2014–15, HC 258.

House of Commons Education Committee (2016) *The Role of Regional Schools Commissioners*, London: The Stationery Office.

Howson, J. and Sprigade, A. (2008) *14th Annual Report on the State of the Labour Market for Senior Staff in Schools in England and Wales*, London: Education Data Surveys at TSL Education Limited.

Hubbard, L., Mehen, H. and Stein, M. (2006) *Reform as Learning*, New York, NY: Routledge.

Husbands, C. (2015) Which Knowledge Matters Most?, in J. Simons and N. Porter (eds), *Knowledge and the Curriculum A Collection of Essays to Accompany E. D. Hirsch's Lecture at Policy Exchange,* 43–50, London: Policy Exchange.

Hutchings, M. (2015) *Exam Factories? The Impact of Accountability Measures on Children and Young People*, London: National Union of Teachers.

Hutchings, M., Greenwood, C., Hollingworth, S., Mansaray, A., Rose, A., Minty, S. and Glass, K. (2012) *Evaluation of the City Challenge Programme*, Research Report RR215, London: DfE.

Huysman, M. (1999) Balancing biases: a critical review of the literature on organizational learning, in M. Easterby-Smith, J. Burgoyne and L. Araujo (eds), *Organizational Learning and the Learning Organization*, 59–74, London: Sage.

Institute for Government (2012) *The Development of Quasi-markets in Secondary Education.*

Institute of Education Sciences (2015) *Search Funded Research Grants and Opportunities*, http://ies.ed.gov/funding/grantsearch/index.asp.

Jaffer, N. (2015) *Guardian*, 20 June 2015, 6.

James, C., Brammer, S., Conolly, M., Fertig, M., James, J. and Jones, J. (2011) School governing bodies in England under pressure: the effects of socio-economic context and school performance, *Educational Management Administration and Leadership*, 39 (4): 414–34.

Jensen, B., Hunter, A., Sonnemann, J. and Burns, T. (2012) *Catching Up: Learning from the Best School Systems in East Asia*, Melbourne: Grattan Institute.

Jensen, B., Sonnemann, J., Roberts-Hull, K. and Hunter, A. (2016) *Beyond PD: Teacher Professional Learning in High-Performing Systems*, Washington, DC: National Center on Education and the Economy.

Johnson, L. and Campbell-Stephens, R. (2010) Investing in diversity in London schools: leadership preparation for black and global majority educators, *Urban Education,* 45 (6): 840–70.

Jones, R. and Treanor, J. (2014) Who do we want to bank with? John Lewis, of course, http://www.bbc.co.uk/corporate2/insidethebbc/howwework/reports/trust_and_impartiality.html.

Kamp, A. (2013) *Rethinking Learning Networks: Collaborative Possibilities for a Deleuzian Century*, London: Peter Lang Publishers.

Kaparou, M. and Bush, T. (2007) Invisible barriers: the career progress of women secondary school principals in Greece, *Compare*, 37 (2): 221–37.

Kärkkäinen, K. (2012) *Bringing about Curriculum Innovations: Implicit Approaches in the OECD*, OECD Education Working Paper No. 82, Paris: OECD.

Kaspersky Lab (2015) The Rise and Impact of Digital Amnesia: Why we need to protect what we no longer remember. https://blog.kaspersky.com/files/2015/06/005-Kaspersky-Digital-Amnesia-19.6.15.pdf.

Kennedy, M. (1999) Infusing educational decision making with research, in G. J. Cizek (ed.), *Handbook of Educational Policy*, 54–81, San Diego, CA: Academic Press.

Kingdon, J. W. (2003) *Agendas, Alternatives, and Public Policies*, 2nd edn, New York: Addison-Wesley.

Kirschner, P. (2015) The disturbing facts about Digital Natives, 20 October. Paul Kirschner: Blog, http://portal.ou.nl/nl/web/pki/blog/-/blogs/the-disturbing-facts-about-digital-natives.

Kivimaki, M. (2015) Long working hours and risk of coronary heart disease and stroke: a systematic review and meta-analysis of published and unpublished data for 603,838 individuals, *The Lancet*, 386 (10005): 1739–46.

Kotter, J. (1996) *Leading Change*, Harvard, MA: Harvard Business Review Press.

Krasikova, D., Green, S. and LeBreton, J. (2013) Destructive leadership: a theoretical review, integration, and future research agenda, *Journal of Management*, 39: 1308–38.

Kunreuther, F. (2003) The changing of the guard: what generational differences tell us about social-change organizations, *Nonprofit and Voluntary Sector Quarterly,* 32 (3): 450–57.

Lacey, C. (1977) *The Socialization of Teachers*, London: Methuen.

Lamothe, L. and Denis, J.-L. (2007) The emergence of new organizational forms: networks of integrated services in health care, in M. Wallace, M. Fertig and E. Schneller (eds), *Managing Change in the Public Services*, 57–74, Oxford: Blackwell Publishing.

Le Grand, J. (2005) Inequality, choice and public services, in A. Giddens and P. Diamond (eds), *The New Egalitarianism*, 200–10, Cambridge, UK: Polity Press.

Leadbeater, C. and Wong, A. (2010) *Learning from the Extremes*, San Jose, CA: Cisco.

Leithwood, K. (1994) Leadership for school restructuring, *Educational Administration Quarterly*, 30 (4): 498–518.

Leithwood, K. and Seashore Louis, K. (2012) *Linking Leadership to Student Learning*, San Francisco: Jossey-Bass.

Leithwood, K., Day, C., Sammons, P., Harris, A. and Hopkins, D. (2006) *Seven Strong Claims about Successful School Leadership*, Nottingham: NCSL.

Leithwood, K., Day, C., Sammons, P., Harris, A. and Hopkins, D. (2006) *Successful School Leadership: What it is and How it Influences Pupil Learning*, Nottingham: NCSL.

Lekka, C. (2011) *High Reliability Organisations*, London: HSE.

Levacic, R. (1995) *Local Management of Schools: Analysis and Practice*, Buckingham: Open University Press.

Levacic, R. and Woods, P. (2000) The impact of quasi-markets and performance regulation on socially disadvantaged schools. Paper presented at the annual meeting of the *American Educational Research Association*, 24–28 April, New-Orleans, LA.

Levin, B. (2008) *How to Change 5000 Schools*, Harvard, MA: Harvard Educational Press.

Levin, B. (2013) *Confident School Leadership: A Canadian Perspective*, Nottingham: NCSL.

Levin, H. M. (2015) Issues in educational privatization, in H. F. Ladd and M. E. Goertz (eds), *Handbook of Research in Education Finance and Policy*, 411–22, New York and London: Routledge.

Lilly, J., Peacock, A., Shoveller, S. and Struthers, D. (2014) *Beyond Levels: Alternative Assessment Approaches Developed by Teaching Schools*, Nottingham: National College for Teaching and Leadership.

Lipman-Blumen, J. (2005) *The Allure of Toxic Leaders: Why we Follow Destructive Bosses and Corrupt Politicians – and how we can Survive them'*, New York: Oxford University Press.

Little, A. (2015) *An Intelligent Person's Guide to Education*, London: Bloomsbury.

London Borough of Tower Hamlets (2000/2001) *Strategic Plan for the Education Service 1998-2002: Year 3 implementation*, London: Borough of Tower Hamlets.

London Borough of Tower Hamlets (2002a) *Tower Hamlets Council Strategic Plan 2002–2006, Year 1 (2002–2003) Annual Report Learning,* London: Tower Hamlets Achievement and Leisure Scrutiny Panel.

London Borough of Tower Hamlets (2002b) *Strategic Plan for the Education Service 2002-2006*, London: Borough of Tower Hamlets.

London Borough of Tower Hamlets (2006a) *Children and Young People's Plan, 2006-2009*, London: Borough of Tower Hamlets.

London Borough of Tower Hamlets (2006b) *Children and Young People's Plan, 2009-2012*, London: Borough of Tower Hamlets.

London Borough of Tower Hamlets (2012a) *Children and Families Plan, 2012-2015*, London: Borough of Tower Hamlets.

London Borough of Tower Hamlets (2012b) *Educational Achievements and Progress Briefing, 26 January 2012*, London: Borough of Tower Hamlets.

London Leadership Strategy (2014) *Nine Pillars of Greatness*, London: Department for Education.

Louis, K. S. (2007) Trust and improvement in schools, *Journal of Educational Change*, 8 (1): 1–24.

Louis, K. S., Leithwood, K., Wahlstrom, K. L. and Anderson, S. E. (2010) *Learning from Leadership: Investigating the Links to Improved Student Learning*, Minnesota: The Wallace Foundation.

Lubienski, C. (2009) *Do Quasi-markets Foster Innovation in Education?: A Comparative Perspective*, OECD Education Working Papers, No. 25, Paris: OECD.

Luckin, R., Bligh, B., Manches, A., Ainsworth, S., Crook C. and Noss, R. (2012) *Decoding Learning: The Proof, Promise and Potential of Digital Education*, London: Nesta. http://nesta.org.uk/publications/decoding-learning.

Lumby, J. (2014) School leaders' gender strategies: caught in a discriminatory web, *Educational Management, Administration and Leadership*, 40 (4): 541–57.

Lumby, J. (2015) Distributive leadership: the uses and abuses of power, *Educational Management, Administration and Leadership,* 41 (5): 581–97.

Lumby, J. and English, F. (2010) *Leadership as Lunacy and other Metaphors for Educational Leadership*, Thousand Oaks, CA: Corwin.

Lumby, J. and Azaola, M. C. (2014) Women principals in South Africa: gender, mothering and leadership, *British Educational Research Journal,* 40 (1): 30–44.

Lunenburg, F. (2011) Self-efficacy in the workplace: implications for motivation and performance, *International Journal of Management, Business and Administration*, 14 (1): 1–6.

Lupton, R. and Thomson, S. (2015) *The Coalition's Record on Schools: Policy, Spending and Outcomes 2010-2015*, Social Policy in a Cold Climate, Working Paper 13, Joseph Rowntree Foundation/Nuffield Foundation/Trust for London.

MacBeath, J. (2006) A story of change: growing leadership for learning, *Journal of Educational Change,* 7 (1): 33–46.

MacBeath, J. (2011) No lack of principles: leadership development in England and Scotland, *School Leadership and Management,* 31 (2): 105–21.

MacBeath, J., O'Brien, J. and Gronn, P. (2012) Drowning or waving? coping strategies among Scottish head teachers, *School Leadership and Management,* 32 (5): 421–37.

Macfarlane, R. and Woods, D. C. (eds) (2010) *Going for Great, London Leadership Strategy*, London: Department for Education.

Macfarlane, R. and Woods, D. C. (eds) (2011) *Glimpses of Greatness, London Leadership Strategy*, London: Department for Education.

Macfarlane, R. and Woods, D. C. (eds) (2012) *Growing Greatness, London Leadership Strategy*, London: Department for Education.

Macfarlane, R. and Woods, D. C. (eds) (2013) *Generating Greatness, London Leadership Strategy*, London: Department for Education.

Macfarlane, R. and Woods, D. C. (eds) (2014) *Gathering Greatness, London Leadership Strategy*, London: Department for Education.

Macfarlane, R. and Woods, D. C. (eds) (2015) *Unleashing Greatness, London Leadership Strategy*, London: Department for Education.

MacGilchrist, B., Myers, K. and Reed, J. (2004) *The Intelligent School*, 2nd edn, London: Sage.

Male, T. (2006) *Being an Effective Headteacher*, London: Paul Chapman.

Malen, B. and Vincent Cochran, M. (2015) Beyond pluralistic patterns of power: research on the micro-politics of schools, in B. S. Cooper, J. G. Cibulka and L. D. Fusarelli (eds), *Handbook of Education Politics and Policy*, 2nd edn, 3–36, New York and London: Routledge.

Malik, K. (2015) After years of assimilation our societies appear more fragmented, *Observer*, 15 November: 5.

Marquand, D. (2014) *Mammon's Kingdom: An Essay on Britain, now*, London: Allen Lane.

Marsh, C. (2009) *Key Concepts for Understanding Curriculum*, London: Routledge.

Matthews, P. (2014) *Professional Accountability – Redesigning Schooling 7,* London: SSAT.

Matthews, P. and Sammons, P. (2004) *Improvement Thorough Inspection?* London: Ofsted.

Matthews, P. and Hill, R. (2010) *Schools Leading Schools ii: The Growing Impact of National Leaders of Education*, Nottingham: NCSL.

Matthews, P. and Berwick, G. (2013) *Teaching Schools: First Among Equals?*, Nottingham: National College for Teaching and Leadership.

Matthews, P. and Headon, M. (2015) *Multiple Gains – An Independent Evaluation of Challenge Partners' Peer Reviews of Schools,* London: IOE Press.

Matthews, P., Rea, S., Hill, R. and Gu, Q. (2014) *Freedom to Lead: A Study of Outstanding Primary School Leadership in England*, London: DfE.

Maxwell, B., Connolly, P., Demack, S., O'Hare, L., Stevens, A. and Clague, L. (2014) *TextNow Transition Programme: Evaluation Report and Executive Summary*, https://educationendowmentfoundation.org.uk/uploads/pdf/EEF_Evaluation_Report_-_TextNow_Transition_-_October_2014.pdf.

McCray, C. R. and Beachum, F. D. (2010) An analysis of how the gender and race of school principals influences their perceptions of multicultural education, *International Journal of Education Policy and Leadership,* 5 (4): 1–10.

McIntosh, J. (Chair) (2015) *Final Report of the Commission on Assessment without Levels,* London: Department for Education.

McKinney, S. E., Berry, R. Q., Dickerson, D. L. and Campbell-Whately, G. (2007) Addressing urban high-poverty school teacher attrition by addressing urban high-poverty school teacher retention: why effective teachers persevere, *Educational Research and Reviews,* 3 (1): 1–9.

McLendon, M. K., Cohen-Vogel, L. and Wachen, J. (2015) Understanding education policymaking and policy change in the American states: learning from contemporary policy theory, in B. S. Cooper, J. G. Cibulka and L. D. Fusarelli (eds), *Handbook of Education Politics and Policy*, 2nd edn, 86–117, London: Routledge.

Mehta, S. and Maheshwari, G. (2014) Toxic leadership: tracing the destructive trail, *International Journal of Management,* 5 (10): 18–24.

Micklewright, J., Jerrim, J., Vignoles, A., Jenkins, A., Allen, R., Ilie, S., Bellarbre, B., Barrera, F. and Hein, C. (2014) *Teachers in England's Secondary Schools: Evidence from TALIS 2013 Research report*, Institute of Education, University of London.

Mincu, M. (2014) Inquiry paper 6: teacher quality and school improvement – what is the role of research? In the British Educational Research Association/The Royal Society for the encouragement of Arts, Manufactures and Commerce (eds), *The Role Of Research In Teacher Education: Reviewing The Evidence*, https://www.bera.ac.uk/wp-content/uploads/2014/02/BERA-RSA-Interim-Report.pdf.

Ministry of Education, New Zealand (2015) *Best Evidence Synthesis Programme* https://www. educationcounts.govt.nz/topics/BES.

Mintrop, H. and Trujillo, T. (2007) The practical relevance of accountability systems for school improvement: a descriptive analysis of California schools, *Educational Evaluation and Policy Analysis*, 29: 319–52.

Mitchell, D. E. (1996) Institutional theory and the social structure of education, in R. L. Crowson, W. L. Boyd and H. B. Mawhinney (eds), *The Politics of Education and the New Institutionalism*, 167–88, London: RoutledgeFalmer.

Mohrman, S., Tenkasi, R. and Mohrman, A. (2003) The role of networks in fundamental organizational change, *Journal of Applied Behavioural Science*, 39 (3): 301–23.

Monaghan, R. (2015) Education technology is nothing – without people, *EdTech Digest*, 17 August, https://edtechdigest.wordpress.com/2015/08/17/ education-technology-is-nothing-without-people/.

Mongon, D. and Leadbetter, C. (2012) *School Leadership for Public Value: Understanding Valuable Outcomes for Children, Families and Communities*, London: Institute of Education.

Moorosi, P. (2012) Mentoring for school leadership in South Africa: diversity, dissimilarity and disadvantage, *Professional Development in Education,* 38 (3): 487–503.

Mourshed, M., Chijioke, C. and Barber, M. (2010) *How the World's Most Improved School Systems Keep Getting Better*, London: McKinsey&Co.

Mowbray, D. (2013) *Guide to Corporate Resilience*, Cheltenham: MAS Publishing.

Muijs, D. (2015) Improving schools through collaboration: a mixed methods study of school-to-school partnerships in the primary sector, *Oxford Review of Education*, 41 (5): 563–86.

National Association of Head Teachers (2014) *Commission on Assessment*, Haywards Heath: NAHT.

National Audit Office (2015) *Funding for Disadvantaged Pupils*, https://www.nao.org.uk/wp-content/ uploads/2015/06/Funding-for-disadvantaged-pupils.pdf.

National College for Leadership of Schools and Children's Services (2009) *School Business Management Competency Framework: A Guide to Continuous Professional Development for SBMs*, Nottingham: National College.

National College for Teaching and Leadership (2014) *School Business Management Competency Framework*, Nottingham: National College.

National College for Teaching and Leadership/Department for Education (2013) *System Leadership Supported Schools Impact Analysis.*

Neill, S. (1976) The national diffusion network: a success story ending?, *Phi Delta Kappan*, 57 (9): 598–601.

Nelson, J. and O'Beirne, C. (2014) *Using Evidence in the Classroom: What Works and Why?* Slough: NFER.

Nelson, R., Spence-Thomas, K. and Taylor, C. (2015a) *What Makes Great Professional Development: Research Case Studies*, Nottingham: NCTL.

Nelson, R., Spence-Thomas, K. and Taylor, C. (2015b) *National Research Themes Project, Final Report*, Nottingham: NCTL.

New Schools Network website http://www.newschoolsnetwork.org/what-are-free-schools/ free-school-facts-and-figures.

Newcomb, W. S. and Mansfield, K. C. (2014) *Women Interrupting, Disrupting, and Revolutionizing Educational Policy and Practice,* Charlotte, NC: Information Age Publishing, Incorporated.

Nielsen, K., Yarker, J., Randall, R. and Miner, F. (2009) The mediating effects of team and self-efficacy on the relationship between transformational leadership and job satisfaction and psychological well-being in healthcare professionals, *International Journal of Nursing Studies,* 46 (9): 1236–44.

Nonaka, I. and Takeuchi, H. (1995) *The Knowledge Creating Company: How Japanese Companies Create the Dynamics of Innovation*, New York: Oxford University Press.

Northouse, P. G. (2009) *Leadership: Theory and Practice*, 5th edn, London: Sage.

O'Brien, J. (2011) The potential of continuing professional development, in C. Chapman, P. Armstrong, A. Harris, D. Muijs, D. Reynolds and P. Sammons (eds), *School Effectiveness and Improvement Research, Policy and Practice,* 106–11, London: Routledge.

O'Shaughnessy, J. (2012) *Competition Meets Collaboration: Helping School Chains Address England's Long Tail of Educational Failure,* London: Policy Exchange.

O'Sullivan, F., Thody, A. and Wood, E. (2000) *From Bursar to School Business Manager: Reengineering Leadership for Resource Management*, London: Financial Times/Prentice Hall.

Oates, T. (2015) So who says that a 12 year-old should learn that? confused issues of knowledge and authority in curriculum thinking, in J. Simons and N. Porter (eds), *Knowledge and the Curriculum: A Collection of Essays to Accompany E. D. Hirsch's Lecture at Policy Exchange*, 65–83, London: Policy Exchange.

OECD (2011a) *PISA in Focus* 2011/9 (October).

OECD (2011b) *School Autonomy and Accountability: Are they Related to School Performance? PISA in Focus*, Paris: OECD.

OECD (2013a) *Teaching and Learning International Survey*, Paris: OECD.

OECD (2013b) *Synergies for Better Learning: An International Perspective on Evaluation and Assessment*, PISA, Paris: OECD.

OECD (2013c) *PISA 2012 Results: Excellence Through Equity, Giving Every Student the Chance to Succeed, Vol 2*, Paris: OECD.

OECD (2014) *TALIS 2013 Results: An International Perspective on Teaching and Learning*, Paris: OECD.

OECD (2015a) *Education Policy Outlook 2015: Making Reforms Happen*, Paris: OECD.

OECD (2015b) *PISA in Focus 51: What do Parents Look for in their Child's School?* Paris: OECD.

OECD (2015c) *Students, Computers and Learning: Making the Connection*, Paris: PISA.

OECD (2015d) *Education Policy Outlook 2015: Making reforms happen*, Paris: OECD.

Ofsted (1996) *The Teaching of Reading in 45 Inner London Primary Schools*, London: Ofsted.

Ofsted (1998a) *Inspection of Tower Hamlets Local Education Authority*, London: Ofsted.

Ofsted (1998b) *School Evaluation Matters*, London: Ofsted.

Ofsted (2000) *Inspection of Tower Hamlets Local Education Authority*, London: Ofsted.

Ofsted (2005) *Annual Performance Assessment of London Borough of Tower Hamlets Council's Education and Children's Social Care Services 2005*, London: Ofsted.

Ofsted (2006) *Annual Performance Assessment of Services for Children and Young People in the London Borough of Tower Hamlets 2006*, London: Ofsted.

Ofsted (2007) *Annual Performance Assessment of Services for Children and Young People in the London Borough of Tower Hamlets 2007*, London: Ofsted.

Ofsted (2008) *Annual Performance Assessment of Services for Children and Young People in the London Borough of Tower Hamlets 2008*, London: Ofsted.

Ofsted (2009) *Twelve Outstanding Secondary Schools – Excelling Against the Odds*, London: Ofsted.

Ofsted (2010a) *Developing Leadership: National Support Schools Strategies used to Develop Leadership Potential and Effectiveness in Schools*, London: Ofsted.

Ofsted (2010b) *Good Professional Development in Schools*, London: Ofsted.

Ofsted (2010c) *Twelve Outstanding Special Schools – Excelling Through Inclusion*, London: Ofsted.

Ofsted (2010d) *Twenty Outstanding Primary Schools – Excelling Against the Odds*, London: Ofsted.

Ofsted (2011) *Evaluation of London Challenge*, London: Ofsted.

Ofsted (2013a) *The Report of Her Majesty's Chief Inspector of Education, Children's Services and Skills 2012-13: Schools*, London: Ofsted.

Ofsted (2013b) *Unseen Children; Access and Achievement 20 Years on*, London: Ofsted.

Ofsted (2015a) *School Inspection Handbook*, London: Ofsted.

Ofsted (2015b) *The Annual Report of Her Majesty's Chief Inspector of Education, Children's Services and Skills 2014/15*, London: Ofsted.

Ofsted (2015c) *Common Inspection Framework: Education, Skills and Early Years*, London: Ofsted.

Ofsted (2015d) *The Annual Report of Her Majesty's Chief Inspector of Education, Children's Services and Skills*, London: Ofsted.

Ogunbawo, D. (2012) Developing black and minority ethnic leaders: the case for customized programmes, *Educational Management Administration and Leadership,* 40 (2): 158–74.

Ogus, A. I. (2004) *Regulation, Legal form, and Economic Theory*, Oxford and Portland, OR: Hart.

Olssen, M., Codd, J. and O'Neill, A. (2004) *Globalisation, Citizenship and Democracy*, London: Sage.

Orton, J. D. and Weick, K. E. (1990) Loosely coupled systems: a reconceptualization, *The Academy of Management Review,* 15 (2): 203–23.

Osborne-Lampkin, L., Folsom, J. S. and Herrington, C. D. (2015) A *Systematic Review of the Relationships Between Principal Characteristics and Student Achievement* (REL 2016–091), Washington, DC: U.S. Department of Education, Institute of Education Sciences, National Center for Education Evaluation and Regional Assistance, Regional Educational Laboratory Southeast.

Padilla, A., Hogan, R. and Kaiser, R. (2007) The toxic triangle: destructive leaders, susceptible followers and conducive environments, *Leadership Quarterly*, 18: 176–94.

Painter, A. (2014) 'Core values', https://www.thersa.org/discover/publications-and-articles/journals/issue-1-2014/.

Payne, C. M. (2008) *So Much Reform, So Little Change: The Persistence of Failure in Urban Schools,* Harvard, MA: Harvard Educational Press.

Pellegrino, W. and Hilton, L. (eds) (2012) *Education for Life and Work: Developing Transferable Knowledge and Skills in the 21st Century.* Center for Education; National Research Council, Washington, DC: National Academic Press.

Philipsen, M. I. and Bostic, T. B. (2010) *Helping Faculty Find Work-life Balance: The Path Toward Family-friendly Institutions,* San Francisco, CA: John Wiley.

Phillips, S. and Sen, D. (2011) Stress in headteachers, in J. Langan-Fox and C. L. Cooper (eds), *Handbook of Stress in the Occupations*, 177–200, Cheltenham: Elgar Press.

Plank, D. N. and Keesler, V. (2009) Education and the shrinking state, in G. Sykes, B. Schneider and D. Plank D (eds), *Handbook of Education-Policy Research*, 694–704. New-York: AERA/ Routledge.

Porritt, V. (2009) Evaluating the impact of professional development, *Education Journal*, 116: 8–9.

Pryce Jones, J. (2010) *Happiness at Work – Maximizing Your Psychological Capital for Success*, Chichester: Wiley Blackwell.

Puusa, A., Kuittinen, M. and Kuusela, P. (2013) Paradoxical change and construction of identity in an educational organization, *Educational Management, Administration and Leadership*, 41 (2): 165–78.

Pyhältö, K., Pietarinen, J. and Soini, T. (2015) When teaching gets tough – professional community inhibitors of teacher-targeted bullying and turnover intentions, *Improving Schools,* 18 (3): 263–76.

Radnor, H., Ball, S. and Vincent, C. (1998) Local educational governance: Accountability and democracy in the United Kingdom, in R. J. S. Macpherson (ed.), *The Politics of Accountability: Educative and International Perspectives*, 120–33, Thousand Oaks, CA: Corwin Press.

Ranson, S. (2012) Schools and civil society: corporate or community governance, *Critical Studies in Education*, 53 (1): 29–45.

Rayner, S. (2014) Playing by the rules? the professional values of head teachers tested by the changing policy context, *Management in Education*, 28 (2): 38–43.

Rea, S., Hill, R. and Sandals, L. (2011) *System Leadership: Does School-to-School Support Close the Gap?,* Nottingham: NCSL.

Rea, S., Hill, R. and Dunford, J. (2013) *Closing the Gap: How System Leaders and Schools Can Work Together*, London: National College for Teaching and Leadership/Department for Education.

Reed, L. C. (2012) The intersection of race and gender in school leadership for three Black female principals, *International Journal of Qualitative Studies in Education,* 25 (1): 39–58.

Rhodes, C. and Brundrett, M. (2010) Leadership for learning, in T. Bush, L. Bell and D. Middlewood (eds), *The Principles of Educational Leadership and Management*, 2nd edn, 153–75, London: Sage.

Richardson, R. (2015) British values and British identity: muddles, mixtures and ways ahead, *London Review of Education,* 13 (2): 37–48.

Riley, K. (2013a) Walking the leadership tightrope: building community cohesiveness and social capital in schools in highly disadvantaged urban communities, *British Educational Research Journal*, 39 (2): 266–86.

Riley, K. (2013b) *Leadership of Place, Stories from the US, UK and South Africa*, London: Bloomsbury.

Riley, K. (2017) *Place, Belonging and School Leadership: Researching to Change School Cultures*, London: Bloomsbury.

Robertson, I. and Cooper, C. (2011) *Wellbeing – Productivity and Happiness at Work*, Basingstoke: Palgrave Macmillan.

Robinson, K. (2001) *Out of Our Minds*, Oxford: Capstone.

Robinson, V. (2011) *Student-centred Leadership*, San Francisco: Jossey-Bassey.

Robinson, V. (2013) Leadership where it counts: making a bigger difference to your students, *School Leadership Today*, 5 (2): 63–8.

Robinson, V., Hohepa, M. and Lloyd, D. (2009) *School Leadership and Student Outcomes: Identifying what Works and why: Best Evidence Synthesis*, Wellington, New Zealand: Ministry of Education.

Robinson, V., Lloyd, C. and Rowe, K. (2008) The impact of leadership on student outcomes: an analysis of the differential effects of leadership types, *Educational Administration Quarterly*, 44 (5): 635–74.

RSA (2014) *Schools with Soul: A New Approach to Spiritual, Moral, Social and Cultural Education*, London: RSA.

Rudd, P., Poet, H. and Featherstone, G. (2011) *Evaluation of City Challenge Leadership Strategies: London Area Report*, Slough: NFER.

Sacred Heart Catholic School Website http://www.sacredheart.southwark.sch.uk/.

Sahlberg P. (2011a) http://www.no-straight-lines.com/blog/ what-makes-the-finnish-education-system-work/.

Sahlberg, P. (2011b) *Finnish Lessons*, New York: Teachers College Press.

Salokangas, M. and Chapman, C. (2014) Exploring governance in chains of academy schools, *Educational Management, Administration and Leadership*, 42 (3): 372–86.

Sandals, L. and Bryant, B. (2014) *The Evolving Education System in England: A 'Temperature Check'*, London: Department for Education.

Santamaría, L. J. and Jean-Marie, G. (2014) Cross-cultural dimensions of applied, critical, and transformational leadership: women principals advancing social justice and educational equity, *Cambridge Journal of Education*, 44 (3): 333–60.

Sassen, S. (1991) *The Global City: New York, Tokyo and London*, Princeton, NJ: Princeton University Press.

Saunders, L. (2015) 'Evidence' and teaching: a question of trust?, in C. Brown (ed.), *Leading the use of Research and Evidence in Schools*, 40–53, London: IOE Press.

Schein, E. (2010) *Organizational Culture and Leadership*, San Francisco: Jossey-Bass.

Schleicher, A. (2011) *Building a High-Quality Teaching Profession: Lessons from around the world*, Paris: OECD.

Schleicher, A. (2015) School technology struggles to make an impact, BBC Business, 15 September, http://www.bbc.co.uk/news/business-34174795.

Schleicher, A. (ed.) (2012) *Preparing Teachers and Developing School Leaders for the 21st Century: Lessons from around the World*, Paris: OECD.

Scott, P. (1989) Accountability, responsiveness and responsibility, in R. Glatter (ed.), *Educational Institutions and their Environments: Managing the Boundaries*, 11–22, Milton Keynes: Open University Press.

Scott, W. R. (2001) *Institutions and Organizations*, 2nd edn, London: Sage Publications.

Seashore Louis, K. (2015) Linking leadership to learning: state, district and local effects, *Nordic Journal of Studies in Educational Policy*, 1: 30321, http://dx.doi.org/10.3402/nstep.v1.30321.

Sebba, J., Kent, P. and Tregenza, J. (2012) *Powerful Professional Learning: A School Leader's Guide to Powerful Professional Development*, Nottingham: NCTL.

Selvarajah, S. (June 23 2015) Headhunters for headteachers: schools pay firms up to £50,000 to find leaders, *The Guardian*. Retrieved from http://www.theguardian.com/.

Selznick, P. (1957) *Leadership in Administration*, New York: Harper and Row.

Selznick, P. (1996) Institutionalism: old and new, *Administrative Science Quarterly*, 41 (2): 270–7.

Sergiovanni, T. J. (1992) *Moral Leadership: Getting to the Heart of School Improvement*, San Francisco, CA: Jossey-Bass.

Shah, S. (2008) Leading multi-ethnic schools: adjustments in concepts and practices for engaging with diversity 1, *British Journal of Sociology of Education*, 29 (5): 523–36.

Shah, S. and Shaikh, J. (2010) Leadership progression of Muslim male teachers: interplay of ethnicity, faith and visibility, *School Leadership and Management*, 30 (1): 19–33.

Shakeshaft, C. (1993) Women in educational management in the United States, in J. Ouston (ed.), *Women in Educational Management*, 47–63, London: Longmans.

Shakeshaft, C., Brown, G., Irby, B. J., Grogan, M., Ballenger, J. and Klein, S. S. (2007) Increasing gender equity in educational leadership, *Handbook for Achieving Gender Equity Through Education*, 2: 103–29.

Siraj-Blatchford, I., Sylva, K., Muttock, S., Gilden, R. and Bell, D. (2002) *Researching Effective Pedagogy in the Early Years* (Research report RR356), London: Institute of Education, University of London.

Slavin, R. (2002) Evidence-based education policies: transforming educational practice and research, *Educational Researcher*, 31 (7): 15–21.

Sleeter, C. (2001) Preparing teachers for culturally diverse schools: research and the overwhelming presence of whiteness, *Journal of Teacher Education*, 52 (94): 94–106.

Smith, A. (2011) *High Performers: The Secret of Successful Schools*, Carmarthen: Crown House Publishing.

Smith, D. (1993) The head and the bursar, in P. Anthony and R. Pittman (eds), *Head to Head: How to Run a School: Fifteen HMC Heads Offer their Advice*, 2nd edn, 29–30, Saxmundham: John Catt Educational Ltd.

Smith, J. (2011) Agency and female teachers' career decisions: a life history study of 40 women, *Educational Management Administration and Leadership*, 39 (1): 7–24.

Smith, W. C. (ed.) (2016) *The Global Testing Culture: Shaping Education Policy, Perceptions, and Practice*, Oxford: Symposium Books.

Smithers, A. and Robinson, P. (2003) *Factors Affecting Teachers' Decisions to Leave the Profession*, Research Report RR430, London: DfES.

Smrekar, C. (1996) *The Impact of School Choice and Community: In the Interest of Families and Schools*, NY: State University of New York Press.

Smythe, J. and Wrigley, T. (2013) *Living on the Edge: Rethinking Poverty, Class and Schooling*, New York: Peter Lang Publishing.

Southworth, G. (2002) Instructional leadership in schools: reflections and empirical evidence, *School Leadership and Management*, 22 (1): 73–91.

Southworth, G. (2004) Learning-centred leadership, in B. Davies (ed.), *The Essentials of Leadership*, 75–92, London: Sage.

Southworth, G. (2009) Learning centred leadership, in B. Davies (ed.), *The Essentials of School Leadership*, 2nd edn, 91–111, London: Sage.

Southworth, G. (2010) *School Business Management, a Quiet Revolution*, Nottingham: NCSL.

Spence-Thomas, K. (2010) How to make innovative and strategic connections, *Professional Development Today*, 13 (3): 30–4.

Spillane, J. P., Healey, K. and Kim, C. (2010) Leading and managing instruction: formal and informal aspects of elementary school organization, in A. Daly (ed.), *Social Network Theory and Educational Change*, Cambridge, MA: Harvard Education Press.

Spillane, J. P. (2007) The making and effects of education policy: commentary/policy, politics, institutions, and markets, in S. H. Fuhrman, D. K. Cohen, F. Mosher (eds), *The State of Educational Policy Research*, 129–36, Mahwah, NJ: Lawrence Erlbaum.

Spillane, J and Hunt, B. (2010) Days of their lives: a mixed-methods, descriptive analysis of the men and women at work in the principal's office, *Journal of Curriculum Studies*, 2010, 1–39.

St. Stephen's Primary School Website http://www.ststephensinf.org.uk/.

Starratt, R. J. (2007) Leading a community of learners: learning to be moral by engaging the morality of learning, *Educational Management, Administration and Leadership*, 35 (2): 165–83.

Stoll, L. (2015a) Using evidence, learning and the role of professional learning communities, in C. Brown (ed.), *Leading the use of Research and Evidence in Schools*, 54–65, London: IOE Press.

Stoll, L. (2015b) *Three Greats for a Self-Improving School System – Pedagogy, Professional Development and Leadership: Teaching Schools R&D Network National Themes Project 2012-14* Research Report.

Stoll, L., Brown, C., Spence Thomas, K. and Taylor, C. (2015) Perspectives on teacher leadership for evidence-informed improvement in England, *Leading and Managing*, 21 (2): 75–89.

Stoll, L., Harris, A. and Handscomb, G. (2012) *Great Professional Development which Leads to Consistently Great Pedagogy: Nine Claims from Research*, Nottingham: NCTL.

Stoll, L. and Stobart, G. (2005) Informed consent? issues in implementing and sustaining government-driven educational change, in N. Bascia, A. Cumming, A. Datnow, K. Leithwood and D. Livingstone (eds), *International Handbook of Educational Policy*, 153–72, Dordrecht: Kluwer.

Stoten, D. (2015) Virtue, ethics and toxic leadership: tackling the toxic triangle, *Education Today*, 65 (1): 3–6.

Strand, S. (2015) *English as an Additional Language and Educational Achievement in England*, https://educationendowmentfoundation.org.uk/uploads/pdf/EAL_and_educational_ achievement2.pdf.

Strike, K. A. (2003) Liberty, democracy, and community: legitimacy in public education, in W. L. Boyd and D. Miretzky (eds), *American Educational Governance on Trial: Change and Challenges – the 102nd Yearbook of the National Society for the Study of Education (NSSE)*, 37–56, Chicago, IL: Chicago University Press.

Suggett, D. (2015) School autonomy: necessary but not sufficient, *Evidence Base,* 1. The Australian and New Zealand School of Government.

Supovitz, J. (2015) Teacher data use for improving teaching and learning, in C. Brown (ed.), *Leading the use of Research and Evidence in Schools*, 117–25, London: IOE Press.

Supovitz, J., Daly, A. and del Fresno, M. (2015) #CommonCore: How Social Media Is Changing the Politics of Education. Retrieved from http://www.hashtagcommoncore.com.

Sutton Trust (2011) *Improving the Impact of Teachers on Pupil Achievement in the UK – Interim Findings*, London: Sutton Trust.

Swaffield, S. and MacBeath, J. (2008) Leadership for learning, in J. MacBeath and N. Dempster (eds), *Connecting Leadership and Learning: Principles for Practice*, 32–52, London: Routledge.

Tan, E. (2014) Human capital theory: a holistic criticism, *Review of Educational Research*, 84 (3): 411–45.

Teaching and Learning Research Programme (2015) TLRP Homepage, http://www.tlrp.org/index.html.

TES (2015) TES Teaching Resources, https://www.tes.com/teaching-resources.

The Cantle Report (2001) *Community Cohesion: A Report of the Independent* Review Team, London: Home Office.

Timperley, H. (2011a) Knowledge and the leadership of learning, *Leadership and Policy in Schools,* 10 (2): 145–70.

Timperley, H. (2011b) *Realizing the Power of Professional Learning*, Maidenhead: Open University Press.

Timperley, H. and Robertson, J. (eds) (2011) *Leadership and Learning*, London: Sage.

Timperley, H., Wilson, A., Barrar, H. and Fung, I. (2007) *Teacher Professional Learning and Development: Best Evidence Synthesis Iteration*, Wellington: New Zealand Ministry of Education.

Tinker, R. (2015) *Stakeholder Schools: Why Collaboration is Key to the Next Phase of School Reform*. Available online https://www.fabians.org.uk/publications/ england-needs-a-national-constitution-for-schools-says-fabian-report.

Tinsley, T. and Board, K. (2014) *The Teaching of Chinese in the UK*, Alcantara Communications.

Tschamien-Moran, M. and Hoy, W. K. (2000) A multidisciplinary analysis of the nature, meaning, and measurement of trust, *Review of Educational Research*, 71: 547–93.

Tschannen-Moran, M. (2004) *Trust Matters: Leadership for Successful Schools*, San Francisco, CA: Jossey-Bass.

Uhl-Bien, M. and Carsten, M. (2010) Being ethical when the boss is not, in G. Robinson Hickman (ed.), *Leading Organisations: Perspectives for the New Era*, 365–76, London: Sage.

UNHCR (2015) Figures at a Glance, http://www.unhcr.org/pages/49c3646c11.html.

Veljanovski, C. (2010) Economic approaches to regulation, in R. Baldwin, M. Cave and M. Lodge (eds), *The Oxford Handbook of Regulation*, 17–38, Oxford, UK: Oxford University Press.

Vickers, I. (2016) *The Good New Habits Book*, Auckland: Sancta Maria College.

Waldegrave, H. and Simons, J. (2014) *Watching the Watchmen: The Future of School Inspections in England*, London: Policy Exchange.

Walton, M. (2007) Leadership toxicity – an inevitable affliction of organisations, *Organisations and People,* 14 (2): 19–27.

Waslander, S., Pater, C. and van der Weide, M. (2010) *Markets in Education: An Analytical Review of Empirical Research on Market Mechanisms in Education* (working paper 52), Paris: OECD.

Waters, M. (2013) *Thinking Allowed on Schooling*, Carmarthen: Crown House.

Wermke, W. and Hostfalt, G. (2014) Contextualising teacher autonomy in time and space: a model for comparing various forms of governing the teaching profession, *Journal of Curriculum Studies*, 46 (1): 58–80.

West-Burnham, J. (2015) Moral leadership http://www.unrwa.org/userfiles/file/leading_4_the_ future/module1/moral-leadership%20West%20Burnham.pdf.

West-Burnham, J. and Harris D. (2015) *Leadership Dialogues*, Carmarthen: Crown House Publishing.

Wey Smola, K. and Sutton, C. D. (2002) Generational differences: revisiting generational work values for the new millennium, *Journal of Organizational Behavior,* 23 (4): 363–82.

What Works Network (2014) What Works? Evidence for decision makers [Online], accessed 29 October 2015, https://www.gov.uk/government/uploads/system/uploads/attachment_data/file/378038/What_works_evidence_for_decision_makers.pdf.

Whitty, G. (2002) *Making Sense of Education Policy*, London: Paul Chapman.

Whitty, G. (2008) Twenty years of progress? English education policy 1988 to the present, *Education Management, Administration and Leadership*, 36 (2): 165–84.

Whyte, W. H. (1956) *The Organization Man*, New York: Simon and Shuster.

Williams, D. (2005) *Toxic Leadership in the US Army, unpublished Master of Strategic Studies dissertation*, US Army War College.

Williams, J. C. and Segal, N. (2003) Beyond the maternal wall: relief for family caregivers who are discriminated against on the job, *Harvard Journal of Law and Gender,* 26: 77.

Wilson, M. (1997) *Women in Educational Management: A European Perspective,* London: Paul Chapman Educational Publishing.

Wilson-Starks, K. (2003) *Toxic Leadership*, Colorado Springs: Transleadership Inc.

Wong, K. K. (2015) Federalism and equity and accountability in education, in B. Cooper, J. Cibulka and L. Fusarelli (eds), *Handbook of Education Politics and Policy*, 2nd edn, 37–61, London: Routledge.

Wood, E., O'Sullivan, F., Rix, S. and Al-Bahrani Peacock, D. (2007) *The Baseline Study of School Business Managers*, Nottingham: NCSL.

Woodin, T. (ed.) (2015) *Co-operation, Learning and Co-operative Values: Contemporary Issues in Education*, London: Routledge.

Woods, C. (2014) *Anatomy of a Professionalization Project: The Making of the Modern School Business Manager*, London: Bloomsbury.

Woods, C., Armstrong, P., Bragg, J. and Pearson, D. (2013) Perfect partners or uneasy bedfellows? competing understandings of the place of business management within contemporary education partnerships, *Educational Management Administration and Leadership*, 41 (6): 751–66.

Woods, D., Husbands, C. and Brown, C. (2013) *Transforming Education for all: The Tower Hamlets Story*, London: IOE Press.

Woods, P., Woods, G. and Gunter, H. (2007) Academy schools and entrepreneurialism in education, *Journal of Educational Policy*, 22 (2): 237.

Woods, P. A. and Simkins, T. (2014) Understanding the local: themes and issues in the experience of structural reform in England, *Educational Management, Administration and Leadership*, 42 (3): 324–40.

Wright, N. (2001) Leadership, 'bastard leadership' and managerialism: confronting twin paradoxes in the Blair education project, *Educational Management and Administration,* 29 (3): 275–90.

Yeung, K. (2010) The regulatory state, in R. Baldwin, M. Cave and M. Lodge (eds), *The Oxford Handbook of Regulation*, 64–86, Oxford, UK: Oxford University Press.

Young, M. D. and McLeod, S. (2001) Flukes, opportunities, and planned interventions: factors affecting women's decisions to become school administrators, *Educational Administration Quarterly,* 37 (4): 462–502.

Young, P. and Young, K. H. (2010) Perceptions of female and male superintendents for a middle school principalship as moderated by sex and national origin of applicants, *Leadership and Policy in Schools,* 9 (4): 441–61.

Yukl, G. (2002) *Leadership in Organizations*, 5th edn, Upper Saddle River, NJ: Prentice-Hall.

Zavadsky, H. (2010) *Bringing School Reform to Scale: Five Award Winning Urban Districts*, Harvard, MA: Harvard Educational Press.

Zemke, R., Raines, C., Filipczak, B. and Association, A. M. (2000) *Generations at Work: Managing the Clash of Veterans, Boomers, Xers, and Nexters in Your Workplace,* New York, NY: Amacom.

Index